101

Management
Models
Marijn Mulders

Noordhoff Uitgevers Groningen | Houten

Cover design: G2K Designers, Groningen/Amsterdam
Cover illustration: iStock

If you have any comments or queries about this or any other publication, please contact:
Noordhoff Uitgevers bv, Afdeling Hoger Onderwijs, Antwoordnummer 13, 9700 VB Groningen,
e-mail: info@noordhoff.nl

0 1 2 3 4 5 / 14 13 12 11 10

© 2010 Noordhoff Uitgevers bv Groningen/Houten, the Netherlands

ISBN 978-90-01-78316-7

NUR 801

Preface

Management Models

Management models: many students become familiar with them during their studies. However, a model only comes to life if someone works with it. In practice, when students complete a practical assignment, it often turns out that they don't know which model they should apply in a certain situation. The management books they study include models but these are often dispersed over several chapters and consequently more difficult to find and compare. Furthermore, due to current developments in education and trade and industry it is no longer necessary to learn all the knowledge and its application by heart. It is no longer possible to view everything separately because all the processes and corporate functions within the enterprise are interlinked. To gain more insight into how the activities in an enterprise are mutually related, it is wise to follow the modelling approach. There now seem to be many hundreds of models that can offer support. But not all the models are as relevant and applicable, so it is difficult to select a suitable model from their ever-growing numbers.

This book has been written as a reference work and serves to find one or more models that can be used for the development of a research or advice project. A large number of much tried and tested models and a number of new, promising models have been put together.

101 Management Models

The list of 101 models came about on the basis of:

- Feedback from users of the Dutch edition of this book: according to teachers and professionals, a number of models should absolutely be present.
- The many years experience in the business community with which models have been used and applied.
- An assessment of models that are (as yet) little used but will perhaps become more important in the future.

Models and instruments

A frequently used definition of the concept of 'Models' is a simplified reflection of reality. A model attempts to imitate or describe reality. They make you think. The 101 management models are not all models. Instruments are also included in the book. An instrument is an aid to determining a certain result, investigating a question or implementing a solution, for example.

All the same, model or instrument, the selection in this book gives the user a modelling insight into the problem and offers tools to put the models into practice.

Target group

101 Management Models is a concise and accessible reference work for bachelors and masters students who regularly have to apply models in research or advice projects. For them, this book provides an excellent reference work for the rapid selection of the correct model for the development of their assignments. This book is also very practical for entrepreneurs, managers and advisors from trade and industry, to support their decisions and recommendations with the aid of the models.

Web site

With this book there is a supporting web site available for students and teachers: www.managementmodels-englishedition.noordhoff.nl. This site offers handy tools for the application of the models. Furthermore, the figures of the models can be downloaded as PowerPoint presentations.
For teachers, cases and their solutions are available.

Finally, I hope that everyone will use this book with pleasure, not only in their studies but also at work.

Marijn Mulders RI

Haaren, July 2010

Contents

Preface *3*

How do I use 101 Management Models? *9*

1   360° feedback *13*

2   AAA Triangle *16*

3   Activities schedule *20*

4   Activity Based Costing *23*

5   Balanced Scorecard *26*

6   BART *29*

7   BCG Matrix *32*

8   Belbin Team Roles *36*

9   Benchmarking *39*

10   Blue Ocean Strategy *42*

11   Brainstorm *47*

12   Brand Asset Valuator *51*

13   Business Intelligence *55*

14   CAGE Distance Framework *58*

15   Colour Print Thinking *63*

16   Competence management *67*

17   Competing Values Framework, Quinn *70*

18   Competitive Forces, Porter *74*

19   Competitive Positions, Kotler *78*

20   Competitive Strategies, Kotler *82*

21   Competitive Strategies, Porter *85*

22   Complaints Management *88*

23   Conflict Handling *91*

24   Confrontation Matrix *94*

25   Core Competence *97*

26   Core Marketing System *101*

27   Core Qualities *104*

28   Costs-Benefits Analysis *108*

29   Cultural Dimensions, Hofstede *111*

30   Customer Order Decoupling Point *114*

31   Customer Pyramid, Curry *118*

32   Customer Relationship Management *122*

33   Customer Satisfaction *126*

34   Customer-Value Profiles *129*

35   Decision Table *133*

36   Deming Circle *136*

37   DESTEP *139*

38   Diamond, Porter *143*
39   Employability Scan *146*
40   Entry Mode Decision *149*
41   F-PEC scale *153*
42   Functional and process management *156*
43   Gantt Chart *159*
44   Global Sourcing *162*
45   GPS for Enterprises *165*
46   Growth Strategies, Ansoff *168*
47   Image and Identity *171*
48   Industrial column *175*
49   INK / EFQM *178*
50   Intelligence Pyramid *181*
51   International Market Research *184*
52   International Pricing Strategy *187*
53   ITIL V3 *191*
54   Karasek's Job Strain Model *195*
55   Knowledge management *199*
56   Kraljic Matrix *203*
57   Lead time/net time *207*
58   Levers of Control *211*
59   MaBa Analysis *215*
60   Managerial Grid *218*
61   Mergers and Takeovers *222*
62   Multichannel Marketing *226*
63   Organisation Chart *230*
64   Organisational Climate Index *234*
65   Organisational growth, Greiner *237*
66   Organisational Management *241*
67   OSO model *246*
68   Pareto Analysis *250*
69   Performance matrix for family businesses *253*
70   Physical Distribution *256*
71   PMT, Abell & Hammond *260*
72   Positioning *263*
73   PRINCE2 *266*
74   Product Life Cycle *269*
75   Progress reporting *273*
76   Purchasing Process *277*
77   RASCI Matrix *280*
78   Ratio Delay Studies *283*
79   Research method *287*
80   Resource Based View *291*
81   Sales Funnel *295*

82   Segmentation *298*
83   SERVQUAL *302*
84   Seven-S Model *305*
85   SIT Method *309*
86   Situational Leadership Theory *312*
87   SIVA *315*
88   Six Sigma *319*
89   Stakeholder Management *322*
90   Strategic Alignment Model *326*
91   Strategy Clock *330*
92   Strategy Map *333*
93   Supplier Selection *337*
94   SWOT *341*
95   Talent Branding *345*
96   Target marketing *350*
97   Team Buying Team Selling (TBTS) *353*
98   The Ten Steps Plan *356*
99   Two Factory Theory *360*
100   Value Chain, Porter *364*
101   Value Stream Mapping *367*
        Index by Discipline *371*
        Index by Objective *374*
        Index by Research or Advice Project *378*
        Index by Author *381*
        Index by Keyword *383*
        Glossary Dutch-English *389*
        Glossary English-Dutch *391*

How do I use
101 Management Models?

Structure

The structure within which the models are described is the same for every model and comprises the following subjects:

Name of model

The title of the model is the name under which it is best known. Other information that is given for each model:

1 Author: the name of the person who developed the model, if known.
2 Year developed: year in which the model was developed.
3 Also known as: the name under which this model is also known.
4 Purpose: the intention with which the model was developed.

Background

The background gives the context in which the model can be used and also the background of the model.

Application

In the application it is described how the model is applied in practice.

Result

Under result is indicated what the model ultimately produces.

Focus areas

The focus areas indicate what must be paid attention to in the use of this model. This concerns the limitations of the model.

Literature

This concerns references to sources that give more information about the model. The first reference relates as far as possible to the original book.

Indices

This book was written as a reference work and is used to find one or more models that can be used in the development of a research or advice project. If it is already known which model will be used, you can use the table of contents in alphabetical order to find in which chapter the model is described in. If the name of the model is unknown, you can search via various indices at the back of the book for which model applies to the problem in your question.

The following indices are included at the back of the book:
- by Discipline
- by Objective
- by Research or advice project
- by Author
- by Keyword

These indices are further explained hereafter.

Discipline

This matrix indicates for each model for which area of application the model was originally developed. The following areas of application are used:
- ■ General management. Models that can be used at different times and places in a research project.
- ■ Strategy. Models applicable to the strategy of the enterprise with a planning horizon from three to five years.
- ■ Marketing. Models applicable to the marketing aspects of the enterprise with a planning horizon from one to five years.
- ■ Sales. Models for account and sales management.
- ■ Purchasing. Models that can be used in purchasing.
- ■ Project & Planning. Models that can be used for project execution and project planning.
- ■ Production. The realisation of the products of the enterprise.
- ■ Quality. Concerning integrated quality assurance.
- ■ Logistics & Distribution. Models for logistics and distribution.
- ■ Information management. Models that can be used in the (computerised) information processing of the enterprise.
- ■ Financial. Models concerned with the flow of money in an enterprise.
- ■ HRM & HTM. Human Resource Management and Human Talent Management. Models used for personnel matters.
- ■ Internationalisation. Models that can be used in the international activities of the enterprise.

Objective

This index gives direction to the purpose for which the model can be used.

Research or advice project

Education and trade and industry are coming increasingly closer to each other and students and entrepreneurs increasingly carry out projects together. Consequently, more and more attention is paid to the manner in which these projects are carried out. A model for structuring such a project is given hereafter.

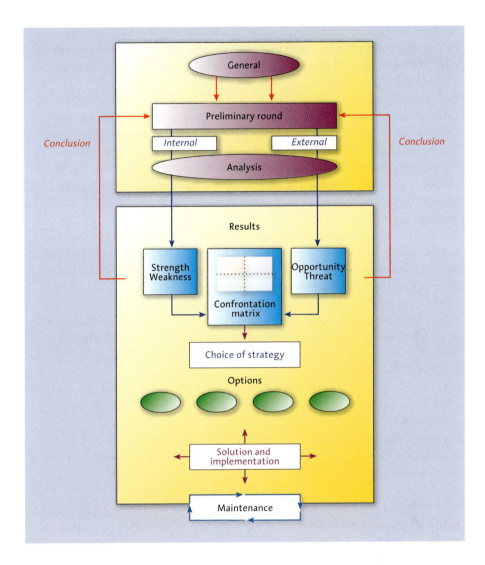

1 General

Projects that can be applied prior to or as the result of a research or advice project

2 Preliminary study

During the preliminary study, a question is formulated to define and give direction to the whole of the research. The question is composed of three parts:

- Background: the background reflects the events that led to the setting up of this research. What led to the current situation and symptoms?
- Problem determination: the problem determination always begins with a question. For example: how can we increase turnover? When can a new product be introduced to the market? The problem determination guides your thoughts for the third step, the terms of reference.

- Terms of reference: the terms of reference always begin with a verb. For example: write a business plan that leads to increasing the turnover by 25% within three years. The terms of reference must be formulated according to SMART.

3 *Analysis: external research*

External research is performed before internal research. If the market has no need for the solution the enterprise has to offer, it makes no sense to carry out internal research. The external research provides an answer to the question of the market possibilities for the enterprise to achieve the declared mission. The results of the external research are formulated within the opportunities and threats for the enterprise.

4 *Analysis: internal research*

The internal research within the enterprise comprises an analysis of different components to establish whether the enterprise is actually capable of carrying out the mission formulated in the question. The results of the internal analysis are expressed in the strengths and weaknesses of the enterprise.

5 *Choice of strategy*

On the basis of the internal and external research, an analysis can take place and an interpretation of the findings to establish the further strategy of the enterprise.

6 *Solution and implementation*

After the correct strategy has been determined, it will have to be further developed into a concrete solution that can subsequently be implemented.

7 *Maintenance*

After the implementation of the chosen solution, aftercare and monitoring must take place to establish whether the activities have also actually led to the desired results. If this is not the case, changes will have to be made.

Name of author

In this index, users will find the models ordered by the name of the author of the model, if known.

Keyword

In this index, users will find the models ordered according to the names they are commonly known by.

Glossaries

At the back of the book, two glossaries are available; one from Dutch to English and a glossary from English to Dutch. This supports the use of the book in both Dutch and English classes.

1
360° feedback

Author	P. Ward
Year developed	1985
Also known as	Multi Rater Feedback
Objective	Awakening process to arrive at own development

Model

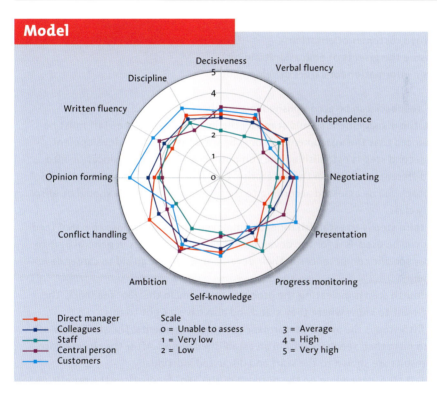

Legend:
- Direct manager
- Colleagues
- Staff
- Central person
- Customers

Scale
- 0 = Unable to assess
- 1 = Very low
- 2 = Low
- 3 = Average
- 4 = High
- 5 = Very high

Background

The purpose of 360° feedback is learning and development. If used properly, 360° feedback is an excellent aid for providing people with information about what kind of conduct is seen as strong and which behaviours should be changed.

General management | Strategy | Marketing | Sales | Purchasing | Project & Planning | Production | Quality | Logistics & Distribution | Information management | Financial | HRM & HTM | Internationalisation

The 360° feedback process has the purpose of collecting perceptions of the behaviour of the employee and the consequences of such behaviour for managers, business contacts, colleagues, members of the project team, internal and external customers and suppliers. It is a method of assessing the functioning of employees by allowing a number of people in their direct environment to give feedback. These can be direct colleagues, subordinates and managers, but also customers, suppliers or family members. Next to the fact that others make an assessment, the person in question fills in his own score. In this way, a complete picture of the employees in question is obtained.

Application

360° feedback can be used to:
- develop employees
- make competences measurable
- improve customer orientation
- measure the effects of education/training
- obtain information for career development

360° feedback can be accomplished in a number of steps:
1 First, the management should stand by the instrument and the staff must be convinced that the instrument will only be used for their own development.
2 The second step is establishing the competences and their classification into the different roles within the enterprise. Everyone who participates in this 360° feedback will be assessed according to these competences. This should be absolutely clear.
3 The third step is to establish for each employee for what purpose the 360° feedback will be used. Is it for the development of the employees in general, is it to follow specific competences in their development or is it an aid to career development?
4 The fourth step is indicating the process steps used in the 360° feedback. The staff want to know where they stand and also have a right to this.
5 The fifth step is the actual performance of the assessments. The staff allow others to fill in their feedback within an established period. After the closing date, the results are shown to the staff and discussed individually.
6 The last step, depending on the purpose of the 360° feedback, is the repetition of the research within a certain period of time, to establish the development of the employees.

Multi-rating
Multi-rating (assessment by more than one person) has a greater degree of acceptance than assessment by a single rating (assessment by one person). The fact that the assessment is performed by several people and not just by the manager gives a better chance of acceptance.

Self-assessment

Besides the fact that several people participate in the assessment, the people in question will have to assess themselves.

Due to this, people are able to compare the picture they have of their own functioning against the opinions of others. Statistical research shows that people almost always assess themselves more positively than the assessors. This is because people like to draw a positive picture of themselves and tend to adjust their self-image to the wishes of the people in their environment. Here, it is true that the difference between self-assessment and the assessment of others is smaller with successful people than with people who are less successful. This means that self-assessment is characterised as hardly successful.

Digital

360° feedback can be excellently performed digitally because there are nowadays sufficient electronic aids available.

Result

The result of 360° feedback is insight into the functioning of employees in their current work situation. This information can then be used by employees, in consultation with the manager, to set up a personal development plan (PDP) and develop themselves in this manner.

Focus areas

The instrument is not suitable to completely replace assessment, since a corrective element is lacking. It must all the same be avoided that a relationship arises between the 360° feedback and the payment structure. The results depend on how long a person has worked in a certain position. In the event of a short period working in a position there is a risk that the model is filled in as the pattern of expectation that others have of the role. This does not always agree with the actual functioning. The objectivity of 360° feedback is highly dependent on those who fill in the assessments. Allowing only friendly colleagues to fill in the assessment gives a one-sided view.

Literature

- http://www.custominsight.com/360-degree-feedback/
- http://www.hr-survey.com/360Feedback.htm
- http://www.360degreefeedbackbestpractice.co.uk/

2
AAA Triangle

Author	P. Ghemawat
Year developed	2001
Also known as	–
Purpose	Internationalisation strategy

Model

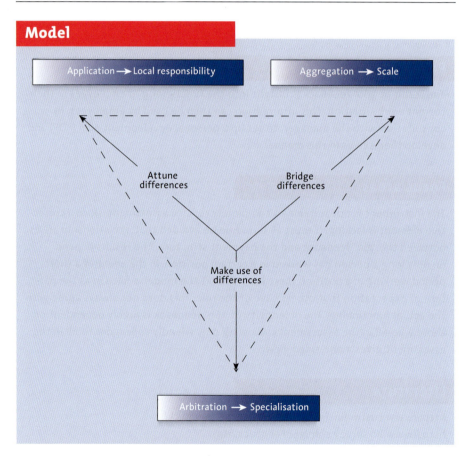

Application → Local responsibility

Aggregation → Scale

Attune differences

Bridge differences

Make use of differences

Arbitration → Specialisation

Background

On the basis of the great differences that arise between countries when doing international business, people can be inclined not to start up or expand international activities. Opting for the easy way out is a big temptation. This easy way consists in choosing the same approach for every country and responsibility is delegated to the country manager. This country manager must be able to take advantage of the local demand in the country concerned. However, in this way, control of the activities in these countries is given to someone else. With the aid of the AAA Triangle, these problems can be resolved.

There are sufficient strategies for setting up competitive strategies in these countries and bridging the differences between the countries. These strategies are divided into three categories:

- adaptation
- aggregation
- arbitration

Every enterprise will do something with each of the strategies. They will, however, have to choose which strategy is best for them to take as a starting point for international activities.

Application

In order to be able to make a choice from the three possible strategies, they are first described.

Adaptation
Adapting to the local demands of the markets in different countries seems the most logical solution. This is true. It is also a very expensive solution, however. Adapting products or services to local demands usually produces no extra functionality from which the extra costs can be regained. The management can set priorities for adaptation on the following five categories:

- Variation: variation of products, policy, positioning and so forth.
- Focus: limit variation by focusing on part of it, for example, products, services, number of countries, segments and so forth.
- Outsourcing: outsource activities to partners.
- Design: design flexible, adaptable products, make the product modular and so forth.
- Innovation: spread ideas to other countries, recombine elements of the business model of the home country and so forth.

There are thus many more strategies to choose from than just adapting the product or service to local demand.

Aggregation
Standardisation of the regional and international activities to create increases in scale. Due to this, products or services can be realised at lower unit cost. Moreover, in this way the differences between the different countries are bridged. There are six regional strategies:

- regional focus
- regional portfolio

- regional distribution points
- regional platforms
- regional mandates
- regional networks

A aggregation strategy is more than an extra regional head office and the addition of an extra layer of management.

Arbitration
Consciously opting to outsource part of the value chain in another country or region. Arbitration is searching for regions with a specialisation in workers instead of searching for increase in scale by means of standardisation. For example, production becomes cheaper by outsourcing it to China because wages there are lower.

It is tempting to try all three strategies at once. This is hardly possible, however. The three are in conflict with each other. Therefore, an 'A' will first have to be chosen and thereafter, a limited focus on another 'A'. Entrepreneurs can select the international strategy and set priorities with the aid of the following table, starting from the sector in which they work and the purposes of the enterprise.

	Adaptation	Aggregation	Arbitration
Competitive advantage Why internationalisation?	Achieving local relevance by a national focus on the use of a limited scale.	Achieving scale through international standardisation.	Achieving an international specialisation.
Configuration Where shall we begin?	Especially in other countries that have a resemblance to the home country, to limit the effects of the cultural, administrative, geographic and economic differences.		In countries that are different to discover the differences.
Coordination How must we accommodate the international activities in the organisation?	Per country, with attention paid to local presence.	Via sectors, regions or segments, with attention paid to horizontal relations for scale across the borders.	Via functions, with attention paid to vertical relationships, even across organisational boundaries.
Management For what extremes should we beware?	Extreme variety or complexity.	Too much standardisation.	Too specialised.
Obstructers of change For whom must we beware, internally?	Rigid country managers.	All powerful unit, regional or account managers.	Managers in key positions.
Corporate diplomacy How must we tackle corporate diplomacy?	Discuss points for attention, taking sensitivity into account, given the attention paid to developing a local presence.	Avoid homogenisation or hegemony.	Discuss the exploitation of suppliers, distribution channels and intermediaries who are most sensitive to political disturbances.
Corporate strategy What strategic handholds do we have?	Selection of scope: • variation • decentralisation • division • modularisation • flexibility • partnership • recombination • innovation.	Regions and other national divisions: • product or sector • position • platform • competence • sector of the customer.	• culture (home country effects) • government measures (levies, laws) • geographic differences (distance, climate) • economic (price differences, knowledge).

Result

The international strategy of the enterprise is structurally organised and elaborated. The enterprise will focus at least one 'A' and a second 'A' to a lesser extent. The resources and budgets are focused on this. This means the risks of failed internationalisation are lower. The enterprise is thus assisted in making the correct choice between standardisation of the product or service around the world or precisely adapting the product or service or adapting the product or service for every region to local market demands.

Focus areas

Organisations that wish to internationalise can make use of various models for support. Whatever model is followed, two aspects are important in all situations: Cultural differences. These perhaps sometimes seem small but nevertheless, they can constitute a significant barrier when doing business. See, for example, Cultural Dimensions, Hofstede.
Entry mode decision. This concerns the manner in which the enterprise starts up its activities abroad: carefully via export or an immediate large investment in production facilities. See Entry Mode Decision.

Literature

- http://www.ghemawat.org/

3
Activities schedule

Author	**Developed in practice**
Year developed	–
Also known as	–
Purpose	**Establishing the sequence of activities and their responsibilities in processes**

Model

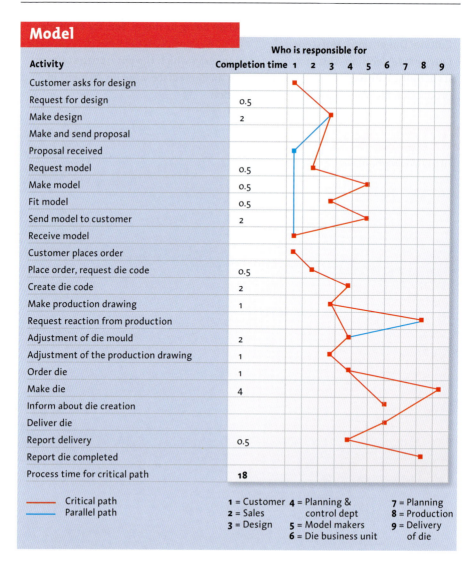

Who is responsible for

Activity	Completion time	1	2	3	4	5	6	7	8	9
Customer asks for design										
Request for design	0.5									
Make design	2									
Make and send proposal										
Proposal received										
Request model	0.5									
Make model	0.5									
Fit model	0.5									
Send model to customer	2									
Receive model										
Customer places order										
Place order, request die code	0.5									
Create die code	2									
Make production drawing	1									
Request reaction from production										
Adjustment of die mould	2									
Adjustment of the production drawing	1									
Order die	1									
Make die	4									
Inform about die creation										
Deliver die										
Report delivery	0.5									
Report die completed										
Process time for critical path	**18**									

—— Critical path
—— Parallel path

1 = Customer
2 = Sales
3 = Design
4 = Planning & control dept
5 = Model makers
6 = Die business unit
7 = Planning
8 = Production
9 = Delivery of die

Background

Any enterprise that wishes to achieve its objectives will do this on the basis of a number of successive processes. Enterprises for which the processes have not yet been described as a whole and those who have set up the different functions for every business unit, will be slowed down when they wish to switch to a process-oriented structure. The shared processes will have to be attuned to ensure that the staff perform the correct activities and that no gaps or double activities arise. By setting up an Activities Schedule it becomes clear who is responsible for which activity in a process.

Application

To come to the correct steps in a process, this process must be completely written out. The example represents the realisation of the design for a new cardboard box, from the request by the customer up to and including the moment that production can be commenced. The design process for a new cardboard box comprises the following activities:

1 *Establish and describe the activities*
This is shown on the vertical axis of the model. These activities concern all actions that are necessary to get from the first request of a customer to the moment that everything is ready for the final production run for the product.

2 *Placing the activities in order of execution*
Activities that can be performed simultaneously, are placed together. These are called parallel activities. The other activities, which cannot be placed in parallel, constitute the critical path of the process. This is the shortest possible completion time for this process on the basis of the activities that must be performed.

3 *Establish who is responsible for each activity*
This is the horizontal axis of the matrix. This concerns not only internal business units or people, but also the outsourced activities. After all, these also determine the lead time. In this way, someone can always be addressed if activities are not carried out in accordance with the agreements.

4 *Indicate lead time*
The lead time concerns the number of days or hours from the start to the moment the activity is completed. The hours and days of the successive activities are totalled. This is the shortest possible time in which this process can be carried out and is called the critical path.

Result

The Activities schedule provides the enterprise with the possibility to better attune the business processes to each other and so shorten the lead time. Furthermore, the enterprise obtains insight into the responsibilities for each activity in a process. When deviations arise, the correct staff can consequently be addressed, which should lead to improvements.

Focus areas

With large and complex processes, it is necessary to divide them into in subprocesses to keep sufficient oversight.
Enterprises that are radically changing their products or methods of production will have to spend extra time keeping these Activities schedules up-to-date.

Literature

None.

4

Activity Based Costing

Authors	Cooper and Kaplan
Year developed	1988
Also known as	ABC, Activity Based Management
Purpose	Assigning costs to activities that incur costs

Model

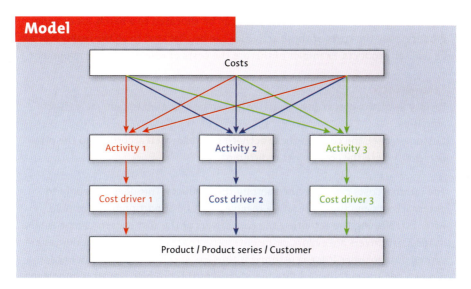

Background

In the calculation of the cost price, overhead costs are often allocated to the products purchased via an apportionment formula. In this way, products that are sold a lot are disproportionately expensive, while it is precisely these products that ensure the efficient use of the production facilities. After all, with large volumes the cost per item goes down. In contrast with this, the products that take a disproportionate amount of effort and incur overheads are too cheap. The model for ABC analysis (Activity Based Costing) deals with this problem because the actual costs are allocated to the products. This is done by establishing what actual activities and resources contribute towards the realisation of the product. After all, the activities and resources needed to make the product incur the costs and not the products themselves. The different products also require different activities and resources for production. Therefore, it is also reasonable to allocate the corresponding costs to that product.

A primary condition for making effective use of ABC is listing the processes and activities of the enterprise.

It must also be known where these costs can be allocated, the cost objects. Cost objects are items (product, product series, customer, business unit, person, means of transport) for which a separate cost determination is required. In order to calculate the costs in the correct manner, the activities must be classified. For example, when a machine has to be re-tooled for a new series, the costs of re-tooling should be reckoned over all the products in the series.

Costs can be divided into:

Internal costs
- Unit level: the costs of these activities can be allocated per product.
- Batch level: the costs of these activities can be allocated to a batch, lot or series.
- Product level: the costs of these activities can be allocated to all the realised or to be realised products. Examples of this are the costs of research and development.

External costs
- Facility level: the costs of these activities can be allocated to general research activities.
- Customer level: the costs of these activities are allocated according to the product level, where the cost object is different.

The internal costs can be divided among the products. This does not apply to external costs and these therefore receive a certain apportionment formula. After establishing the activities, the cost drivers or the cost causers can be established. Cost drivers are events in the enterprise that ensure that the activities are carried out. An order from a customer is thus a cost driver. The customer orders a product and the enterprise subsequently makes this product. Now it is important to know how many customer orders there are in total, to establish the total cost.

Assessment of the costs is performed as follows:
- Multiply the costs by the cost drivers (for example, number of orders times the cost of one order).
- The results of the previous step are allocated to the cost objects.
  Two types of costs are excluded from ABC because otherwise, a misleading picture can arise. These are the costs of unused capacity or overcapacity and the costs of general research. After all, these costs cannot be linked to one of the existing cost objects. A separate cost object has to be defined for this.

To apply ABC correctly, the following steps must be carried out:
1. Determine the cost objects.
2. Determine the processes of the enterprise with the corresponding activities.
3. Determine the resources or means of production, such as machines, people, computers and buildings, which can be partly or wholly linked with an activity.

4 Determine the costs of the resources.
5 Determine the cost drivers.
6 Calculate the costs of the activities.
7 Calculate the total costs per cost object.

An extra important contribution with the aid of ABC can above all be obtained by implementing ABC in companies that satisfy a specific situation, namely:

- companies that have large overheads
- companies that arbitrarily allocate costs to the products with an apportionment formula
- companies where the overhead costs are not proportional to the use of resources by products
- companies in a highly competitive market
- companies with a large variety of products and production processes with large and small series
- companies with many different sales activities for many distribution channels and customers

Result

The result of ABC is a finely-meshed allocation of costs to cost objects, such that hidden costs become visible and insight is obtained into the drivers of overhead costs. Insight is obtained into the actual costs, so that a revised pricing policy can be implemented, with which the enterprise's competitive position can be improved.

Focus areas

With the reallocation of costs via ABC, it becomes clear at what cost products are made. It can occur that after reallocation some products become significantly more expensive and it is not possible to pass the higher price on to customers. The amount of detail for cost drivers and cost objects can lead to a too complex system. A good supporting information system can resolve this problem.
If it turns out that a product is too expensive on the basis of the ABC, due to special customer specifications or a small series, it cannot immediately be supposed that this product should therefore be phased out. This is particularly the case when these products are sold along with other products to the same customer. For this reason, the total package of this customer should be reviewed.

Literature

- Kaplan R., Anderson, S. (2007). *Time-Driven Activity-Based Costing*. Harvest Books.
- http://www.accountingcoach.com/
- http://hbswk.hbs.edu/item/4587.html

General management

Strategy

Marketing

Sales

Purchasing

Project & Planning

Production

Quality

Logistics & Distribution

Information management

Financial

HRM & HTM

Internationalisation

5

Balanced Scorecard

Authors	**Kaplan and Norton**
Year developed	**1996**
Also known as	**Business Balanced Scorecard, BSC, BBSC**
Purpose	**Development of organisational strategy and focusing activities on it**

Model

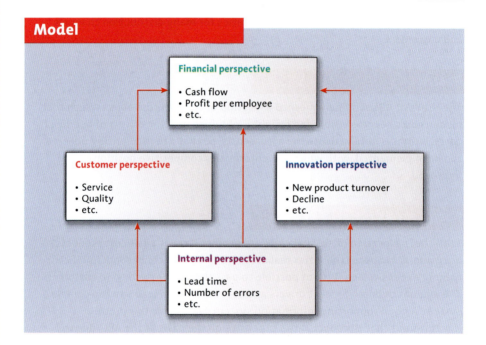

Background

Due to the many changes in the environment of the enterprise, for example, with customers, competitors, suppliers and the authorities, an enterprise must continuously check whether the necessary activities are being performed for the execution of its strategy. Formerly, the book value of an enterprise was based on its financial position. Nowadays, there are many more aspects on which an enterprise is valued. For example, their relationship with their customers, well-trained and motivated personnel, innovation in products and services, modern information technology and properly implemented processes that are attuned to each other. Due to this, it is becoming increasingly difficult to establish how the enterprise is actually doing on the basis of financial figures alone. The financial figures are after all derived from the activities of the enterprise and are thus by definition behindhand. With the aid of the Balanced Scorecard, the results of the enterprise can be monitored from several angles.

Application

The Balanced Scorecard (BSC) comprises four perspectives: customer, internal organisation, innovation and financial. Together, these perspectives provide a clear picture of the long-term vision of the enterprise. The BSC is a top-down method with which the goals and objectives of the enterprise can be determined from the vision and mission. For each perspective, the key factors that contribute towards the achievement of the mission and vision of the enterprise are established. These are called the critical success factors of the enterprise and they are made measurable with the aid of performance indicators.
Setting up the BSC proceeds according to the following steps:

1 *The management forms a mission and vision*
An enterprise can only nominate success factors when there is a vision and a mission. In this vision and mission, it must be established which customers will be approached with which instruments and for what purpose. This concerns the core values and right to exist of the enterprise, which are translated into measurable factors.

2 *Establishing the success factors*
The success factors are established by the management of the enterprise. This occurs on the basis of the vision and mission. For each of the four perspectives, the managers will have to ask the question: when do we think we will be successful? The answers to this question are the potential critical success factors.

3 *Arrangement of the BSC*
The potential critical success factors are discussed and evaluated by the management team. Factors selected on the basis of consensus form the basis for the critical success factors.

4 *Establishing performance indicators*
The established critical success factors are made measurable in order to establish whether the objectives are actually being achieved by the strategy. To make a critical success factor measurable, use is made of several performance indicators. For example:

> An enterprise has the critical success factor: customer satisfaction. This is represented on a scale from one to ten and the objective is to score an eight. First, it is established what the components of customer satisfaction are. This could be, for example, the number of times the telephone rings before someone answers and the number of minutes of waiting time before the right person comes on the line. Establishing these components takes place through research among the customers. These two components are measurable with regard to a norm. If they fulfil the norm, then the score is

eight on a ten-point scale. If they score better or worse, then the score becomes correspondingly lower or higher. Adding together and dividing by two produces the score for customer satisfaction.

Success factor	Performance indicator	Grade	Target value	Masured value	Result
Customer satisfaction		Figure	8		6
	Answering phone	Number	< 3	4	5
	Waiting at counter	Minutes		6	4
	Referred on	Number	<= 3	2	8
			2		

The four perspectives of the BSC are therefore developed until a few critical success factors have been determined for each perspective. It is advisable to select no more than three or four success factors per perspective.

Result

With the aid of the BSC, the enterprise can orient on the goals and objectives that are derived from the strategy. Because these have been made measurable, the implementation of the strategy can be properly monitored for the enterprise and timely measures can be taken.

Focus areas

Setting up the first version of the BSC is very time-consuming. Establishing the norms is a difficult activity. Make sure with the first measurements that the norms are correct and adjust them if necessary.
The risk exists that signals not included on the Balanced Scorecard will be ignored because they are not measured and guided.

Literature

- http://www.balancedscorecard.org
- http://www.scorecardsupport.com/

6

BART

Author	M. Mulders
Year developed	2005
Also known as	Budget Activities Resources & Time
Purpose	Drafting the planning for an implementation plan

Model

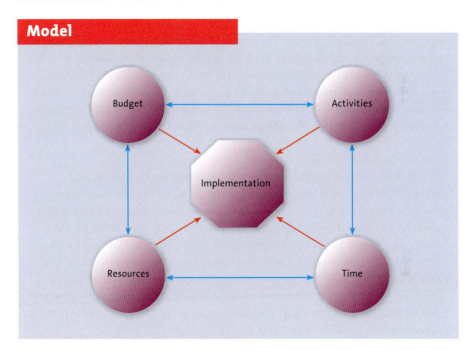

Background

Many assignments are drafted by companies to do research into new markets, new products, customer satisfaction, etc. These assignments are executed by internal staff or by outside parties if the enterprise has too little capacity. Three questions are posed by the client, in many cases the management of the enterprise:

a What will I get?
b When will I get it?
c How much will it bring in?

The BART model helps to bring the answers to these questions to light and implement them in a structured fashion.

BART stands for Budget, Activities, Resources and Time. These are the components that determine the answers to the client's questions. These components immediately provide a plan to implement the given solution in a structured fashion. The following steps are executed:

1 Drafting the budget

The budget comprises two different components. One component concerns the costs of the project. These costs are drafted on the basis of known and lesser known facts. After all, the project has not yet been carried out and nobody can see into the future. As the drafter of the project does more cost calculations, the costs will come closer to reality than if someone less experienced does this. The counterpart of the costs side is the realisable value side. The client will be less interested if the project costs more than it delivers, unless investment has to take place for strategic reasons. The cost side concerns all the costs incurred for the project. These costs will have to be calculated and estimated one by one. In general, this is not a big problem. More difficult is the realisable value side. It is more difficult to estimate what income a project will generate because it often concerns the development of the market. An estimate will still have to be made, however, if the third question is to be answered (see Costs-Benefit analysis).

2 Establishing the activities

The activities concern the tasks that must be carried out by internal and external staff to achieve the objectives of the project. They will have to be established one by one. The activities are often mutually related and therefore cannot be carried out randomly. Some activities can only start when another activity has been finished. To perform the activities, hours are worked by internal or external staff. For both there is an hourly rate. This is important for the calculation of the costs. As soon as there are several activities carried out by several people and various relationships arise among them, it is usually wise to make a plan. Using a Gantt Chart for example, an overview is obtained into the sequence of the activities (see Gantt Chart).

The products are realised due to the activities carried out in the project. An answer is thereby given to the first question of the client: What do I get? These products are related to the costs involved in the project. If the costs of adapting the product are very high and the adaptation itself is only small, the client will not easily accept the costs with respect to what will be delivered, even apart from what it ultimately delivers.

3 Establishing the resources

For each activity it is established what and how much resources are needed. The resources are not only the staff who carry out the activities, but often also workplaces, equipment, acquisition of software licenses, rental of cars and office sundries. These resources are included in the project planning, to establish when the resources are needed. This can often be done via the same planning package that puts the activities in a Gantt Chart. The costs of the resources are added to the total costs.

4 Establishing net time and lead time
The aspect of time gives an answer to the question 'When can I calculate whether the project will deliver a profit from the efforts that have been made?' This is the date of completion (When do I get it?) plus the time necessary to recover the costs. Two aspects of time should be taken into account here. The first aspect is the net time and the second aspect is the lead time. The net time is the number of hours needed by the staff to finish the project. The lead time is the calendar time that elapses between the start of the project and the completion of the last component (see Lead time/net time).

Result

The result of this model provides the enterprise with a structured and calculated planning to implement the solution to a problem.

Focus areas

The planning is a plan and an estimation of the expectations in the future. With every plan it is possible to deviate from the planning due to unforeseen circumstances. The enterprise must be flexible enough to accept changes to the plan. At the same time, limits must be set on the number and level of changes to the plan. The model does not provide for this. Consideration by the management of the enterprise is necessary for this.

Literature

None.

7

BCG Matrix

Author	**Boston Consulting Group**
Year developed	**1970**
Also known as	**Portfolio diagram, BCG Analysis, Growth Share Matrix**
Objective	**Portfolio analysis**

Model

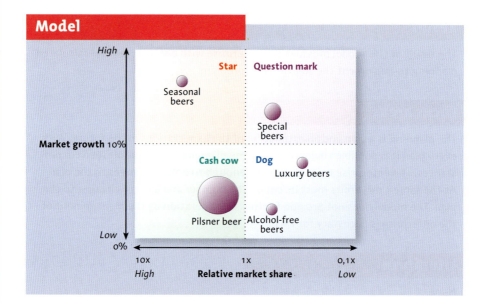

Background

Almost all enterprises offer several products or services on the market because one product or service poses a risk to continuity. If there is no more demand for that product, the company goes bankrupt. It is therefore important to have the products and/or services properly balanced in terms of the contribution of a product to the enterprise. A product could be in the introductory phase and require a great deal of investment, while another product or service lasts longer and as yet generates only limited profits. A balanced portfolio with respect to the products and services is then crucial for the enterprise.

The model comprises quadrants in which the products and services are placed, on the basis of market share and market growth. The quadrants stand for:

- *Star*

  These are products with a relatively high market share in a growing market. The potential of these products is great with respect to their contribution to the profits of the enterprise. Investment in these products and services is almost self-evident, because these are the products and/or services that will in the future make up a significant part of the product portfolio.

- *Cash cow*

  These are products with a high market share that make a good contribution to the profits. The market is no longer growing, however, and investment in these products and services is not wise, unless it concerns retention of position and profitability.

- *Question mark*

  These are products with a small market share in a rapidly growing market. The potential of these products and services can be great, but is very uncertain. Before there is any investment in these products, more information will have to become available to establish whether investment would be justified.

- *Dog*

  These products and services are at the end of their lifecycle and it is not wise to invest in them. If these products and services ultimately start to make a loss, they should be disposed of or disinvested (taken off the market).

The axes of the model comprise two aspects: *relative market share* and *market growth*.

The relative market share is the ratio of the market share of the largest competitor. If a competitor has a market share of 30% and the enterprise 10%, then the relative market share of 10/30 is 0.3. Only if the enterprise is the market leader could the relative market be more than 1. The larger the market share, the better the enterprise can profit from scale and experience.

The market growth of a product is measured with the total growth of the market. Rapidly growing markets give a better competitive position and improved long-term prospects. If the market growth is greater than 10%, there is high market growth. This can moreover differ somewhat per sector.

A matrix is thus formed in which the products are depicted as circles. The size of a circle shows the relative turnover of this product with respect to the turnover of all products.

Implications of using the matrix

- The extra turnover from the Cash cows should be used for selected Question marks and Stars. The objective is to consolidate the Stars in their current position and convert the Question marks into Stars, to make the portfolio more interesting.

- The Question marks with the weakest or most uncertain turnover must be disinvested in order to deploy the resources elsewhere.
- If there are too few Cash cows, Stars or Question marks in an enterprise, it is advisable to supplement them by means of acquisitions, to obtain a more balanced portfolio, for example. Stars and Question marks ensure healthy long-term growth and profits. The Cash cows ensure sufficient resources to be able to invest in Stars and Question marks.
- If the product is a Dog, the enterprise must get rid of it.
Development in the BCG matrix can lead to further success or to radical failures.

Success

The path of success runs from the Question mark to the Star. A product in the Question mark quadrant is developing positively in the market, due to which market share will increase. At a certain time, it will exceed the limit of 1.0 of relative market share, continue to follow market growth in the same way, namely above 10%, and end up in the Star quadrant. This can be attained due to the fact that the cash flow from the Cash cows is invested in the various Stars. Subsequently, the enterprise can also use the budget that becomes available from the Cash cows to retain its relative market share, while market growth becomes less and ends up under 10%. In this position, the product can generate a great deal of cash flow to again invest in the Question marks and Stars. The enterprise now has the challenge of further developing the products that are Cash cows by means of adaptation, so that they can again become stars. These adjustments can be related to a new design or improved or added functionality.

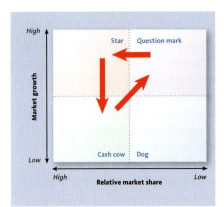
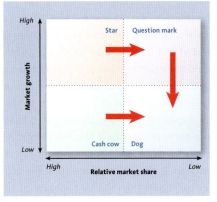

Success — Failure

Failure

The development of products can also unfortunately lead to failure. A Question mark of which the market share does not increase, should be closed down. This product can never be a Cash cow and will cost more money than it ultimately makes. A product that has developed from a Question mark into a Star but has falling market share, will also never become a Cash cow. Here too, it is advisable to get rid of the product.

Lastly, a situation can arise where no new adaptations for a product can be done, ultimately growth declines and market share becomes less than 1.0. The product then comes in the category of Dog. The enterprise does not invest in the product anymore. As long as profit is still being made on the product, it will remain in the range. But when this also declines, the product is taken out of circulation.

Result

The result is an overview of the products and services on the basis of which the priorities of the products and/or services can be set. Furthermore, this makes it possible for the enterprise to allocate budgets to where they can be of most use for the future growth and profitability of the enterprise.

Focus areas

Although the model can be very concretely filled in, it must not be blindly followed. If there are relationships in the sector that make it uninteresting to invest in this area, this should be taken properly into account.

Furthermore, units like market share and market growth are limiting. A product that is not put on the market has by definition a low market share and low growth. This product is then characterised as a Dog, while it should actually be characterised as a Question mark.

In a saturated market a demand for replacement can arise where a good competitive position is possible while market growth is almost zero. With sophisticated marketing strategies, it is then as yet possible to achieve a good turnover for a product-market combination (PMC).

Literature

- http://bcgmatrix.org/

8

Belbin Team Roles

Author	M. Belbin
Year developed	1993
Also known as	Belbin Self-Perception Inventory, Belbin types
Objective	Working in teams successfully

Model

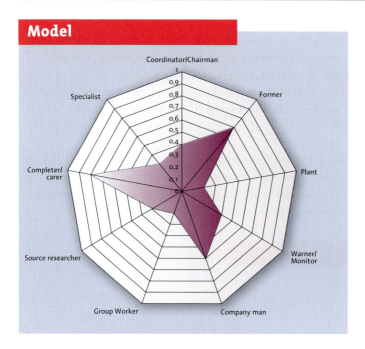

Background

Belbin developed a model in which success and failure factors are established in relation to the personalities of the people who have to work in a team. With this model – which comprises nine team roles – insight is obtained into the team dynamics and mutual interplay among team members. Every team member exhibits a certain behaviour. The foundations for this behaviour lie in, for example: personality, mental skills, current values and motivation, learning roles and experiences. The team roles constitutes the recognition that every team member has strong and less strong sides in his/her own role. People that form a team are complementary to each other.

Application

Belbin distinguishes nine team roles.

Type (of team role)	Abbreviation	Typical characteristics	Positive qualities	Admissible weaknesses
Chairman	VZ	calm, controlled, lots of self-confidence	assesses everyone who can contribute without prejudice on their merits and acts accordingly, very goal-oriented	not a shiner in intellect or creative aptitude
Former	VM	lots of energy, extravert, dynamic	driven and motivated to do something about inertia and ineffectiveness	impatient, quickly irritated, tendency towards brusqueness
Plant	PL	individualistic, serious, unorthodox	geniality, imagination, intellect, knowledge	in an ivory tower and tends to disregard practical details or protocols
Monitor	MO	sober, little emotion, cautious	good judgement, skilled, business-like, critical	lacks inspiration and the ability to inspire others
Company man	BM	conservative, dutiful, predictable	organisational talent, common sense, practical, hard worker, self-discipline	lack of flexibility, not open to ideas that have not proved their worth
Group worker	GW	socially-oriented, mild and sensitive	responds positively to people and situations and promotes team spirit	indecisive at times of crisis
Source researcher	BO	extrovert, enthusiastic curious, communicative	good at making social contacts and exploring new developments; responds well to challenges	quickly loses interest after the first enthusiasm is over
Carer	ZD	accurate, orderly, conscientious, tense	can finish things well, perfectionist	has the tendency to worry too much about small things, unable to let go
Specialist	SP	focused only on professional area	a great deal of professional knowledge	not interested in others

Every person can perform at least two roles without problems. There are always at least two roles that do not match anyone, however.

Someone's profile can be established with the aid of standard questionnaires.

It is extremely important in team formation to first establish which roles are needed. Almost everyone has two preferred roles in which he or she automatically functions. It must be acknowledged that some roles are contradictory and, due to this, conflicts may arise. If an assignment should require this combination of roles, an extra role will have to be added to keep possible conflicts manageable. In this way, self-guided teams are formed that can carry out projects on the basis of the assignment formulation.

Result

Teams that are in balance as far as the personality characteristics necessary to carry out the project successfully are concerned. The management thereby has an instrument to carry out projects with less supervision and risk.

Focus areas

The model does not take into account the hierarchical relationships that may exist between the team members. This often leads to a situation in which subordinates are less inclined to demonstrate their initiative and they wait and see what the manager does.
The model likewise ignores the possible chemistry between the various players. If people do not like each other, it makes no sense to put them in a team.
The starting point of the model is that the staff have sufficient expertise, training and experience with regard to the subject of the project. This does not always turn out to be true.
The questionnaires make use of mandatory choices even if people do not agree with a single proposition. Due to this, people can easily be seen as an extreme type. Through the use of scoring with ten sentences and the combination of team roles, this extreme is cancelled out.

Literature

- Belbin, M. (1997). *Changing the way we work*. Butterworth-Heinemann.
- www.belbin.com
- http://www.belbin.info

9
Benchmarking

Author	Hollensen
Year developed	1998
Also known as	Competitive Benchmarking
Objective	Creating a better performance with the competition's customers

Model

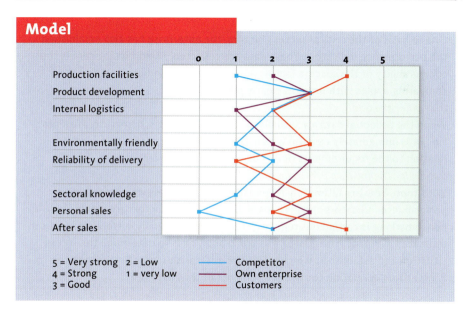

5 = Very strong   2 = Low
4 = Strong   1 = very low
3 = Good

Competitor
Own enterprise
Customers

Background

Benchmarks are used to mutually compare enterprises. In benchmarking, the enterprise is not only compared with the competition, but also with the needs of the customers. This makes it possible to establish what the core competences of the enterprise are, what critical success factors the enterprise has and where the enterprise is behind compared to the competition and does not fulfil the customers' needs. The future is also reviewed with benchmarking, so that the enterprise can focus in a more goal-oriented fashion.

General management
Strategy
Marketing
Sales
Purchasing
Project & Planning
Production
Quality
Logistics & Distribution
Information management
Financial
HRM & HTM
Internationalisation

Application

Benchmarking comprises the following steps:

1 *Determine what benchmarking will be applied to*

The enterprise comprises a quantity of processes, from sales, via planning and production, to purchasing. First of all, the enterprise must establish to which process(es) benchmarking will be applied. When this has been established, the critical success factors for comparison are established. This involves the critical success factors of the selected processes.

2 *Determine the benchmark partners*

At least three parties are included in the benchmark: the enterprise itself, the 'best-in-class' competitor and the customer concerned. It is extremely difficult to find the 'best-in-class' competitor because different success factors have to be compared.

3 *Determine the method of collecting data and collect it*

On the basis of the critical success factors, the enterprise has also established the performance indicators. These data are collected. The difficulty here is the comparability of the success factors and performance indicators. The risk of comparing apples with oranges clearly plays a role here.

4 *Determine the gap*

When the collected data are visualised according to the schematic representation, it is immediately clear on which aspects the enterprise scores less well in relation to the requirements of its customers and the competition.

5 *Determine the future performance levels*

With those who are ultimately responsible for the processes involved, new performance indicators and perhaps also new success factors are established. If benchmarking is carried out regularly, for example annually, a trend analysis can ultimately be made. The goal of this trend analysis is to determine the future situation and establish at which times the enterprise scores better than the competitors in relation to the requirements of the customers.

6 *Make the benchmarking findings known and ensure they are accepted*

The findings will have to be supported by all the staff in the enterprise. The managers who participate in the project must involve the staff in the developments resulting from the project.

7 *Draft an action plan*

To achieve any new success factors and performance indicators, action plans are drafted that will be carried out under the responsibility of the process owners.

8 *Implementation*

In the last step, implementation is addressed. This involves: implementing the action plans, measuring the results and the annual performance of the benchmarking.

Result

Insight into the core competences of the enterprise, the critical success factors and the points on which the enterprise is behind compared to the competition and does not fulfil the requirements of the customers. This insight can encourage the enterprise to lower costs, increase the effectiveness of the enterprise and better fulfil the requirements of the customers. Due to this, turnover and profits can increase.

Focus areas

One of the most difficult aspects in such comparisons is the comparative value of the selected criteria. If the data on enterprises do not correspond, a situation will arise in which apples and oranges are being compared to each other. Partners that participate in the benchmarking must therefore fulfil the following criteria:
- financially comparable
- comparable size
- comparable industry
- comparable structures
- comparable market

Many businesses that have carried out benchmarking stop after the comparison and thus leave the possibilities to improve their position in the market unused.

Literature

- http://www.hutchins.co.uk/Ar_Bench.aspx
- http://www.answers.com/topic/benchmarking

10

Blue Ocean Strategy

Authors	W. Chan Kim and M. Mauborgne
Year developed	2005
Also known as	The Blue Ocean, reconstructionist view
Objective	Finding a creative strategy for new, competition-free markets

Model

Red Ocean Strategy	Blue Ocean Strategy
Competing on the existing market	Create markets without competition
Defeat the competition	Make the competition irrelevant
Exploiting an existing need	Create and capture new demand
Market value versus cost choice	Break with the value versus costs choice
Use all resources for differentiation OR low costs	Use all resources for differentiation AND low costs

Background

Businesses are always confronted with competition in the market. A company then has the choice of taking on the competition or opting for other products/ services and/or other markets. If the company takes on the competition, we speak of a 'red ocean', which is equal to heavy competition. The ocean is coloured red from the 'bloodshed' between the competitors. The red ocean is characterised by an existing and known market where the boundaries and competition are accepted. The counterpart to this is the 'blue ocean', which represents a strategy where a company operates better than the competitor and thus avoids the competition. The blue ocean has clear, sparkling, blue water that is full of fish to be caught. The blue ocean is characterised by a market where the competitor no longer matters and where a new need is created and grasped. This creation of new markets is not yet affected by competition.

General management
Strategy
Marketing
Sales
Purchasing
Project & Planning
Production
Quality
Logistics & Distribution
Information management
Financial
HRM & HTM
Internatio-nalisation

Application

The strategy of the blue ocean is to arrive at value innovation in which the customers receive the highest customer value at the lowest cost. The application of the blue-ocean strategy consists in six principles, of which four are guiding and two are executive.

The four guiding principles

For the formulation of a successful 'blue-ocean strategy', there are four guiding principles. The first principle limits the search risk for new markets. The second sets up the strategic planning, including risk planning. The third focuses on making the market as large as possible and limiting risks of scale. The fourth principle focuses on the business model, paying attention to the business model risk.

1 *Redefining market boundaries*

The first of the four guiding principles is redefining the market by breaking through the existing boundaries and looking for possibilities. A structure for this is the 'six paths framework', six approaches to redefining market boundaries:

- *Looking for alternative sectors*: looking for alternative sectors goes further than looking for substitutes. Substitutes have the same function or customer value. Alternatives are products or services with a different form but the same objective. For example, a restaurant and a cinema. They have completely different functions but fulfil the same objective for the customer, namely an evening's entertainment.

- *Looking at businesses in other strategic groups in the sector*: businesses in the same sector but in another group are usually not each other's competitors. For example, extremely luxury cars and small, cheap cars. By offering a luxury car for a low price, a new market is created.

- *Looking at the role of the buyers*: if you look at the business column, there are several players with an interest in a certain product or service. If we look further to the client's customer, other needs can arise than just those of the direct client. Due to this, new markets can be discovered. For example, the insulin syringe that is always sold to doctors with needles and ampoules. By looking at the users, a new need arose: an insulin syringe without needles and ampoules with automatic dosing.

- *Looking at a complementary product and service range*: companies often focus only on the product or service they provide. For example, a cup of coffee. Enjoyed in a restaurant or café this is just a drink of coffee. Enjoyed in Starbucks, it is a whole experience. By focusing more on the wider needs of the purchasers, more products and/or services can be offered.

- *Reconsideration of the functional/emotional orientation in the sector*: companies focus on the functional or emotional aspects or a combination of the two. Usually, these aspects were once established on the basis of customer needs and built up further in the course of time. On the one hand, there are customers who more and more fulfil the expected pattern of businesses and on the other, there are businesses that more and more take the customer's needs into account. This creates a spiral: the functional businesses become more functional and the emotional businesses more emotional, resulting in an unsuitable product or service for too high a price.

- *Looking at a different time*: many companies develop step-by-step on the basis of customer needs. In this way, they miss the trends that arise in the world; trends in different areas, such as technology, sustainability and the environment. By better following the trends and trying to establish what developments these trends cause in the market, new markets can be tapped in a timely fashion.

2 Looking at the broad perspective

This strategy is not based on figures. Drawing a strategy picture leads to better creativity from the staff in the company. This strategy comprises the following steps:

- *Visual awareness*: every employee must be aware of the strategy and has to realise that the current strategy is probably not the correct one. It will have to be established on which points the strategy has to be adapted.
- *Visual investigation*: this step embraces researching what the customers are up to, not only customers, but also non-customers. It is important for this that a broad enough view is taken. For example, among the cinema-goers there are many young parents who need a babysitter. By offering this on the spot, a larger target group is created.
- *Visual strategy presentation*: the new strategy is presented on the basis of 'the four actions framework': scrubbing, strengthening, weakening and creating. This grid indicates which aspects of the strategy will change.
- *Visual communication*: the new strategy is explained to all levels in the company on the basis of a picture that is as simple as possible. The management explains the strategy to their subordinates, who do the same thing in turn.

3 Reaching further than the existing demand

Reaching further than the existing demand goes into enlarging the market. In order to always be distinctive from the competitors, there is often further segmentation. In this way, there can be a better response to specific customer needs. But many small target markets arise, which are too expensive to be approached separately. To enlarge markets on the other hand, companies can better focus on the correspondence between what customers and non-customers appreciate. The non-customers are divided into three groups:

- *The minimum customers*: these are customers who make minimal use of the range and will soon not be customers any longer.
- *The non-customers who refuse to become customers*: these customers will not become clients because the range is unacceptable or too expensive.
- *The non-studied customers*: these are customers on which the company is absolutely not oriented because it is presumed that these customers will not purchase any products or services.

For each group of non-customers, a strategy can be devised to make them into customers.

4 Build up the strategy in the correct order
Now that the blue ocean has received sufficient form, it is important to build a robust business model to subsequently realise sufficient profit from the company model. Four aspects are important for this:

- *Customer value*: what added value does the product or service provide for the customers? This is the most important question. If this question cannot be answered, the idea can go into the icebox or there has to be a great deal more discussion to find added value for the customer.
- *Price*: against customer value is a price. The price must be cost-covering but also affordable for customers.
- *Costs*: with the costs aspect one cannot assume cost price plus the margin, but one should assume cost price less the margin, the target cost price. This is an important starting point for keeping the costs of one's own organisation as low as possible.
- *Adoption*: if the blue ocean is to be successful, this strategy will have to be adopted by three important groups: the employees, the partners and the public.

Executive principles
The two executive principles concern apportionment leadership and a fair process. Apportionment leadership gives the manager a handle with which to implement the change in the organisation. With the fair process, implementation is integrated into the strategy to motivate everyone in the organisation to follow the strategy.

5 Apportionment leadership
In order to implement changes, companies have to clear four hurdles. The first is making it clear that change is necessary, the cognitive hurdle. The second hurdle is formed by the limited resources within the company. The third hurdle is the motivation of the staff. And the last hurdle is political in nature.

6 Fair process
With changes in a company, all the staff must be involved in the process of change because otherwise, opposition can be expected from the staff. When the process is clear to and accepted by everyone, the outcome of the process will also be accepted. To accomplish this, three principles are important: involvement, explanation and clarity.

Result

The company achieves a value innovation by means of the blue ocean strategy. This value innovation is striving for differentiation and cost savings. The company distinguishes itself from its competitors in this way. It can enter different and new markets from which turnover and profits can be achieved.

Focus areas

A good blue ocean can only be successful when a thorough analysis of the customers has taken place. This means research not only into customers, but also non-customers and even customers who in the first instance would not be thought at all suitable for the current offer that the company is bringing onto the market. Here too, it is clearly about the perceptions of the customers and not how all competitors approach the market. After a thorough analysis of the market, the company can indicate what the needs of the customers are. Often, the company can even do this better than the customers themselves. This is a crucial condition to achieving a blue ocean and properly inputting the parameters in the 'four actions framework'.

Literature

- Chan Kim, W., Mauborgne R. (2005). *Blue Ocean Strategy*. Harvard Business School Press.
- http://www.blueoceanstrategy.com/

11

Brainstorm

Author	Alex Osborn
Year developed	1938
Also known as	–
Objective	Generating and developing ideas

Model

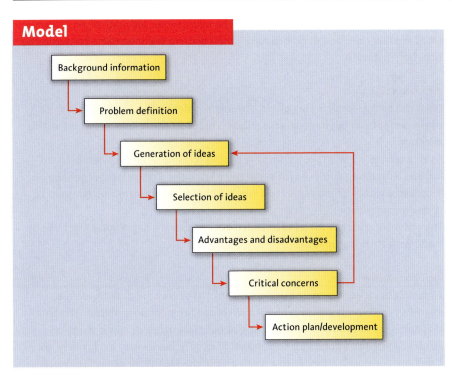

Background

Indefinable concepts such as quality and user-friendliness are difficult to elaborate and concretise. The resolution of problems in group context often leads to long meetings with exclusively contradictory standpoints or interminable discussions. By using the brainstorm model, enterprises can tackle these problems in a structural and controlled manner and develop them into a step-by-step plan with which everyone can agree.

Application

The brainstorm consists in a seven-step approach that leads to a concrete, feasible plan. To allow the brainstorm to proceed properly, a facilitator is appointed. This person is responsible for the process and may not interfere with the session substantively.

The seven steps of the brainstorm are:

1 Background information

In this phase, every participant receives the background information against which the problem occurs. This is important for a proper understanding of the problem. This information consists in the events of the previous period. The events that have led to the current situation are presented in chronological order. Subsequently, the symptoms are presented so that everyone knows to what situations, problems or challenges the events have led. Last of all, it is indicated what actions and decisions have taken place in the meantime to tackle the situation in question.

2 Problem definition

From the background, in this phase a problem is defined on the basis of which those present can begin generating ideas. This problem definition begins with a question.

As an example we will take a company that as a result of intense competition has had a declining turnover for a number of months. The question could be: 'How can we as a company create a better competitive position with regard to the new competitor?'

The school of thought for all the participants is now the same and a start can be made with thinking up ideas.

3 Idea generation

To generate ideas, it is extremely important that everyone puts forward as many as possible suggestions to obtain a broad range of possibilities. The participants may not enter into discussion about the quality or applicability of an idea. This will be done at a later stage. The participants may exclusively ask questions for clarification. With a small group, the facilitator can write the ideas down. If the group is larger than ten people, it should have a different method for collecting the ideas. For example, by writing all the ideas on Post-it memos and handing them in.

Everyone may write down as many ideas as they can think of, where each idea is written on a separate Post-it memo.

4 Idea selection

When no more new ideas are being thought up, the thing is to select the best idea. First of all, all the ideas relating to the same topic are grouped together. Each collection of ideas receives its own name. Subsequently, the categories of ideas are prioritised. From the category of ideas with the highest priority, a number of ideas is selected that can be developed in the time available.

5 Advantages and disadvantages

For each category of ideas, the advantages and disadvantages are detailed. Here too, there may be no substantive discussions. However, as many as possible advantages and disadvantages are detailed, so that proper consideration can be given to them. On the basis of this activity, priorities can be reviewed and possibly adjusted. This occurs exclusively on the basis of the advantages that each idea brings with it. The disadvantages are reviewed in the following step.

6 Working on critical concerns

Now the advantages and disadvantages have been detailed, for each idea – starting with the idea with the highest priority – it is established whether there are any critical concerns present. Critical concerns are disadvantages which ensure that the idea cannot be implemented. These disadvantages are properly considered and a solution is sought. The correct method for this is to express these disadvantages by means of a question, which begins with 'How can we...' or 'I would like...' For example: with an idea it turns out to be an disadvantage that many of the staff do not have the correct training. The question could be: 'Who can train so many staff to work with these machines within so much time?' All the questions can subsequently be settled by determining what actions to carry out. These actions are listed and put with the idea concerned. In this way, the ideas are discussed one-by-one.

7 Action plan and development

The list of questions just created leads to actions by people to find the answers to the questions. The importance of this step is to divide the actions established among the staff. It is also established at what time or date the answers must be provided. In the following workshop, the ideas are again reviewed one-by-one on the basis of their order of priority. For each idea it is established whether there are critical concerns and if they can be resolved. If a critical concern remains, then this idea can unfortunately not be implemented and it is crossed off the list. As soon as there is an idea for which all the critical concerns have been resolved, further development can follow.

Result

The result is a solution for a certain problem that is supported by the staff involved. The structure of the brainstorm method ensures a result and avoids becoming stranded in endless discussions.

Focus areas

In practice, one single brainstorming session is hardly ever enough. It often turns out that as many as three sessions are necessary for the brainstorming itself and then another one for the follow-up. Because arriving at ideas is in many cases a creative process, the facilitator must control the process tightly to prevent too much digression.

Literature

- Cory T. (2003). *Brainstorming*. iUniverse.

12

Brand Asset Valuator

Authors	J. Young & R. Rubicam
Year developed	2003
Also known as	Brand valuation method, BAV
Objective	Understanding and managing brands

Model

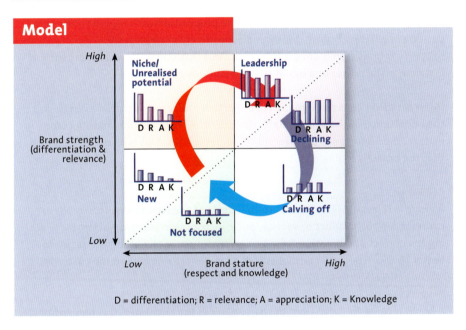

D = differentiation; R = relevance; A = appreciation; K = Knowledge

Background

Building a brand is not a simple task. A great deal of time, energy, effort and money are expended on the realisation of a brand. Moreover, a great deal of care is put into maintaining the value of the brand for the enterprise. Brands often mean quality and certainty to customers. For enterprises and marketers, brands mean a way to differentiate themselves. A brand is a promise the enterprise makes to its customers about what the service or product will produce for that customer.

Enterprises correctly ask themselves what value a brand will have for the enterprise in the future. To answer this question, we look at the stature of the product and the strength of the brand. It is important that the scores for these two variables (stature and strength) are above the dotted line in the figure. This score is established by looking at the differentiation, relevance, appreciation and knowledge the customers assign to this brand. The strength of the brand indicates to what extent the brand can still grow, while the stature indicates what the current strength of the brand is. To arrive at a correct assessment of the brand, the consecutive steps that can be taken are explained under Application.

Application

The Brand valuation method is based on four pillars: differentiation, relevance, appreciation and knowledge. An enterprise can build up a brand in this order.

Differentiation

If a brand wants to be successful, then the name must distinguish itself from all other names in this category. Differentiation comprises three distinctive components:

- *Different*: this concerns deviating from the proposition with regard to the competition in whatever sense, for example, positively or negatively.
- *Unique*: a proposition is unique if it stands out in originality and authenticity.
- *Distinctive*: the power of a brand to command a high price.

Differentiation does not diminish in importance, it remains crucial even if the importance of the other pillars increases. However, when brands become mature, the importance of differentiation diminishes. This is also a direct signal that the brand is fading and its value decreasing.

Relevance

A brand is relevant if it responds to the needs of the customers. This need is expressed in the product or service, price, distribution and promotion. By selecting the correct combination from this marketing mix, the brand will respond better to the needs and consequently become more relevant to the customer.

Respect

A brand receives respect from *the perception* of the customer. This perception has to do with what the customer expects from the brand and whether the brand lives up to this expectation. These expectations are often in the areas of functionality (does the brand do what it should do?) and quality (does the brand do what it should do well and is the brand durable?).

Knowledge

The extent of the customer's knowledge about a brand indicates that this customer also knows what the brand stands for. Customers cannot be forced to gain knowledge about a brand. The highest objective that a brand can achieve is that the customers want to do this themselves. The previous three pillars are conditions if a customer wishes to gain knowledge about a brand.

The four pillars can be summarised in two aspects: brand strength and brand stature. The strength of a brand indicates its growth potential and its stature indicates the current strength of the model. From this arises a matrix with the following meanings:

New brand

A new brand has distinctive power but is still unknown to the customers. Because the customers do not (yet) know the brand, its relevance is low. This naturally also applies to appreciation and knowledge.

Development of the brand

The enterprise will have to carry out (promotional) activities to bring the brand to the attention of customers. From this, customers can see whether it is a differentiated brand and if it is relevant for them to use. This quadrant is called the niche quadrant. Some brands remain in this quadrant and are very relevant to a small group of customers.

Leadership

The leadership position is the most profitable position in the matrix, where all four of the pillars score highest. It is therefore important for enterprises to remain in this quadrant.

Loss

Brands that end up in this quadrant have lost their differentiation and relevance because the market is changing, customers have other needs or the competition is offering the same thing. Usually, appreciation and knowledge are still high but that is only of historical significance. No brand can be built up on the basis of this latter fact.

The relationships among the four pillars can be characterised as follows:
- *Differentiation is greater than relevance*: this is a good development. The brand can grow further because it is distinctive. Moreover, by growing it can better fulfil the needs of the customer.
- *Appreciation is greater than knowledge*: this shows that appreciation is great and the customer wants to know more about the brand itself and will consequently buy.
- *Relevance is greater than differentiation*: the first signal that the brand is losing market share or will soon do so. The brand no longer distinguishes itself from other brands.
- *Knowledge is greater than appreciation*: customers know a lot about the brand but the brand no longer meets the expectations of the customers. Loyal customers still remain loyal. However, with persistently bad results, theywill also change to another brand.

Result

The model gives clear direction for the development of a brand. The enterprise knows which activities have to take place to bring the brand into the Leadership quadrant or keep it there.

Focus areas

The Brand Asset Valuator (BAV) has been compared to a large number of other brand valuation methods. Because exclusively the Young & Rubicam Group has access to the data base, comparison can exclusively take place at a price. Otherwise, the enterprise itself will have to make a comparison with analogous brands in the same sector.

Literature

- Shaw, R., Mazur, L. (1997). *Marketing Accountability*. Pearson Professional ltd.
- Tollington, T., Tollington, T. (2002). *Brand Assets*. John Wiley & Sons.
- Meek, H., Meek, R., Palmer, R., Parkinson, L. (2007). *Managing Marketing Performance*. Elsevier ltd.

13
Business Intelligence

Author	I. Ansoff
Year developed	1991
Also known as	BI, Strategic Business Intelligence
Objective	The collection, interpretation and translation of data into goal-oriented decision making

General management
Strategy
Marketing
Sales
Purchasing
Project & Planning
Production
Quality
Logistics & Distribution management
Information management
Financial
HRM & HTM
Internationalisation

Model

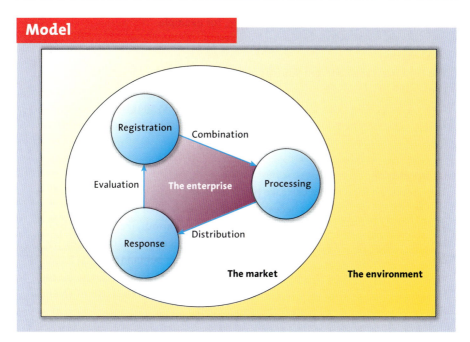

Background

Due to the quantity of information available nowadays, it turns out that taking decisions on the basis of this information has become increasingly complex and more difficult. Decisions are meanwhile also taken more quickly because the pace of trade and industry has increased enormously. Furthermore, globalisation has made sure that these decisions do not exclusively affect the local market, but the whole world. Finding, selecting and interpreting the correct information to guide the enterprise has consequently become the primary objective of Business Intelligence (BI). This information comes not so much from the immediate environment of the enterprise (the market), the Core marketing system (see Core Marketing System), but from the environment outside it.

Application

BI is implemented by carrying out the following steps.

1 Collection

Data are collected from existing systems that are present in the enterprise. These data are supplemented with information that is found by the staff or is registered. This can occur via search campaigns on the internet, in books, magazines, newspapers, etcetera. Data that come from customers and competitors are also collected. Moreover, information is obtained from the 'rumours in the corridors'. It is thus important to not too quickly exclude data that do not seem relevant. Only after carefully considered filtering may data be excluded because they are too old, inaccurate or not reliable, for example.

2 Presentation

The data from the different sources are subsequently combined and integrated and stored in a shared location. By this, a shared source for decision making is created. Detailed data are aggregated into useable sets that remain orderly. These sets of data are visualised such that their interpretation can take place quickly.

3 Interpretation

The interpretation of data can take place when it gains meaning for the processor of the data. For this, it is necessary that the context of the data is known. The context is indicated by variables such as place, period, size, quantity or largeness. The internalisation of the data can take place when the context is clear. Internalising means owning the message that is behind the data. To this end, objectivity should be assured. With the aid of these data, it can be established whether the current picture needs to be adjusted on the basis of the new data or not; this is called review and enrichment.

4 Checking

The new insights must be checked. For example, if market share is declining and turnover increasing, the market could have become larger or perhaps a mistake has been made in the processing of the data. If it turns out that everything is correct after checking, the data can be enriched with information about the newly created situation. If, for example, market share is declining because of two new competitors, an investigation into these two competitors will have to be started. By discussing the newly created situation with others, subtle distinctions in the interpretation can be added. The information that is now available will have to be stored for further use. This use can be immediately or at a later date.

5 Distribution

Not all information can simply be sent to the staff of the enterprise. Dependent on the need of the staff in the enterprise and the topicality of the data, it can be determined when which information can be sent to what places or positions within or outside the enterprise.

6 Anticipation

Now, it is up to the enterprise to make the right decisions on the basis of the information received and guide the enterprise to achieve its stated objectives. The data used in BI have to comply with a number of requirements allowing decision making based on it. The categories for this are time (timeliness, frequency), content (relevance) and form (for example, the sequence).

To give all the data from BI proper form, it is wise to store them in computerised information systems, so that they can be viewed from different angles. This concerns systems such as data warehouses and portals. Moreover, it is advisable to convert the information obtained via BI into success factors and performance indicators, as with the Balanced Scorecard (see Balanced Scorecard).

Result

With proper use of BI, the result is a strong competitive advantage and the ability to take decisions much more quickly and effectively. Due to this, the objectives of the enterprise will be achieved sooner.

Focus areas

BI projects are often department, process and even business unit transcending. Furthermore, BI projects always relate to the strategy and management of an enterprise and the technology involved. Furthermore, they have a high political content. Starting up a BI project should therefore be carefully planned.

Literature

- Howson, C. (2007). *Successful Business Intelligence*. McGraw-Hill.
- Miller, G., Bräutigam, D., Gerlach, S.(2006). *Business Intelligence Competence Centers*. John Wiley & Sons.
- Williams, S., Williams, N. (2007). *The Profit Impact of Business Intelligence*. Elsevier inc.

14
CAGE Distance Framework

Author	P. Ghemawat
Year developed	2001
Also known as	–
Objective	Determining which international markets to enter

Model

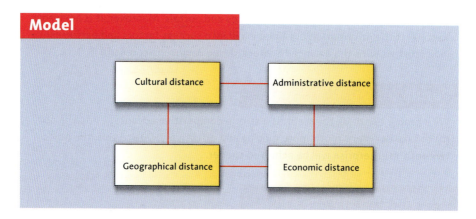

Background

To determine which country is most interesting for an enterprise, a countries portfolio analysis is often performed. For each country, in circles, consumption per capita and income per capita are set against each other. In this way, an overview is created of the potential markets for the enterprise. The size of the circle reflects the potential of the product concerned. The diagram (see pag 59) is an example of this. This diagram has been compiled for an American fast-food restaurant.

The success that enterprises achieve in foreign markets cannot solely be based on a countries portfolio analysis. Its success is partly influenced by the following four distances:
- cultural distance
- administrative distance
- geographical distance
- economic distance

In general, the greater the distance, the lower the success rate. Ghemawat developed the CAGE Framework to be able to evaluate international markets on the basis of the four said distances, as well as with analytical tools.

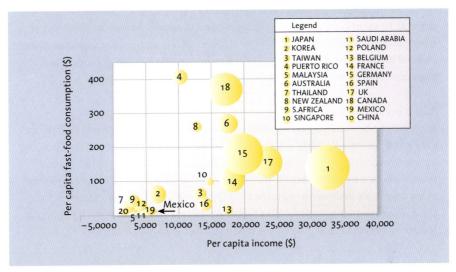

Source: Ghemawat, 2001

Application

Due to information technology, the world seems to be becoming ever smaller. This indeed applies to information. But for doing business, this is this a false supposition and can even be dangerous. The distance in the four areas can play an important role in international expansion. Enterprises can be more successful with international activities if they take these distances into account via the CAGE Framework of Ghemawat.

Cultural distance	Administrative distance	Geographical distance	Economic distance
different languages	lack of colonial background	physical distance	differences between rich and poor
different ethics	lack of shared regional trade support	lack of national borders	other differences, such as costs or quality of natural resources, financial resources, labour forces, infrastructure, information or knowledge
other religious beliefs	lack of a joint currency	different time zones	
lack of confidence	political hostility	differences in climate/disease	
other values and standards			

With the aid of the CAGE model, the impact can be determined of the different distances on the international activities of the enterprise.

Cultural distance

Interaction between people is often based on their cultural background. Differences in religion, race, social standards and language can create a huge distance. Some aspects are very clear, for example language. Others are much more difficult to assess and bridge, for example social values that are not defined anywhere but are rooted deep within the culture. Often, choices are based on these cultural differences. It is then important to know which cultural aspects are important if a product or service is to be sold in a different country.

Administrative distance

Associations between countries based on history or political considerations are very good for mutual trade relations. A common unit of currency makes trading between countries much more insightful. Due to this, more is traded. If countries introduce import charges, this will have a negative effect on imports from other countries. Moreover, a stable country is important for good trade relations. Countries where corruption and social unrest reign are much less popular for doing business with. The risk is much greater in these countries.

Geographical distance

The greater the distance, the more difficult it is to do business. It is, however, not only the actual distance in kilometres that makes doing business more difficult, but also the size of the country, distances to the border, access to waterways and oceans are important. The transport and communications infrastructure plays an important role in doing international business when it involves geographical distance.

Economic distance

The welfare and income of the consumers is still the most important attribute when it involves economic distance. Countries with a low per capita income do less business on an international basis than countries with a high per capita income. On the other hand, countries with a low per capita income trade more with wealthier countries than with poorer countries. Enterprises that rely on scale, experience and standardisation, can better seek countries with a similar economic profile.

In the following table an overview is given of the sectors or products that are influenced by the four different distances.

Cultural distance	Administrative distance	Geographical distance	Economic distance
products with a large language content (TV)	sectors where government involvement is too high: • manufacturers of consumer goods (electricity) • companies with many employees • large suppliers to the government • national companies of which people are proud • important to national security (telecoms) • miners of raw materials (oil, iron) • high costs (infrastructure)	products with a low value to weight or bulk ratio (cement)	basis of the need changes based on income level (cars)
products on the basis of cultural or national identity (food)		delicate products or ones that rot (fruit, glass)	high standardisation and scale are important (mobile telephones)
variations in product characteristics such as: • size (cars) • standards (electrical equipment) • packaging		communication and connectivity are important (financial services)	remarkable differences in cost of labour and other cost factors
		local supervision and operational requirements are high (many services)	distribution and corporate systems (insurances)
products with country-specific qualifications (wine)			companies that must be reactive (devices for the home)

Besides the application of the four distances for each country, the CAGE Framework will have to be applied to each sector. For each sector or product, each of the four distances can exercise a certain influence on the product or sector concerned. For example, geographical distance: if the physical distance is very great, then for a product like cement (low-value, high-weight) a different choice will have to be made than for an expensive product with a low weight (watches).

Result

If the countries portfolio analysis is extended with the four distances, a big difference in market attractiveness can occur. The same example of the fast-food restaurant, taking into account the four distances, is shown in the following diagram.

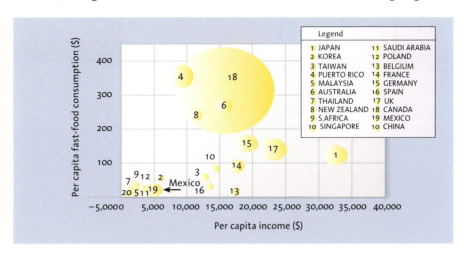

It turns out that the market attractiveness of Mexico has increased considerably while Japan (1) and Germany (15) are almost equally interesting. Canada (18) is now the most attractive market.

Focus areas

The CAGE Framework can have a huge effect on determining the market attractiveness of different countries. A complete analysis of market attractiveness can only be performed if the size of the market, market growth and the intensity of the competition are taken into account.

Literature

- Ghemawat, P. (2001). *Distance still matters: the hard reality of global expansion.* Harvard Business Review, 79 (8), 137-147.
- Ghemawat, P. (2007). *Redefining global strategy.* Boston: Harvard Business School Press.

15
Colour Print Thinking

Author	Leon de Caluwé
Year developed	1997
Also known as	Thinking in colours
Objective	Streamlining of changes in enterprises

Model

Five change types

Background

Every enterprise consists in personnel that think in a certain way. This constitutes the culture of the enterprise. The founder of the enterprise is the establisher of this culture, unless the personnel have further expanded it. When taking on new personnel, it must be established whether they fit into the culture of the enterprise. When adapting the enterprise as a result of market changes, for example, a change process will have to be initiated. How the personnel deal with change is related to the culture of the enterprise and their own way of thinking. When contradictions arise in these patterns of thinking, the implementation of change is difficult and the chances of success are small. To gain insight into these thinking patterns, De Caluwé has divided them into five groups and given them different colours.

The following five patterns of thinking are distinguished:

- *Yellow*: gathering together of interests, setting and effectively striving for complex objectives.
- *Blue*: establishing the result in advance, specification of requirements, successive performance of activities and steering in the light of the result to be achieved.
- *Red*: the use of HRM instruments and organisational science elements to change the 'soft' aspects of an organisation.
- *Green*: people are changed or moved by motivating them to learn. The outcome is highly dependent on learning ability.
- *White*: everything changes automatically and change is a permanent process. Steering is based on inner certainty instead of the external certainties. Interpretation plays an important role.

By establishing the most dominant colour of the enterprise, the change programme can be designed via this route.

Application

	Things/people wil change if you...
Yellow	• bring interests together • force them to adopt (certain) standpoints/opinions • create win-win situations/form coalitions • demonstrate the advantages of certain ideas (power, status)
Blue	• formulate a clear result/objective in advance • make a good, phased plan from A to B • monitor the steps well and steer on that basis • keep everything as stable and controlled as possible • reduce complexity as much as possible
Red	• provoke them in the right way, for example by means of punishment or inducement • use advanced HRM instruments for pay, motivation, promotion, status • give people something back for what they give to you
Green	• make them aware of new opinions/own shortcomings (consciously unskilled) • are able to motivate them to see/learn/do new things • can create suitable collective learning situations
White	• assume that the will and wishes and the 'natural way' of people themselves adds meaning • allow the individual energy of people to appear • want to see dynamics/complexity • take away any barriers • use symbols and rituals

The starting point for thinking in colours is establishing the culture within the enterprise and thereby searching for the correct intervention techniques, in order to carry out a change process successfully. The above overview indicates in which way changes can be realised with the various colours.

For the enterprise, via the questionnaires the 'thinking' and 'actions' of the enterprise are now established in a certain colour. Change processes in an enterprise take place not only at the individual level, but also at the level of groups of and the organisation. The table below gives an overview of what intervention techniques in a colour are applicable to the individual, the group of the whole organisation.

Dominant colour	Individual	Group	Organisation
Yellow	**Personal commitment statement** out-placement, protegé constructions	**Confrontation meetings** third-party strategy, top structure	**Improving the quality of the work** strategic alliances, CAO negotiations
Blue	**Management by objectives** hygienic working, working with an agenda	**Working in projects** archiving, decision making rules	**Strategic management** business process, redesign, investigation, auditing
Red	**Career development** recruitment and selection, task enrichment/ task expansion	**Social activities** team roles, management by speech	**Remuneration in organisations** mobility and diversity, triple ladder
Green	**Coaching** intensive clinic feedback discussions, mirroring	**Teambuilding** gaming intervision	**Open systems planning** parallel learning structures, quality circles
White	**T-groep** personal growth, networking	**Self-governing teams** open-space meetings, making explicit mental models	**Search conferences** rituals and mysticism, tearing down sacred places

Result

A greater chance of a successful change programme because the intervention techniques that are applied are attuned to the culture within the enterprise, the group and the individual.

With changes, four factors play an important role:
- the objective of the change
- the change environment
- the customer/client
- the changer

If all four factors are the same colour, this undoubtedly leads to an easy mutual relationship and to improvements. If they are different, this can cause tensions. How can they be made productive? And how many differences can a change programme tolerate? Another challenge is to be found in further exploration of culture-specific methods of approach to change. If in the uncertainty-avoiding cultures blue thinking is dominant and in power differences accepting cultures yellow thinking? And: how can you use the palette of colours to design and guide (complex) change programmes? A white approach cannot be adopted in cases of acute danger to survival. A blue approach will not be successful in a highly political environment.
It is also clear that the systematic input of (blue) self-governing teams (substantively seen, a white concept) will not be a successful approach.

Literature

- Caluwé, L., Vermaak H. (2003). *Learning to change*. Sage Publications Inc.
- Sims, R. (2002). *Changing the Way We Manage Change*. Greenwood Publishing Group Inc.

16
Competence management

Author	M. Nieuwenhuis
Year developed	2006
Also known as	—
Objective	Deploying staff optimally on the basis of knowledge, training and skills

Model

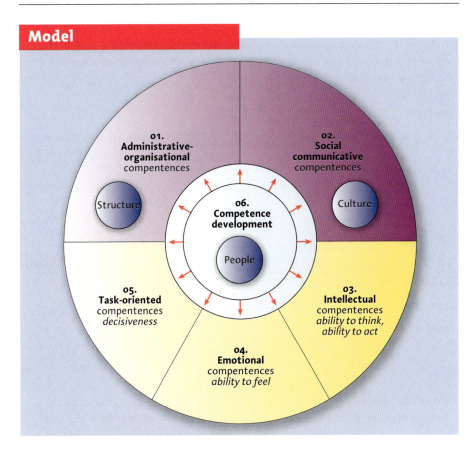

Background

To be able to do their work, the personnel in an enterprise carry out activities. These activities must be carried out in a correct manner. For this, knowledge, experience and skills are indispensable. Enterprises therefore invest in the personnel to improve their knowledge, experience and skills. The sum of the knowledge, experience and skills are called the competences of an employee.

Application

The competence model describes the different competences that employees must have to be able to do their work (activities) in the correct manner. For each activity or set of activities (role), a competence profile is needed. In this way, for each role a theoretically perfect competence profile is compiled (we speak rather of roles than the somewhat older word functions). This competence profile is then compared with the competence profiles of the employees.
Compiling a competence profile comprises the following steps:

1. Compile the necessary competences for each role.
2. Compile a competence profile for each employee.
3. Determine for each role what the employee must at least fulfil.
4. Determine for each role what the maximum deviation from the other competences in the profile may be.
5. Determine for each role which employee matches the competence profile. The other way around is also possible. Determine for each employee which profiles match for each role.

Example

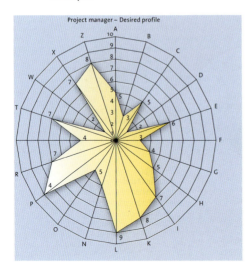
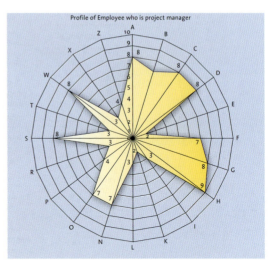

In the example, above is shown the desired competence profile of the skills a project manager must have. In the diagram on the right are the skills of a staff member in relation to the role of project manager. From the two diagrams it appears that these profiles are each other's opposite. This establishes that the role of project manager is not the desired role for this person.

Explanation competence profile			
A Need to perform	F Need to be supportive	L Leading role	S Striving for harmony
B Need to belong to group	G Role of hard worker	N Need to finish things off	T Work rhythm
C Personal organisation	H Planning & integration	O Need for new personal relationships	W Need for rules
D Attention to detail	I Decisiveness	P Need to lead	X Need to be noticed
E Emotional control	K Need to be assertive	R Conceptual thinking	Z Need to change

Result

By comparing the competence profiles of individual employees with the profiles of the roles desired in the enterprise, the employees can be optimally deployed. The employees will be able to do their work with more motivation because the role fits within their potential. A motivated employee quite simply performs better. This benefits the productivity of an enterprise.

Furthermore, it is a big advantage for the enterprise to work in this way. Because thinking is not in terms of functions and tasks, employees can be deployed in a flexible manner in the different roles within the enterprise. After all, it is easy to establish that the competence profiles of the roles correspond with the competence profiles of the employees.

Focus areas

When there is a switch from functions to roles with competence profiles, it could be that the employees rationally understand that they fit in some roles and not in others. On the other hand, it could be that employees cannot cope with it emotionally. These employees will then need extra guidance to find a new role within or, if desired, outside the enterprise.

If the requirements in relation to the correspondence between the profiles of employees and roles are set too high, it could be that nobody is found for a certain role.

Literature

- www.similarminds.com/big5.html

General management
Strategy
Marketing
Sales
Purchasing
Project & Planning
Production
Quality
Logistics & Distribution
Information management
Financial
HRM & HTM
Internationalisation

17
Competing Values Framework, Quinn

Author	R. Quinn
Year developed	1994
Also known as	Model of Competing Values, Quinn Model, Competing Values Model
Objective	Effective leadership

Model

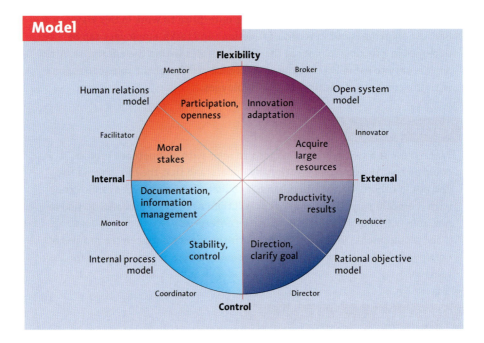

Background

To achieve a highly dynamic environment for organisational effectiveness, Quinn has combined four models into the model of the competing values. The four models he used are:

- Rational objective model
- Internal process model
- Human relations model
- Open system model

These four models are in theory contradictory to each other. But for the manager, it is necessary to be able to change management styles to run the enterprise successfully according to the situation. The model derives it name from this discordance: the model of the competing values.

Application

The relationships between the models can be shown in two dimensions. This is represented by the two axes of the model. The vertical axis runs from flexibility to control; while the horizontal axis runs from internal to external. Each model now fits in one of the quadrants.

For each quadrant, Quinn has defined two management roles, which have been translated into the behaviour of the manager.

Rational objective model
- *Producer.* Task-oriented, shows great involvement, is motivated and has energy and personal effort. Accepts responsibility, brings assignments to a good conclusion and has high productivity.
- *Director.* Makes expectations clear via processes like planning and setting objectives. Defines problems, selects alternatives, indicates what must be aspired to, defines tasks and roles, establishes rules and policy and gives instructions.

Internal process model
- *Coordinator.* Maintains structure and flow in the system, is reliable; you can count on him/her. Focused on workload reduction such as arranging, organising and coordinating the efforts of the personnel; is focused on coping with crises and pays attention to technological, logistics and household matters.
- *Monitor.* Knows what is happening, sees that everyone keeps to the rules and that everyone achieves his/her objective. Is a good analyst, is strong in administration with regard to reports and overviews, makes inspection rounds.

Human relations model
- *Mentor.* Involved human role, a sympathetic approach to human development. Is considerate, helpful, sensitive, approachable, open and fair. Gives compliments.
- *Facilitator.* Encourages collaboration, brings about cohesion and teamwork, resolves conflicts. steers towards processes.

Open system model
- *Broker.* Keeps himself occupied with the relationship between the organisation and the outside world. Image, presentation and reputation are important elements. Negotiates and sells well.
- *Innovator.* Focuses on making adaptations and changes possible, recognises the changes in the environment and important trends and can cope well with uncertainty and risks. The innovator has vision, notices needs in the market and devises a way to satisfy them.

The eight roles indicate what is expected from someone in a position of leadership. Next to these expectations, leaders also need skills to be productive in their roles. The skills that belong to the roles in question are shown in the table.

Broker	1	building and maintaining a power base
	2	negotiating about stakes and consensus
	3	presenting ideas
Innovator	1	living with change
	2	creative thinking
	3	management of changes
Producer	1	productive working
	2	promoting a productive work environment
	3	time and stress management
Director	1	developing and communicating a vision
	2	defining ojectives and goals
	3	designing and organising
Coordinator	1	project management
	2	designing tasks
	3	cross-functional management
Monitor	1	managing information bij thinking critically
	2	coping with a profusion of information
	3	managing core processes
Stimulator	1	team building
	2	using participative decision making
	3	managing conflicts
Mentor	1	having insight into yourself and others
	2	effective communication
	3	development of employees

With the aid of questionnaires, it can be established which profile someone has. A role will never come out exactly the same. One role will be dominant however, with regard to the other roles. With the use of this model by Quinn, the first step in establishing your own profile is made. The second step is understanding and knowing the other roles in the model and estimating their value. The third step is mastering the leadership roles that do not occur or are not dominant in your own profile. The last step is the application of the roles that a certain situation requires.

Result

Leaders will be able to apply the roles when required for a certain situation. The leaders lead the enterprise to the desired results in this way and thereby represent the interests of the personnel and the environment of the enterprise.

Focus areas

Although this topic concerns people's competences, this is reduced by the model to putting people in boxes. In many countries this can be handled well. There are, however, countries where the culture plays such a strong role and the distance between managers and employees is so great that the application of this model has no effect whatsoever.

The model represents a snapshot. Here, the risk arises that after the snapshot, no development programme follows in which people can gain more skills with regard to the other roles and they consequently lapse deeper into the dominant role.

Literature

- Cameron, K., Quinn, R., Degraff, J., Thakor, A. (2007). *Competing Values Leadership*. Edward Elger Publishing Ltd.
- Quinn, R., Cameron, K. (2006). *Diagnosting and Changing Organizational Culture*. John Wiley and Sons Ltd.
- http://competingvalues.com

18
Competitive Forces, Porter

Author	Porter
Year developed	1998
Also known as	5 forces Porter
Objective	Sector analysis

Model

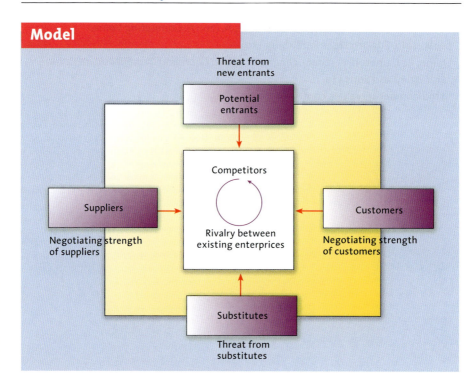

Background

An entrepreneur wishing to do business in a demarcated market or sector, is confronted with what the customers want, what the suppliers can offer, how intensive the competition is, what new entrants there are and by which substitutes the product can be replaced. Due to this, the sector can suddenly look much less attractive or precisely more attractive. With the aid of Porter's Five forces model, this is mapped out.

The model shows the relationships of the five fields of force operating in a sector. These forces are:

The negotiating strength of the suppliers

The strength of the suppliers is determined by the number of suppliers on the market and the negotiating position these suppliers have. If there are many suppliers and thus little negotiating strength, the prices of raw materials, semi-manufactures and materials are low. If there are few suppliers with a strong negotiating position, then the prices for raw materials, semi-manufactures and materials will be high. The negotiating strength of the supplier is high if:

- the supplier has more than enough customers
- the costs of changing suppliers are high
- the supplier supplies a successful brand
- the supplier itself develops the activities that the customer now supplies
- there is an oligopoly or monopoly on the suppliers' side

The negotiating strength of the customers

The strength of the customers is determined by the number of customers and the extent to which these customers are critical in their purchasing. With a large number of customers who are not critical, the negotiating strength of the customers will not be high. If there are few customers who are very critical, their negotiating strength is high. The negotiating strength of the customers is high if:

- there are few customers or if it concerns a relatively big customer
- there are alternative purchasing points, which can be switched to relatively easily
- the customer develops activities that the supplier now provides

The degree of mutual rivalry among the competitors

The degree of mutual rivalry among the companies indicates the size of the margin on the products or services. When there is a great deal of competition on the market within the same product range, the competition will try to gain market share on price. Due to this, the margins on the products or services will decline. An alternative is that the competition seeks distinctive power, due to which differentiation arises in the market. If there is little competition, a stable pricing policy can be followed and the margins on the products and services are high. The range remains limited to what is offered on the market. The rivalry between the companies is high when:

- The balance between the competitors is not equal. If everyone is about the same size, a calmer situation is apt to arise than when there are both large and small enterprises. People are then more easily inclined to perform stunts with the price, et cetera.
- The fixed costs must be covered. Prices are lowered to in any case cover the

fixed costs. Due to this, the competition does this too and the sector ends up in a negative price spiral.
- Production capacity is too great. Over-capacity within a sector leads to competition.
- The exit barriers are high. High exit barriers ensure that the competition finds it difficult to expand as a consequence of fierce competition.

The threat of new entrants to the market

If there is a low threshold for entry to the market, many companies can or wish to share the market. There is a low threshold if the investments in costs and time to access this market are low. With a low threshold, there is thus a high threat of entry into the market. Through this, the competition will quickly increase and margins will be put under pressure. With a high threshold, companies will not easily enter the market and the threat of new entrants is low. Companies already operating on the market have less competition and are able to achieve higher margins.

High thresholds for entry are:
- advantages of scale, the extent to which the products are produced
- the required amount of capital for entry
- the age of sector: the older the more difficult for newcomers
- access to distribution channels: independent distribution channels or distribution channels in the hands of manufacturers
- the expected counter action from existing enterprises, for example, a price war
- the degree of free market effect
- differentiation: can the entrant distinguish itself from the competition?

The threat of substitutes on the market

If it is easily possible to replace the products or services with another product or service, there is a considerable threat of new companies entering the market. Due to this, margins will be under pressure and the competition will increase. If it is difficult to replace the existing products or services by another product or service, the threat of substitutes is low. Companies already operating in the market have less competition and are able to achieve higher margins.

Result

The result of this analysis gives insight into the whether the sector is attractive to the enterprise or not. If the power positions, the threats and the rivalry are all low, then it is an interesting sector for the enterprise to enter. If the negotiating strength of the suppliers and customers is high, then the sector is already less attractive. The suppliers and customers are the most important players in the market. If there is great rivalry between the providers on the market moreover, then the chances of successful entry are considerably lower. If, furthermore, there is also great rivalry between the competition, then the sector is no longer interesting. The investment and risks are too high and the payback time is too long.

Focus areas

The model gives insight into the possibilities in the sector. It says nothing, however, about the possibilities the company has to enter the sector. Next to this model, an internal analysis with therefore have to be made to conclude whether the company is able to enter the market or can remain profitable in the sector.

Literature

- Porter, M.E. (1998). *Competitive Strategy*. The Free Press.
- http://www.exed.hbs.edu/assets/shape-strategy.pdf

General management

Strategy ⊗

Marketing

Sales

Purchasing

Project & Planning

Production

Quality

Logistics & Distribution

Information management

Financial

HRM & HTM

Internationalisation

19
Competitive Positions, Kotler

Author	P. Kotler
Year developed	1996
Also known as	Attack Strategies
Objective	Determining competitive strategies

Model

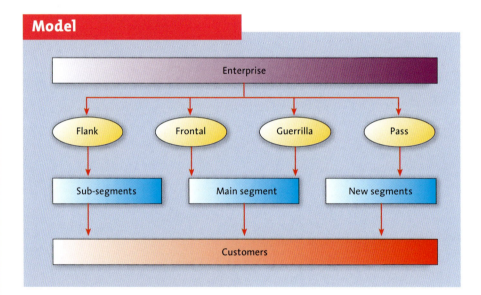

Background

When bringing products and/or services onto the market, an enterprise is after a time always confronted with competition. The objective of an enterprise is not generally to beat the competition. Ideally, it aims to be successful purely by its own strength.

However, it is necessary to set up a competitive strategy to make more explicit your own advantages compared to the competition. To set up a competitive strategy, insight will first have to be obtained into who the competition actually is. A competitor is an enterprise that puts a similar product or service on the market and focuses on the same target group. Subsequently, the correct strategy can be derived in accordance with the model.

The following steps lead to the correct competitive strategy:

1 Competition analysis

The first step in determining the competitive strategy is making a competition analysis. This competition analysis comprises the following:

- inventory of competitors
- establishing the market form:
  - monopoly[1]
  - oligopoly[2] (homogeneous or heterogeneous)
  - polyopoly[3] (homogeneous[4] or heterogeneous[5])
- determining the policy for each competitor

2 Competitor prognosis

To set a competitive course, it is necessary to know the steps the competition will take. If, for example, the market share of a competitor declines, it can be expected that at a given moment action will be undertaken by that competitor to regain market share. But it is also possible that the competitor will divest this part of their business. In both situations, the enterprise must respond. This could, for example, be by setting up far-reaching statistical prediction techniques or at management level 'What-if-scenarios'.[6] If the competition appoints a new director, he will want to implement his own ideas in the enterprise. Target group and positioning can be derived from advertisements and web sites. In these and other ways, the enterprise can establish what the future policy of the competitor will be.

3 Competitive position

After all the information, strengths and weaknesses of the competitor have been collected, they can be compared with your own strengths and weaknesses. In this way, the enterprise can quickly establish on which characteristics it scores better than the competition and so find a unique selling point (USP). To present these characteristics graphically, use can be made of the benchmark method (see Benchmarking).

4 Competitive strategy

Depending on the individual policy of the enterprise, there is a choice from four competitive attack strategies:

- *Frontal attack*

With the frontal attack, the enterprise focuses its strategy on the main segment of the competitor with the intention of decreasing the competitor's market share. The enterprise does this by approaching the target group aggressively. This approach can be applied in different areas. One of the most important approaches is to offer a lower price than the competitor. The enterprise, depending on the product or service and the target group, can also make use of other aspects of the marketing mix, such as a major advertising offensive. With the frontal attack, the enterprise should take into account a forceful and harsh reaction from the competitor. They will not just allow themselves to be driven out of an established market. It is thus important to prepare a frontal attack well and continue it for a long period. In this way, in order to retain market share, price wars or advertising wars arise. The risk that the enterprise takes is that the competition will counter attack the most important segment of the enterprise and could force the enterprise onto the defensive. This competitive strategy requires a great deal of investment and entails risks. If the enterprise succeeds in winning the attack, the market lies open and the enterprise can become the market leader.

- *Flanking attack*
Enterprises with less budget and little capacity to take the initiative and which are therefore not strong enough to attack the market leader directly, will often opt to attack the less important segments of the competitor. There is a focus on specific characteristics of the requirements of the customers in these segments. In this way, a product or service can be packaged in a different way. The enterprise can opt to set up more distribution points in the neighbourhood of the customers. In this manner, the enterprise is able to slowly gain more and more market share in various segments with respect to the market leader. The risk that the enterprise runs is that the market leader does not accept that market share is taken away from its sub-segments and, hence, reacts forcefully.

- *Passing attack*
The enterprise can opt to approach market segments that have not yet been approached by the competition. There is then (still) no competition in these segments and a lead can quickly be built up. All the instruments in the marketing mix are deployed for this segment.

- *Guerrilla attack*
A guerrilla attack also focuses on the main segments of the competition and is usually carried out by enterprises that are less substantial and generally smaller in size. These enterprises usually implement short, attention-catching campaigns via sales promotion. In this way, a limited amount of sales is taken away from the competition. Because the much larger competitor will be sluggish, it will be unable to react quickly and the campaign is already over before a new strategy is set up.

Result

The result is a solid strategy for the way in which the enterprise can best approach the segments with regard to the competition. Moreover, it becomes clear to the enterprise what investment is needed to secure a place in the market in the segments concerned.

Although the competitive approach represents a clear strategy, the efforts that must be made to inventory the competition may not be underestimated. This is expressed by the work in relation to the collection of information on all the competitors. This collection of information takes a long time.

This also means that it takes a long time before the correct strategy can be determined.

Literature

- Kotler, P., Armstrong, G. (2009). *The Principles of Marketing*. Prentice Hall.
- www.kotlermarketing.com

1 Monopoly: there is only one supplier in the market, there are therefore no competitors.
2 Oligopoly: limited number of suppliers in the market, thus strong influence from competitors.
3 Polyopoly: there are so many suppliers in the market that they hardly influence each other.
4 Homogeneous: products from different suppliers that are indistinguishable from each other.
5 Heterogeneous: products from different suppliers that can be distinguished from each other by their components.
6 What-if-scenarios: working out plans for several possibilities and situations that could occur.

20
Competitive Strategies, Kotler

Author	P. Kotler
Year developed	1996
Also known as	–
Objective	Retaining position in the market

Model

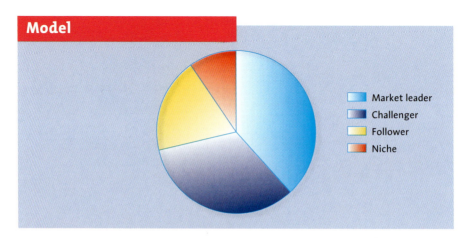

- Market leader
- Challenger
- Follower
- Niche

Background

Almost every enterprise will in time encounter competition on the market. With the arrival of competition, the enterprise must respond to what the other companies in this market do. Failure to respond will force the enterprise out of the market. The reaction to the competition from the enterprise is partly dependent on the position the enterprise occupies in the market. Moreover, the reaction of large enterprises with a multiplicity of products will depend on the product (group) for which the competition arises. Every enterprise has been able to occupy a certain place in the market and will also behave accordingly: as market leader, challenger, follower or niche.

The enterprise will react to competition from this position. A market leader, for example, will be more liable to defend or attack than withdraw from the market.

Left margin navigation tabs:

General management · Strategy · Marketing · Sales · Purchasing · Project & Planning · Production · Quality · Logistics & Distribution · Information management · Financial · HRM & HTM · Internationalisation

Market leader

The market leader is in general a large, dominant enterprise with the capacity to set the tone in the market in relation to price changes, the introduction of new products/services, distribution cover and promotional expenditure. The market leader is carefully watched by its competitors and is challenged, followed or avoided. The market leader will continually and carefully have to pay attention to what is happening in the market. Other companies will try to capture market share in all segments. Due to this, the market leader will have to remain active on four fronts:

- *New demand*
  Market leaders have the biggest advantage when new demand can be created. To this end, the company must achieve a higher degree of penetration within the current target group. In general, this is accomplished through extra advertising and promotion.
- *Expand market share*
  The profitability of enterprises increases when market share increases because there will be a greater return on their investment. Therefore, companies will attempt to increase their market share. To this end, companies do not hesitate to discard products or product groups for the benefit of market share within a specific product group. If several companies do this, it can lead to a marketing war.
- *Improve productivity*
  By improving productivity, the company is attempting to obtain more profit from the same amount of products or services sold. By increasing scale, enterprises can produce more efficiently and, hence, achieve lower costs than the competition. Here it is true that the enterprise must produce as simply as possible; the more complexity in achieving a larger market share, for example, due to related products, the higher the costs.
- *Defend position*
  Market leaders are often attacked because it is easier to steal away part of a large share than of a small one. Certainly if the market leader is occupied with a takeover or a new product introduction. The market leader will then have to defend its position. It can do this by first improving all its weak points, controlling costs, bringing prices into conformity with the market and, subsequently, launching a counter attack as the best form of defence.

Challengers

The challengers usually have a competitive advantage to maintain, for example, lower production costs or product innovations. The challengers have two possibilities for approaching the market:

- *Direct attack on the market leader*
  The challenger takes a big risk. It is often the large returns behind this, however, that motivates this possibility. The enterprise has established a mission and vision in advance and wishes to achieve them.

- *Companies of equal size*

The challenger leaves the market leader alone and attacks companies of equal size, which often operate locally or regionally. The mission and vision are often not fixed and the enterprise wishes to achieve more market share via different attack tactics (see Competitive Positions, Kotler).

Followers

Followers do not take risks by engaging in battles with other enterprises to end up in a weak position. Followers lack the high investments in new products and promotion. They have no teething troubles and they imitate the marketing programmes of the market leader. Due to this, they will not achieve a large market share but due to the lower costs, will still make sufficient profit.

Niche

Niche players focus on a small group of enterprises within a segment with specific needs that cannot be fulfilled by the market leader, due to its large scale (in that situation exceptions are not possible). These are small companies that have insufficient budgets for large-scale promotions and are highly flexible in fulfilling the specific desires of the companies. Due to this specialisation and flexibility, there is nevertheless sufficient profit to be gained on the market for these enterprises.

Result

The result of competitive behaviour is the correct positioning of the enterprise. Due to this, investments are secured and costs are controlled.

Focus areas

With too strong a focus on competitive behaviour, the enterprise loses sight of the market. Because the wishes and requirements of the market are changing more and more quickly, it is more important to follow the market than just focus on competitors.

Literature

- Kotler, P., Armstrong G. (2009). *The Principles of Marketing*. Prentice Hall.
- www.kotlermarketing.com

21
Competitive Strategies, Porter

Author	M. Porter
Year developed	1980
Also known as	Generic strategies Porter
Objective	Establishing a distinctive competitive strategy

Model

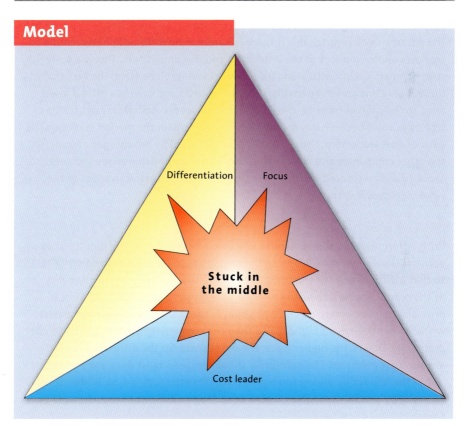

Background

Enterprises that approach the market without a clear strategy and make few choices are less successful than enterprises that do. From many years of research, Porter came to the conclusion that there are three strategic choices. These are the cost leadership strategy, the differentiation strategy and the

General management

Strategy

Marketing

Sales

Purchasing

Project & Planning

Production

Quality

Logistics & Distribution

Information management

Financial

HRM & HTM

Internatio- nalisation

focus strategy. Enterprises who do not opt for one of these strategies are less successful and are 'stuck in the middle' (SITM).

Application

To successfully operate in the market, companies must distinguish themselves from their competitors and have to make choices to this end. Enterprises can opt for the lowest price or a unique approach to the market or for a unique proposition on the market.

Cost leader

For cost leadership, the enterprise will strive for the lowest price in the market. To this end, the enterprise will have to keep the cost price of the product as low as possible. This is achieved by, for example, advantages of scale, low labour costs and technological innovations.

The enterprise can opt for this if there is hardly or no difference between the products and/or services of the enterprise and its competitors. This is a powerful strategy, particularly with standard products and services. Here, the fact that there is only one company that has these low costs and can thus offer a lower price to the market must be closely watched. If several companies opt for this strategy, it will become increasingly difficult to remain the market leader on the basis of cost leadership. Usually, this can be achieved by advantages of scale. If the other companies also opt for this, then stiff competition arises and over-capacity will be created on the market. Due to this, the attractiveness of the whole sector will decline.

Differentiation

With differentiation, the enterprise wishes to distinguish itself from the competition. It can do this by adapting the properties of its products and services so that a difference with the competition is created, where the functionality of the product or service hardly or does not change. By doing this, the enterprise attempts to create a unique position in the market. An important aspect with differentiation is a higher price than the competition, due to the different properties. Due to the higher price, the extra costs for the different properties are also cost effective. The enterprise should ensure that it does not price itself out of the market by asking too high a price. This strategy can be followed successfully by several companies together, as long as different properties can be found.

Focus

With the focus strategy, the enterprise does not focus on the whole target group but only on a few segments. Due to this focus, the enterprise can better serve the customers in this segment or segments because more time and attention can be paid to them. The enterprise will also know better than the competition what is happening with these customers and can take advantage of it.

Hence, customers will be less inclined to switch to the competition. Within the focus strategy, the enterprise also has a choice between differentiation and cost leadership.

'Stuck in the middle'
As a result of his research, Porter suggests that every enterprise must choose from three strategies. If no choice is made, the enterprise cannot distinguish itself from the competition and profitability will decline, unless there is overwhelming demand for the service or product in question. Enterprises that have been in the market for a long time have trouble with the automatic suction effect towards the middle. As long as all the competitors do the same thing and demand is sufficiently great, this will not be a problem. As soon as a newcomer to the market has selected one of the strategies, the enterprise is often too late to respond adequately and loses market share.

Result

The model offers clear positioning of the enterprise in the market with the product or service in question.

Focus areas

The model gives a limited view (costs of differentiation) of reality and is a snapshot. Looking into the future needs of the market and starting from the strength of the enterprise are lacking in this model, though many enterprises put their products and services on the market in this way.

Literature

- Porter, M. (2004). *Competitive Strategy*. Simon & Schuster Ltd.

22

Complaints Management

Author	Developed in practice
Year developed	–
Also known as	–
Objective	Transforming complaints into an improved relationship with the customer

Model

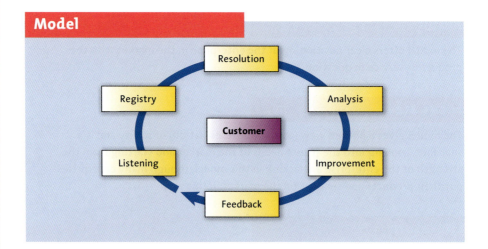

Background

A complaint is an opportunity; a customer contacts you and asks for attention. Therefore, complaints should also be seriously and professionally handled. Complaints Management is not a tiresome secondary phenomenon but a well-considered commercial activity. Complaints from customers provide the enterprise with the possibility to improve its processes from the viewpoint of the customers. Setting up a complaints management procedure has therefore become an important component of delivery according to the needs of the market.

Application

It is a good starting point to see Complaints Management as an improvement process. A process requires an ordered set of activities to achieve its objectives. These activities are further explained below.

1 Listening

The first step is listening to the customer's complaint. Exactly by listening properly and allowing the customer to speak out, the customer feels reassured and taken seriously. Subsequently, questions will have to be asked to find out the cause of the problems. Customers draw conclusions rather quickly when it comes to complaints, while the cause of the problem and the subsequent complaint lies elsewhere and could therefore perhaps be with another supplier. Helping by asking questions and finding out the actual cause of the complaint gives the customer the calm and latitude to remain in discussion. In this step it is important to show understanding for the situation in which the customer has ended up. Do not enter into discussion with the customer: this will have the reverse effect.

2 Registry

As the second step, the complaint will have to be registered in sufficient detail to tackle the matters below. To the customer, this gives a signal that his complaint is being taken seriously. If several people become engaged in dealing with the complaint, everyone is informed of the situation and about what has already been done to resolve the customer's complaint.

For the enterprise, an analysis can later be made of, for example, the types of complaints, when they occur and what the consequences are. On the basis of this analysis, the enterprise can undertake action to prevent repetition and adjust the processes of the enterprise.

3 Resolution

The customer is waiting for the resolution of the problem that has arisen. It is useless to try to indicate that it is someone else's fault, for example. The solution sometimes lies in a very simple action and can then be quickly implemented. If the problem is more difficult, it is better to consult experts and agree with the customer within what time frame the solution can be expected.

If a solution cannot be found right away, it is always advisable to ask the customer if he has a solution in mind. Unreasonable proposals may be rejected. If the customer knows that the solution is on its way, he will be much calmer and give the enterprise the space to resolve the problem. Always indicate to the customer therefore what the solution will be, within what time frame the solution will be available and how any costs incurred will be dealt with.

4 Analysis

On the basis of the collected complaints, processes can be analysed. Especially those processes about which many complaints are received. On the basis of the symptoms and causes indicated by the customers, the process will have to be adjusted. This also applies to the activities belonging to these processes, the quality of the input of the process or the standards fixed for the output of the process. It can also occur that personnel will have to be trained better or more to resolve the problem in question.

5 Improvement

The improvement proposals for processes that come from the analysis are implemented in the enterprise. This can lead to employees having to be trained to carry out the activities in accordance with the quality standards. The improvement process leads to modified results in the enterprise, so that complaints with regard to this topic belong to the past.

6 Feedback

Customers who have reported a complaint highly appreciate being kept informed. They like to get information on the way in which the problem that caused the complaint has been resolved. Moreover, they appreciate knowing when the enterprise will again be operating with standard procedures. It often occurs that for the customers who have reported the complaint, another process is temporarily being used to prevent the problem recurring. When the processes have been adapted, this temporary process will be stopped.

Result

Seriously handling complaints provides the enterprise with the possibility to come into contact with customers. Customers who do not complain, no longer have any confidence in the enterprise and go over to the competition. In that case, it is more difficult to get these customers back. Customers who complain, indicate that they still have confidence in the enterprise but there must be a serious response to the complaint. This means: reacting according to the model and subsequently transforming the complaint into a new opportunity to build up a new relationship with the customer in question and once again do business with each other in the longer term. Handling a complaint well means for the customer that he has been taken seriously, in order that the relationship can further develop.

Focus areas

This model works only with objective complaints, complaints that are demonstrably well founded. This model does not work with subjective complaints, which live only in the assumptions of the customer. The customer actually thinks a mistake has been made but it was not made in the process of the enterprise. Usually, this concerns an expectation of the customer that was not discussed and, therefore, has not been settled. In this case, the customer wrongly assumes that this has been agreed. These complaints require a diplomatic solution.

Literature

- http://www.customerexpressions.com/
- http://customerservicezone.com/Complaint_Handling/
- http://www.gunsalus.net/gunsaluscomplainthandling.pdf

23
Conflict Handling

Author	Thomas Kilmann
Year developed	1974
Also known as	Conflict Styles
Objective	Handling conflicts

Model

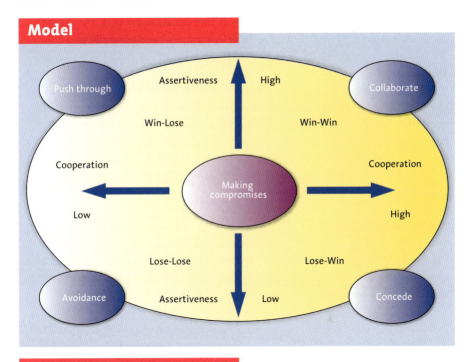

Background

Everyone deals differently with conflicts or opposing interests. After all, conflicts arise if one person wants something and the other wants something else and neither will concede. In this way, every person reacts naturally in a certain way when he or she ends up in a conflict situation. One is out to pursue his or her own objectives, while the other wishes to keep the relationship going and hence, concedes. Due to this, two opposite reactions arise: assertiveness or cooperation. The first ensures a result and depends on the extent to which someone looks after his or her own interests. The second assumes collaboration and an attempt is made to concede the interests of the other.

General management
Strategy
Marketing
Sales
Purchasing
Project & Planning
Production
Quality
Logistics & Distribution
Information management
Financial
HRM & HTM
Internationalisation

The Conflict Handling model recognises fives different styles of conflict handling:

- forcing through
- collaboration
- making compromises
- avoidance
- concession

Forcing through

With forcing through, one's own objectives and interests are foremost. The gain for one's own objective is more important and is usually at the cost of the other. This means there can only be one winner in this situation and that is the person who forces through. In proportion as this situation persists, the conflict becomes increasingly intense and will end in argument and quarrelling.

Collaboration

If not just your own objectives and interests are foremost but also the objectives and interests of the other, there can be collaboration. The interests of all the parties are openly discussed. Furthermore, considerations are made on the basis of which a solution can be found with which everyone can agree. This is not to say that this will proceed without any resistance. Substantial discussions can also occur with collaboration, but the starting point is and remains finding a joint solution.

Making compromises

Searching for an accord in the joint interest is most important here. When making compromises, it is more about everyone having an equal share than a greater whole (or a better solution) being created in total. When making compromises everyone must be prepared to sacrifice part of their principles or interests.

Avoidance

Avoiding discussions, difficult conversations or hard decisions is not about people looking after themselves or concerns about their relationships with others, but more about avoiding the risk of not being thought of as nice. In some situations avoidance is easy and the problem will automatically blow over.

Concession

Concession assumes that the relationship with the other may not be disrupted. In this way, one's own interests are subordinate to the interests of the other. This almost always means that the result of the conflict will be negative for the person conceding. If the other realises this, he will almost always abuse it. Which Conflict Handling style someone uses can be established on the basis of a questionnaire compiled by Thomas and Kilmann. This questionnaire comprises thirty questions. The score can be transferred to a table with the different Conflict Handling styles.

Result

The result of the score indicates which Conflict Handling style the person who filled it in follows as a basic style. Deviation from the basic style is possible, but only in controlled situations. In situations where people have to perform under pressure, they often revert to their basic style. In controlled situations a certain style can be consciously chosen to resolve a conflict or prevent it from escalating. This therefore means that everyone can in principle use all the styles.
For this model there are no right or wrong answers. It concerns a character trait of someone and right and wrong are irrelevant here.

Focus areas

The Thomas-Kilmann model does not take into account cultural differences. Due to this, the model can be less well interpreted if a conflict arises between people from different cultures. On the basis of their cultural background, people can react differently than in the Conflict Handling styles in the model.

Expansion

The Thomas-Kilmann model is a rigid model. That is to say, when answering the questions a choice must be made between A or B. Sometimes, neither answer fits the person. Ron Kraybill has adapted the Thomas-Kilmann model so that this objection can be taken into account. This model is known under the name of The Kraybill Conflict Style Inventory (KCSI). The rigid answers are replaced by a scale that runs from 'fits me' to 'absolutely does not fit me'. The results consist in two lists instead of one. The two lists are produced to give people more insight into how they react under stress. One list is on the basis of stress and one is on the basis of no stress. In this way, someone can see what reaction he/she will have in the different situations.
The test has been adapted to deal with cultural aspects. People have to state whether they come from an individualistic culture (for example: white, North American) or a collectivist culture (for example: black, Spain, India). These people also receive different instructions. Furthermore, the interpretation is more comprehensive and there are handy tips for each profile.

Literature

- Mackay, A. (2006). *Motivation, Ability and Confidence Building in People.* Butterworth-Heinemann.
- http://managementhelp.org/intrpsnl/basics.htm

General management
Strategy
Marketing
Sales
Purchasing
Project & Planning
Production
Quality
Logistics & Distribution
Information management
Financial
HRM & HTM
Internationalisation

24
Confrontation Matrix

Author	Stanford University (supplemented by M. Mulders)
Year developed	1960-1970
Also known as	-
Objective	Determining strategic options on the basis of a SWOT analysis

Model

		Opportunities				Threats				
		Specialisation on broad product knowledge	Lowering costs	Co-makership	Reintegration and practical training	Upcoming development of new technologies	Drastically reduced inflow	Fierce competition in simple types of work	Higher quality requirements	
Strengths	Problem-solving or capacity for thinking along	Y	Y	YY		N				4Y, 1N, 3
	Approach and attitude of personnel			Y	Y					2Y, 0N, 2
	Broadly-oriented machinery inventory	Y	YY	Y	Y	N	N	N	Y	6Y, 3N, 3
	Appreciation for quality and reliability	Y	Y	Y			Y			4Y, 0N, 4
Weaknesses	Professional level of the personnel	Y				N			N	1Y, 2N, -1
	Quantitative supply of personnel		Y	Y			NN			2Y, 2N, 0
	Limited choice of materials		N			N	N		N	0Y, 4N, -4
		4Y, 0N, 4	5Y, 1N, 4	6Y, 0N, 6	2Y, 0N, 2	0Y, 4N, -4	1Y, 4N, -3	0Y, 1N, -1	1Y, 2N, -1	

Y: If the answer to the question in the quadrant is yes
N: If the answer to the question in the quadrant is no
YY: If the answer to the question in the quadrant is convincingly yes
NN: If the answer to the question in the quadrant is convincingly no

Background

The confrontation matrix is filled in on the basis of the previously compiled SWOT analysis (see SWOT). Where the SWOT analysis only reflects a general strategy, the confrontation matrix goes a step further. Here, considered options are selected on the basis of which the enterprise can later determine its strategy. By means of the score on the intersections in the confrontation matrix, it becomes clear to the enterprise what are the most important options, which can be weighed against each other in a decision table (see Decision Table).

Application

Filling in the confrontation matrix and scoring at the intersections proceeds according to the following questions:

- *Opportunities and strengths*: does this strength enable us to utilise this opportunity?
- *Opportunities and weaknesses*: does this weakness prevent us from utilising this opportunity?
- *Threats and strengths*: does this strength enable us to avert this threat?
- *Threats and weaknesses*: does this weakness prevent us from averting this threat?

Three answers are possible for the questions at each intersection:
- If the answer is yes, then a Y is filled in at the intersection.
- If the answer is no, then an N is filled in at the intersection.
- If there is no relationship, the nothing is filled in at the intersection.

It is also possible to use a double Y or N if the relationship is extremely strong. In this fashion, the whole matrix is scored. When all the relationships have been assessed, totalisation takes place. All the Y's are added up, both horizontally and vertically. Then all the N's are added up, both horizontally and vertically. Finally, the sum of the N's is deducted from the sum of the Y's. This produces a score, both horizontally and vertically.

The values can subsequently be deduced from the total scores. The highest value indicates the most important area for attention.

When the highest value horizontally and the highest value vertically are now combined, a strategic option is found. This step is repeated until three or four options have been found, from which a choice can be made for the future strategy of the enterprise. It is also possible to cluster a number of intersections because these subjects are so closely related, they can be included in one option. To produce a proper formulation of the selected options, the following guidelines are followed:

- Describe the option in the form of a question.
- Use the terminology of the opportunities/ threats and strengths/ weaknesses from the matrix.

- Use one of the following verbs according to its place in the confrontation matrix:
  - opportunity and strength: growth
  - opportunity and weakness: reinforce
  - threat and strength: defend
  - threat and weakness: withdraw

The options have now been described. If clustering has taken place, there will be several descriptions in the option. Each option receives a unique name, so that it is recognisable to everyone in the enterprise. The options thus obtained can be assessed via a decision table, on the basis of which the final choice can be made.

Result

The result from the confrontation matrix is a balanced overview of the possible options for the enterprise, on the basis of which further strategy formulation can take place.

Focus areas

The SWOT analysis and the confrontation matrix are models that are indicative for the strategy of the enterprise. The actual actions resulting from the different options and the selected option will have to be further formulated by the enterprise.

Literature

None.

25
Core Competence

Authors	Hamel and Prahalad (supplemented by M. Mulders)
Year developed	1990
Also known as	Core Competitive Ability, Core Competencies, Core Expertise
Objective	Determining the most important competences that contribute towards the results of the enterprise

Model

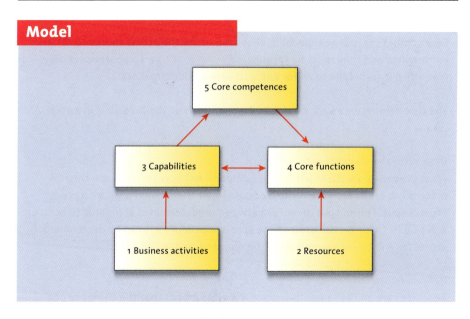

Background

Hamel and Prahalad define core competences as follows:

> 'A core competence is a package of skills and technologies that enables a company to provide the customer with a certain advantage' (1994, p. 205).

If a company is able to define and develop these core competences, a competitive advantage is created. In proportion, as the enterprise exists for longer and grows, the core competences are diluted and companies try everything to generate turnover. In depressed economic times, they then say 'back to the core business'. However, this has become difficult to define. A review of the core competences is then necessary.

General management

Strategy

Marketing

Sales

Purchasing

Project & Planning

Production

Quality

Logistics & Distribution management

Information management

Financial

HRM & HTM

Internationalisation

Application

In addition to their definition, the following aspects are also determinative for establishing a core competence (Hamel and Prahalad 1990; 1994):

- Core competences are *not product-specific*; they constitute a collection of the competitive properties of a series of products or services. A core competence may not be confused with the term core product because a core competence is more comprehensive and specific than a core product.
- Core competences definitely contribute towards the competitive capacity of the organisation.
- Core competences are an *interconnection of skills and technologies*; they form 'the sum of all knowledge present in the relevant skills and organisational units'.
- Core competences produce *fundamental value benefits* on as broad a plane as possible in the eyes of the customer.
- Core competences are unique in the sense that a competitor cannot recognise and then imitate them.
- Core competences are expandable; they constitute the access routes to different markets and they must be formulated as such. 'A core competence is only core when it forms the basis for entry to new product markets.'

The core competences are established on the basis of the following five-step plan:

1 Determine the business activities

What processes are there within the company and how cohesive are they? A process is a set of activities with a certain input that should produce a predefined output. This output must fall between predetermined standards to be acceptable. Later, on the basis of the core competences, it can be determined if processes will be outsourced or can be divested, and which.

2 Determine the resources

Resources are all the tangible and non-tangible means that the company possesses. Resources are grouped into three categories: *physical resources*, such as buildings and machines; *human resources*, such as the knowledge, experience, training and skills of individual employees; and *organisational resources*, such as consultation structures, procedures, control and coordination structures. This concerns determining strategic resources that cannot easily be exchanged between companies. Due to this, these companies have an advantage with regard to their competitors because these resources cannot be directly copied or imitated. A strategic resource must therefore provide additional value, be scarce, sustainable and hard to copy.

3 Determine the capabilities of the company

Capabilities are defined as the skills and technologies a company has available. This concerns the interconnection of knowledge, skills, technologies and individuals. This interconnection produces a large contribution to the trading results, allows the output of processes to fall within the standards, contributes to the added value for the customer and is lodged in processes and procedures. Examples of capabilities are reliable delivery time, customer-friendliness and a stable product. Only capabilities that directly contribute to the products/ services and customer value are counted. Here, attention must also be paid to the fact that some capabilities do not currently contribute but could well do so in the future. Conversely, it also applies that capabilities that now produce a contribution may perhaps no longer be able to do so in the future. Determining these capabilities can best be done by the person ultimately responsible in the department or the owner of the process. To this end, the following formulations are used: 'With the aid of ... (resource) customer benefits are achieved by ... (capability).' By using this formulation, resources are not regarded as capabilities. Example: resource 'IT system'; capability 'giving rapid answers'. The sentence is then expressed: 'With the aid of the IT system, customer benefits are achieved by providing rapid answers.'

4 Determine the core competences

In order to choose from the core competences, five questions are used:

- At which activities is the company good at this time?
- What does this produce in terms of customer value for each activity? Activities without customer value are not counted.
- Is the activity product-specific? All product-specific activities do not count. Product-specific activities cannot be applied to other products or markets.
- What capabilities contribute to the activities per department? Core activities to which fewer than three departments (or divisions) contribute do not count. Activities must be shared by several departments (or divisions).
- Which competitors can copy or imitate this activity in the short term? Activities that are not unique are removed.

5 Determine the core functions

This last step can be seen as a checking step. A function is a defined function for the performance of the activities of the company. A core function is a function that fulfils a strategic value and is unique. That is to say, it cannot be quickly filled by someone outside the company. The control step consists in checking that capabilities are not filled in that are not performed by that department in reality. For each department it is discovered which function performs this capability. If the department does not perform the capability, it could be that it may not be included in the core competences.

Result

The company obtains insight into the competences with which the company can distinguish itself with regard to the competition in the market. Moreover, it provides handholds for determining in which new markets the enterprise can succeed and in which it cannot. Determining the core competences gives the company the insight to achieve a strategic advantage in the long term. Besides establishing the core competences, the company obtains insight into non-critical business processes. These business processes are suitable for out-sourcing to companies for which this activity is regarded as a core competence. This guarantees quality and the company is better able to focus on its own core competences.

Focus areas

When establishing the core competences, no account is taken of the employees who have to support these core competences, in particular the knowledge and skills necessary to support the core competences. It is crucial for a company to ensure that the employees have sufficient skills and knowledge to manage the core competences.

Literature

- Hamel, G., Prahalad, C. (1990). The Core Competence of the Corporation. *Harvard Business Review*, 68, 79-93.
- Hamel, G., Prahalad, C. (1994). *Competing the Future*. Harvard Business School Press.
- http://archiv.tu-chemnitz.de/pub/2008/0085/index_en.html

26
Core Marketing System

Author	**Leeflang**
Year developed	**1993**
Also known as	**–**
Objective	**Establishing the players with a direct influence on the enterprise**

Model

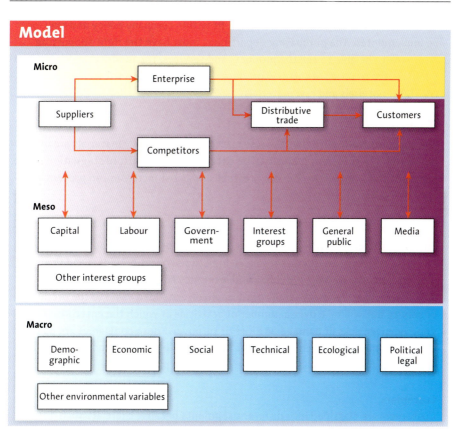

Background

The marketing department of an enterprise is responsible for the positioning of products and services in the market in a proper manner. The task of the marketing management is to communicate the added value of the services and products of the company to the customers, build up further relationships with them and ensure that they are satisfied. It is obvious that they cannot do this alone.

For this, not only are other departments of the enterprise important, but also other players such as suppliers, competitors, distributive trades and the different interest groups, for example, sector organisations. The departments and the players together form the Core Marketing System of the enterprise.

Application

To see what influence the different players have on the enterprise, they are described one by one.

Enterprise

When realising the marketing planning, the marketing department should take into account the other departments within the enterprise such as management, purchasing, production, planning, finance and administration. The top management determines whether the proposals fit within company policy and may be implemented. The purchasing department must have the right supporting resources to be able to sell the products and services. The production department must be able to produce the new products and purchasing must have acquired the right materials and raw materials.

Suppliers

The suppliers make sure that the raw materials and ancillary materials are in stock on time and in sufficient quantity. The enterprise cannot afford stagnation in the supply of these materials. Promptly establishing cost increases can prevent problems or losses.

Distributive trades

These are the players who support the promotion, purchasing and distribution of products and services, such as resellers, logistics services providers and financial services providers (credit providers and insurance companies).
The distributive trades generally produce no direct added value to the product or service but will take over a number of activities at which the enterprise is less good or cover risks of damage and loss of turnover. These companies are paid for their activities. This is a cost item that will have to be closely monitored, because these costs have a direct effect on the price of the product or service.

Customers

Customers are classified into different segments because there are such differences that they cannot be approached in the same way. Each segment sets different requirements for the products and services. Only by doing research among the customers themselves can it be unambiguously established what their current needs are.

Competitors

There are few markets without competitors. Competition in the market keeps the suppliers sharp, due to this they wish to better respond to the needs of the customers and position themselves more strongly with regard to the others. Solely satisfying the needs of the customers is thus not sufficient; the organisation will also have to distinguish itself from the other suppliers on the market by means of the distinctive capacity of their products or services (USP, *Unique Selling Point*).

Interest groups
Interest groups are groups that have an indirect interest in the enterprise that wishes to achieve its objectives. These groups can exercise direct or indirect influence on the activities of the enterprise and so advance the achievement of the objectives or precisely hold them back. The enterprise must take into account seven interest groups:
- financial groups: acquisition of capital
- media groups: news and topical items
- government groups: legal provisions
- action groups: the environment, consumer groups, minority groups, et cetera
- local groups: neighbourhood residents
- public opinion: image of the enterprise
- internal groups: personnel from high to low

Most interest groups cannot be directly influenced but do have an influence on the enterprise itself. It is important that the enterprise knows these players well, to be able to predict what can happen in which situation and so promptly respond to the reactions of the interest groups.

Result

The enterprise obtains insight into the market players involved, such that the enterprise can promptly respond to the reactions of these players. Due to this, it is more predictable if and how the enterprise can achieve its objectives.

Focus areas

The Core Marketing System indicates the interests of the different players in the immediate environment of the enterprise. What the model does not go into is the mutual relationship or dependence of the different players. In this way, a multinational can influence the consumers by advertising. The effects on the distributive trades and retail trade are ignored.

Literature
- Kotler, P., Armstrong G. (2009). *The Principles of Marketing*. Prentice Hall.

27
Core Qualities

Author	D. Ofman
Year developed	1994
Also known as	Core Quality Quadrant, Core Quadrant
Objective	Increasing personal effectiveness

Model

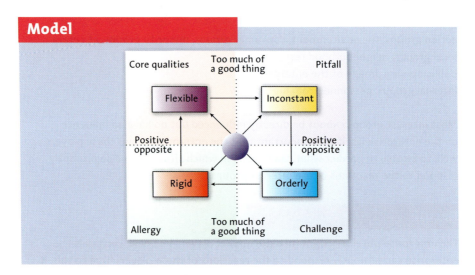

Background

Everyone naturally has strong and less strong sides. The strong sides help you to easily get along with others or perform activities at work. Due to this, pleasure in one's work and private life is created. Unfortunately, the less strong sides sometimes get in the way and everything goes less well. By means of the core quadrant, both sides can be better clarified. The logic of the quadrant is for many a relief, because people begin to realise that someone's pitfall is the result of strength and a great deal can be learned from people to whom one is allergic. In this way, the quality of the one reinforces the challenge from the other. With the aid of the core quadrant, insight is obtained into the behaviour and the background thereof. The less strong sides are seen as a deformation of the strong sides. This makes it easier to accept one's less good sides and work on them.

In a core quadrant, the connection between someone's core quality, pitfall, challenge and allergy becomes visible. These turn out to be all four inevitably bound to each other. They are the logical consequence of each other and together form a quadrant.

Core Qualities

Core Qualities are qualities that belong to the core of a person.
Examples of Core Qualities are:

- decisiveness
- caring
- carefulness
- courage
- enthusiasm
- helpfulness
- receptivity
- tact
- orderliness
- sympathy
- flexibility

A core quality is always potentially present. The distinction between qualities and skills lies primarily in the fact that the qualities come from inside and skills are learned from outside. Skills can be learned, while qualities can be developed.

Deformation or pitfall

Every core quality has a shadow side, also called the deformation or pitfall. The deformation is not so much the opposite of the core quality as a superabundance of it, in other words: the quality has overdosed. Success due to the application of a quality can turn into too much use of this core quality, due to which this 'overdose' becomes a weak point. Decisiveness degenerates into pushiness, caring into patronisation, involvement into obtrusiveness or obsession and sensitivity into sentimentality.

Challenge

As a positive element, in contrast to this pitfall is the challenge. The challenge helps to keep a core quality 'pure'. This can be by constantly keeping in view the challenge that is important for this quality. The challenge is the positive opposing quality of the pitfall. The challenge is the realistic component that keeps the core quality in balance and aims at a certain healthy counterweight. In this way, the pitfall for 'caring' can be patronising; the challenge is then: let loose. With the quality of 'courage', caution (= challenge) can preserve people from recklessness (= pitfall).

Allergy

There is a fourth aspect to all this that is designated with the term allergy. It turns out that people can poorly tolerate when others ask too much from their challenge. The challenge is always an aspiration, it is always something, seen from a certain core quality, that you retain with difficulty. Someone who is naturally very orderly can have as a challenge: flexibility (pliability). If someone makes too great a demand on this flexibility, then the person in question will be unable to tolerate it. He or she will be under stress and there is an 'allergic reaction'. The challenge 'strive for flexibility' (something that is already difficult!) is put too much to the test. This results in an outburst or an apathetic reaction: do nothing about it. Contempt is characteristic for situations in which people are confronted with their allergy. Contempt because the other is lacking on an essential point, namely the point on which the person in question is precisely strong.

In this way, the Core Qualities, pitfalls, allergies and challenges are compiled for everyone. With the core quadrant you can quickly and easily obtain a view of your peculiarities. This insight can help you to learn to recognise possible friction at an early stage. A person who can express his Core Qualities in his work will feel fine and perform better using less energy.

Examples of core quadrants are:

Quality	Pitfall	Challenge	Allergy
decisiveness	pushiness	patience	passiveness
helpfulness	intrusiveness	independence	detachments
sense of perspective	nonchalance	seriousness	melancholia
spontaneity	inconstancy	consistency	straightforwardness
flexibility	blowing with the wind	steadfastness	rigidity
accuracy	minuteness	creativity	confusion

It is possible to step in via any quadrant. Begin with inventorying the qualities and work them out via the pitfall, the challenge and the allergy. Or begin with the challenges, reason back to the pitfall and recognise the quality behind it. Ask friends, family or colleagues for pitfalls. Work back from pitfall to quality and then discover the challenges and allergies.

Core quadrants can be used for:
- performing self-investigation, for example, by compiling a personal SWOT analysis
- analysing conflicts in preparation for a conflict handling interview
- preparation for a performance interview
- drafting a personal development plan

Result

The core quadrant is an aid for your own development. Based on the core quadrants, strategies can be sketched out for dealing with difficult situations. When someone is confronted with his own allergies, rigidity occurs. With the insight gained from this model, such situations can be better handled in time. The model also gives a better view of the quality behind the allergy, due to which more appreciation for the other can be produced.

Furthermore, more insight is obtained into the mechanism of mutually reinforcing allergies. If someone encounters an allergy himself, the chance is great that he or she will revert to a pitfall in reaction. And that only reinforces the allergy of the other. This is a dynamic that often occurs in projects! The situation can be broken through by reacting at that moment from a quality and a challenge. That is the combination that works the best. By reacting from this point of view, it is possible to help both oneself and the other to turn a difficult situation into a fruitful discussion.

Focus areas

There are too many Core Qualities to mention. Furthermore, everyone has his of her own definition for each core quality with its appurtenant pitfalls and allergies. This makes it very difficult to make this objectively measurable and it only remains to sum up a number of correspondences and contradictions. Compiling the Core Qualities often leads to a focus on what is not going well instead of reinforcing what is going well. Moreover, it turns out that the step from inventory of the Core Qualities to actual change is too big a step for many. Because of this, the model of the core quadrants silts up to a static whole instead of something dynamic in which the development van the person is central.

Literature

- Ofman, D. (2001). *Core Qualities*. Scriptum.
- Ofman, D. (2005). *Core Quadrant Game*. Core Quality.
- Ofman, D., Weck, R. van der (2001). *The Core Qualities of the Enneagram*. Scriptum.

28

Costs-Benefits Analysis

Author	Developed in practice
Year developed	–
Also known as	CBA, Break-even Analysis, Payback Period, ROI (Return On Investment)
Objective	Financial justification of projects / investments

Model

Costs	Benefits
· Hours of personnel	· Turnover
· Materials	· Customer satisfaction
· Software	· Higher service levels
· Promotion	· High-quality products
· Machines	· Lower costs
· Buildings	· Fewer personnel
	· Higher capacity utilisation rate

Background

The execution of a project costs money. But a project is usually started to achieve more turnover. In other words: what benefits are there in the financial sense against the costs of the project? Before a project is started, it is important to know if the benefits are higher than the costs. This is called the ROI (Return On Investment) and is an important indicator for the issue of whether the proposed project will actually be carried out. The most simple method of Costs-Benefits Analysis is by establishing all the costs and benefits for each topic. The benefits are more difficult to estimate than the costs. The calculation of the benefits usually assumes expected sales on the basis of an external survey.

Application

A Costs-Benefits Analysis is important if the management has to take a decision whether a certain proposal or project will or will not take place. Although some projects are obligatory due to legal regulations for example, most projects must deliver benefits. The Costs-Benefits Analysis proceeds according to the steps below:

1 Determine the costs on the basis of hours, materials, software, promotion, machines, buildings and unforeseen, among other items.
2 Determine the benefits on the basis of turnover, customer satisfaction, higher service levels, higher-quality products, lower costs, fewer personnel, higher capacity utilisation rate.
3 Determine the ROI (payback period).

1 Determine the costs

The costs consist in various components for which the costs are charged to the project. These are the hours of the personnel on this project, the materials used (such as office articles, rental of PCs, lease of cars, raw materials, et cetera) and the promotion costs (advertising, posters, flyers, brochures, films). Machines that are used for the project are also included as cost items. For buildings the same applies as for machines, if they have been purchased as real estate. It could be that the buildings are rented. In that case, the cost of the rent is charged to the project. When budgeting for the costs of a project, it is wise to include an item (unforeseen) to compensate for disappointments. This item can amount to 10% or 15% of the total project costs, depending on the risks the project runs.

2 Determine the benefits

Establishing the benefits is more difficult than establishing the costs. To cost the project, an analysis of the benefits is necessary. The benefits often consist of less concrete items for which an estimate has to be made. This estimate should be as much as possible based on calculations in which a number of assumptions may be used. The benefits of a project often lie in the area of more turnover, due to higher sales in the market. These sales are calculated on the basis of the assumption that 3% more customers will buy this product, for example. The turnover is then derived from the sales. The benefits with regard to customer satisfaction, quality and service derive from the same assumption for sales. If, there are savings on raw and auxiliary materials or energy due to the project, for example, then these benefits are also credited to the project.

With regard to savings in personnel costs, the enterprise should be cautious. If, in a project for a number of personnel, 10% is saved on their hours, this does not immediately say that the enterprise will incur less costs. After all, these personnel are employed by the enterprise and in general have a fixed salary. How to handle this is a matter for the management and dependent on the financial policy of the enterprise.A higher capacity utilisation rate for machines is easier to calculate, however. Determining assumptions is sometimes very difficult because nobody can see into the future. Use can be made of an estimation technique based on scenarios. The first scenario is the actual scenario in which the assumptions are realised. The second scenario is a pessimistic scenario. Here, the lowest amount possible is assumed, perhaps even zero. The third scenario assumes a positive scenario where the maximum is realised. Averaging these three scenarios generally provides a reliable estimate for the assumption.

3 Determine the ROI

With the Costs-Benefits Analysis, it is about the enterprise knowing whether the project will, in the financial sense, produce more than it costs and when the investments will be paid back. Where with the Costs-Benefits Analysis only all costs and benefits were added up, for the Return On Investment, account is also taken of depreciation periods. The formula for the calculation is:

Payback Period = costs of investment/annual cash flow

Result

The result is a financial foundation on the basis of which the management can make a decision to carry out the project or not.

Focus areas

If the personnel really want the results of a project but they do not compare with the cost and effort, there is sometimes some juggling of the figures and the benefits are too positively estimated. Calculation via the scenarios largely solves this problem but cannot prevent it entirely.

Literature

None.

29
Cultural Dimensions, Hofstede

Author	G. Hofstede
Year developed	1980
Also known as	–
Objective	Providing insight into cultural differences in order to try to bridge them

Model

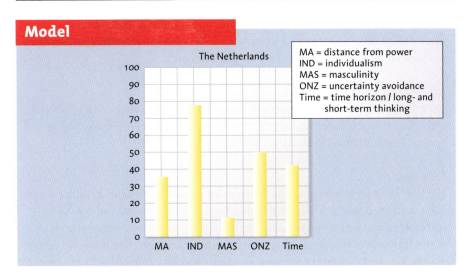

The Netherlands

MA = distance from power
IND = individualism
MAS = masculinity
ONZ = uncertainty avoidance
Time = time horizon / long- and short-term thinking

Background

Doing business does not take place between enterprises but between people. Everyone comes from a certain culture. The standards and values that people maintain are based on the culture from which they originate. It is therefore very important to include the cultural aspects when doing business. Hofstede researched the cultures of seventy countries and, based on this, established four dimensions in cultures. They are distance from power, avoidance of uncertainty, individual versus collective and masculine versus feminine. Later, the time horizon was included.

Application

The application of the model is as follows.

Distance from power

Distance from power is the distance there is between people that the population thinks is normal. In cultures with a large power distance such as Belgium, France and Germany, status products are the most important means of showing people one's position. In cultures with a short distance from power, such as the Netherlands and Denmark, this does not apply.

Individualism

Individualism and collectivism are related trading with people in a culture. With collectivism, people will trade as part of a group, while with individualism they trade as if they are individuals. South Europeans are more collectivist and north Europeans more individualistic.

Masculinity

Masculine cultures consider hard, 'male' aspects such as assertiveness, success and competition, the most important values and standards. With feminine cultures, the 'female', aspects such as quality of life, personal relationships, service and care are the most important values and standards.

Uncertainty avoidance

Uncertainty avoidance as an aspect of culture concerns holding on to structure and rules in unstructured situations. Structured cultures are Germany and south Europe. The Scandinavian countries are more unstructured.

Time horizon

The time horizon is related to the short- or long-term thinking of a culture. Here, it is established that short-term thinking is related to conventional and historical thinking and long-term thinking has a more pro-active and pragmatic view of the future. With the application of Hofstede's model, account is always taken of several cultural differences together. In this way, in a country with a feminine culture, not only do we review the need for safety, but also power relationships and legislation within the culture. After establishing the Cultural Dimensions of one's own culture and those of the other, the following steps can be undertaken. This is necessary to prevent that other cultures are viewed with one's own cultural values in mind and hence, incorrect decisions are taken.

To eliminate this risk, the following steps can be taken:
1 Write the terms of reference in terms of your own culture.
2 Write the terms of reference in terms of the foreign culture.
3 Isolate the influences of your own cultural thinking.
4 Define the terms of reference again for the foreign market's cultural aspects.

Cultural aspects are not about what is better or worse, the emphasis is different. And this is precisely so important for doing business successfully in and with other cultures.
If the Cultural Dimensions of the Netherlands and China are compared, then it is

clear to see where the differences lie. Where the Netherlands is individualistic, the Chinese culture shows great collectivism. This means that doing business in China does not take place with one person but a whole group. It is also important to be included in a group for doing business (*Quanxi*). The Chinese have the highest score in the world in the time dimension. Problems are resolved by time and not so much by the will or power people have.

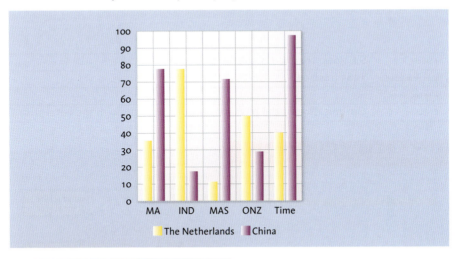

Result

By obtaining better insight into the culture of the country the people come from, the decision-making process becomes clearer. This subsequently leads to better relations and ultimately, more turnover.

Focus areas

The model assumes homogeneous cultures in countries, while in reality, the cultures in countries have a mixed composition. The model was in the first instance set up with regard to only one enterprise, IBM. It is conceivable that the 'culture' of IBM influenced the employees of the enterprise and the backgrounds of the model are consequently incorrect.

Literature

- Hofstede, G. (2003). *Culture's Consequence*. SAGE Publications Inc.
- www.geert-hofstede.com

30
Customer Order Decoupling Point

Authors	S.J. Hoekstra and J.H.J.M. Romme
Year developed	1985 (revised)
Also known as	–
Objective	Optimisation of the physical flow of goods through the enterprise

Model

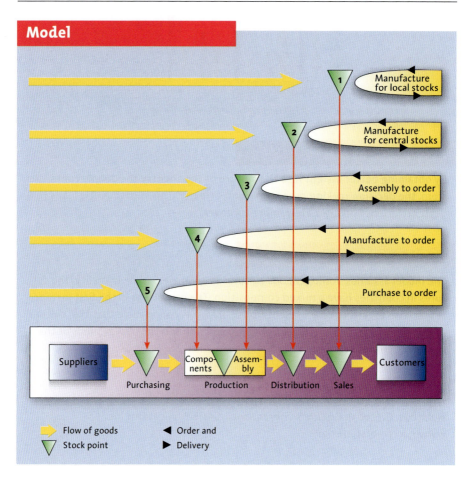

Background

Manufacturing has to be done as cheaply and quickly as possible. To carry out the production from raw materials or semi-manufactures into complete end products as quickly as possible at as low as possible cost, work floors in factories are built as optimally as possible. With the organisation of the work floor, account must thus be taken of the positioning of the machines and the intervening stock points. This arrangement is called the logistics ground form.

It is best if as many as possible products can be produced in succession. Due to the increase in scale achieved, the costs per unit will be lower. This requires a standard product in large quantities. Because customers are increasingly setting requirements, however, it is less possible to produce these large amounts. Manufacturing to customer specifications means more resetting of the machines, different raw materials and/or auxiliary materials or different finishes to products. The more production to customer specifications takes place the earlier in the production or distribution process, the higher the costs. The point at which the standard product changes into a specific (customer-oriented) product is called the Customer Order Decoupling Point or CODP. To deal with them efficiently and make the right considerations between costs and customer requirements, these decoupling points are defined in the model.

Application

There are five different Customer Order Decoupling Points, the stock points 1 to 5 inclusive in the figure:

1 *Production and consignment to stock*: the products are produced as standard products. There are no customer-specific items. The products are sent to and stored in the warehouses and stockrooms of retailers close to the customers. The products are thus locally stored.

2 *Production to stock*: this is also non-customer specific production. The end products are stored in a warehouse at the end of the production line for later shipment to the customers. The products are thus centrally stored.

3 *Assembly (putting together) to order*: products of which purchasing, production, construction and delivery takes longer than the desired delivery time are kept in stock. If this all takes less time than the desired delivery time for the customer, the components are only ordered when the order comes in.

4 *Manufacturing to order*: raw and auxiliary materials are held in stock. They are only produced when there is an actual order. This means that just about every order is customer-specific, unless the delivery time allows for the combination of orders from different customers. In this case, the specifications must be the same.

5 *Purchasing and manufacture to order*: no stocks are held. The order for the raw and auxiliary materials only goes out when the order has been placed by the customer.

The products that are produced for CODP run a stock risk. That is to say, they have already been produced but not yet sold. Products sold after the CODP run a delivery risk and perhaps arrive too late for the customer.

To determine the place of a CODP, the following steps must be undertaken:

1 *Nominate product-market combinations (PMC)*: to directly make a full analysis for each separate product (all suppliers, all production aspects, all distribution aspects and all customer aspects) would take too long and is too expensive because companies usually have a large range of products. Due to this, we look first at the product-market combination. PMCs are groups of similar products that are sold on a specific market. By looking at the PMCs, the analysis is shorter and costs are saved.

2 *Inventory the flows of goods and information*: for each product line/PMC the processing and the stock points must first be mapped out. For each processing or stock point, the (processing) time is established. Bringing to and taking away from the stock points must also be included.

3 *Determine CODP and delivery time*: for each PMC it is now determined where the point is that the product goes from general to specific, or rather, the CODP. Determine subsequently what the delivery time is from the CODP to the customer.

4 *Analyse and determine points for improvement*: the parts before and after the CODP can now be analysed to establish whether improvements can be made in the throughput time. This occurs on the physical flow of goods but also on the flow of information. For all the involved process, supervisors must be present.

5 *Authorities*: indicate who may make which choices in relation to the organisation of the CODP.

Result

The results of correct application are visible in various areas, of which the most important are:

- The enterprise obtains more grip on the production process and costs in this way.
- Production interruptions like urgent orders can then only come from the salesmen and do not arise due to planning problems.
- An important point can be the waiting times for the different processes. If these can be shortened, a faster throughput time is often possible.
- Stock levels become lower, also interim stocks.
- Delivery time becomes shorter.
- Delivery reliability increases.
- Costs go down.

Focus areas

Adjusting the Customer Order Decoupling Point cannot take place just like that. This usually has great consequences for the whole enterprise, for example, in the areas of:

- delivery times
- throughput times
- costs
- prices
- adjusting machines
- different quantities of stocks of end products
- raw materials and auxiliary materials

The management would be wise to organise a project for this with all those involved.

Literature

- Cheng, G., Wan, C., Wang, S. (2010). *Postponement Strategies in Supply Chain Management*. Springer.
- Tseng, M., Piller, T. (2003). *The Customer Centric Enterprise*. Springer-Verlag Berlin and Heidelberg GmbH & Co. KG.
- http://www.essays.se/about/Customer+Order+Decoupling+Point/

31
Customer Pyramid, Curry

Author	J. Curry
Year developed	1998
Also known as	Customer Marketing Method, Customer Profitability Analysis
Objective	Mapping out a customer base

Model

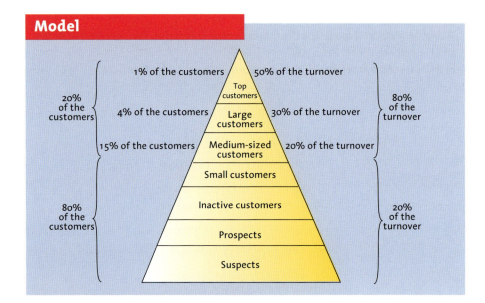

Background

The existing clients (customers) are the most important customers an enterprise has with regard to achieved turnover. It is therefore of interest to get to know and cherish this group of customers. This group of customers ensures the continuity of the enterprise. If loyal customers leave, they will not easily return because the choice to leave was already difficult but unavoidable. While the marketing and sales department is searching for new customers, contact with existing customers is often forgotten. Therefore, it is important to know who the customers are and what turnover they generate. To map this out, use can be made of the Customer Pyramid, also called the Customer Marketing Method.

With the aid of the Customer Pyramid, you can map out which customers account for what proportion of the turnover. From Curry's research, the following statements are true:

- Only 20% of the customers provide 80% of the turnover.
- 80% of the large customers provide 20% of the turnover.
- All the customers provide 90% of the turnover.
- The least marketing budget is allocated to existing customers, while non-customers receive the most.
- There are always customers that can generate more turnover (higher in the pyramid).
- Prospects[7] and Suspects[8] are paid more attention than customers.

Within the ratio of 20% of customers with 80% turnover there is a sub-division into three groups:
- top customers; this is 1% of the customer base with 50% of the turnover
- large customers; this is 4% of the customer base with 30% of the turnover
- medium-sized customers; this is 15% of the customer base with 20% of the turnover

The remaining customers (80%) are divided into the groups below:
- small customers
- inactive customers[9]
- prospects
- suspects

The objective of the method is to move as many as possible customers from the bottom of the pyramid to the top. To this end, a four-step plan has been drafted, comprising four phases:

1 Registration of customer details
To gain insight into the customers they will have to be registered and in such a way that analyses can easily be performed on them. The data that is recorded will have to be established by the enterprise itself. The most important are:
- name, address, city details
- turnover data
- history
- product data
- data from the account manager
- agreements made
- visits

To create a division between top customers and the other customers, turnover limits have to be set. For each segment in the pyramid a turnover limit will have to be established, for example: top customers are always above €200,000, large customers between €100,000 and €200,000, et cetera.

2 Analysis of customer details

Via the information system, the customers will first have to be sorted on their respective turnover. In this way, insight is gained into which and how many customers are in the top segment, how much turnover they generate and what percentage it is of the whole turnover. This is also visible for the other segments. On the basis of the historical data, insight is gained into how the customers in question move in the pyramid: upwards, downwards, new customers or customers that disappear.

3 Planning the activities

New turnover targets are established on the basis of the objectives of the enterprise and the turnover targets of the previous period, usually one year. These turnover targets will have to be divided among the customers concerned by the account managers. It will thus have to be determined what the turnover per customer in the coming period of one year will be. This turnover depends on a number of factors, such as customer share[10] and total size. On the basis of these data the account manager can make predictions about which customers will migrate to a different segment of the pyramid next year. In this way, a migration matrix can be created in which the enterprise can see which customers will end up in which segment of the pyramid next year.

Next to moving existing customers upwards, new customers will have to be recruited. To this end, their needs will have to be properly inventoried so that they can be capitalised on. These companies can also be included in the migration matrix.

Subsequently, the sales and marketing resources can be deployed to achieve the migration matrix.

4 Realisation of the planning

The planning done in the previous phase can now be implemented.

The resources deployed for sales and marketing are divided among the companies in the migration matrix. The budget is divided on the basis of the segment of the customers in the pyramid.

Result

With the Customer Pyramid, the enterprise has available a structured method of dividing the sales and marketing budgets and efforts among those customers who ensure the actual turnover of the enterprise.

Focus areas

A general criticism of the Customer Pyramid is that too much attention is paid to customers of which the company already knows they are top customers. In proportion, too little attention is paid to customers that have the potential to become top customers. The company thereby runs the risk that these customers will be lost.

The model assumes the turnover and not the profitability of a customer for the enterprise.

Literature

- Curry, J. (2000). *The Customer Marketing method.* Simon & Schuster.
- www.customermarketing.com

---

[7] Prospect: a company with which there has been contact in the past year and where the product or service can be offered.

[8] Suspects: companies with which there has not yet been contact, but where there is a possible need for the product or service.

[9] Inactive customers: customers who have generated no turnover in the past year.

[10] Customer share: the share in per cent of the budget of the customer that is spent with the enterprise.

32

Customer Relationship Management

Author	Definition by the Gartner Group
Year developed	2004
Also known as	CRM, Sales Force Automation, Enterprise Relationship Management
Objective	Determining the enterprise's strategy towards customers

Model

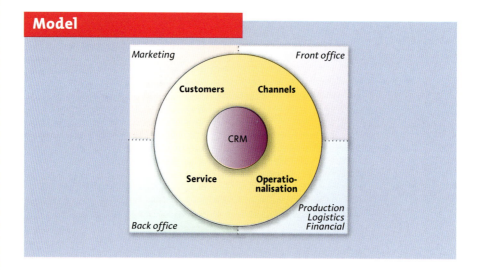

Although maintaining customer relations is already very old, only in 2004 was there a definition that establishes CRM at its actual value: the definition of the Gartner Group:

> 'An IT-enabled business strategy, the outcome of which optimises profitable, revenue and customer satisfaction by organising around customer segments, fostering customer-satisfying behaviours and implementing customer-centric processes.'

The most important aspect of CRM is that it is not a selling system but a strategy in support of processes for the benefit of customer satisfaction. Here, it is important that all personnel have a service-oriented and pro-active attitude towards supporting customers and internal collaboration.

To apply CRM correctly in the enterprise, the following steps must be undertaken.

1 Draft a CRM strategy

Because CRM is not so much a model but a business strategy, everything that is done or input in the area of CRM must fit in with the strategy of the enterprise. The strategy of the enterprise is established in the vision, mission, objectives and strategy.

Thinking from the viewpoint of the market and the customers, the processes in the enterprise will also have to be organised as a process, so that close mutual collaboration is created between the different departments in the enterprise. After all, all the departments contribute towards the realisation of the product or service to the customers. Thus, the enterprise will have to think in terms of the customer and not its own primary process. This means: not product-oriented but market-oriented thinking.

2 Determine customers

In terms of the thinking behind CRM, the organisation will have to select its customers more carefully. After all, it is no longer about 'hit and run', selling something quickly and then back to another customer (pro-active). In terms of CRM thinking, it is about the relationship with the customers. Here the relationship is based on trust and long-term. Due to this, the enterprise will have to invest more in maintaining relationships, even if this does not immediately produce an order with every visit. Precisely because the enterprise has regard for the problems of the customers and deploys its knowledge and personnel to further assist the customer, this will lead to a sustainable relationship where both the enterprise and the customer end up in a win-win situation. It is also true that the enterprise has to maintain contact with the customer on a regular (pro-active) basis, instead of waiting until the customer comes with a question (re-active).

3 Choosing channels

With channels is intended here: the different contacts that the enterprise has with the customers. This is also called Multi-channel management. It is not just the account manager who has contact with the customer. With Team Buying and Team Selling, several people are involved with the customer (see Team Buying Team Selling (TBTS)). On behalf of this customer often also several people are involved. Partners are often involved in the delivery of products or services (for example, the driver from the transport company), which have contact with the customer at different levels in the enterprise. They should be ambassadors for the enterprise because at that moment, they represent the standards of the organisation.

They must radiate the same standards and values as the personnel of the enterprise. Due to far-reaching information technology, customers are able to directly access and view the operational systems of the enterprise. If this does not function well, another communication channel is created from the IT department to the customer.

4 Operationalisation of CRM

It was established earlier that the departments of the enterprise must collaborate with each other very well, because every department contributes towards a sustainable relationship with the customer. This automatically means that the personnel of the enterprise may no longer be managed in a task-focused manner. Task-orientation is simply the performance of their task without taking account of situations that take place elsewhere in the enterprise; nothing more than one's own task needs to be done. In a process (relationship)-oriented enterprise, there is more focus on results and the personnel is deployed on the basis of their competences, knowledge, experience and personality. It is also proper that the personnel have an eye for what happens in the processes preceding their own and what they need to produce for the processes that come after. This applies to both the primary and supporting processes in the enterprise.

5 Provision of service

Support to customers from the enterprise is of great importance for a sustainable relationship. With service there are very many aspects involved, where it is also of great importance that the personnel thinks in terms of the market and the customers and they have a service-oriented attitude. The customer wants one point of contact within the enterprise and does not wish to be sent here, there and everywhere for every subject. The expectation of the customers is that the personnel are informed about the agreements the enterprise has made with its customers. To this end, an information system is needed to store this information and make it accessible. Not only accessible to the personnel of the enterprise, but also (partly) accessible to the customers themselves, so that they can place their own orders, for example.

With the aid of an information system, the enterprise can make analyses of the customer or customer groups. Here, three types of CRM are distinguished:

- *Strategic CRM*
  This CRM system is used to establish what resources can best be used for which business contacts and in what way.
- *Analytical CRM*
  This CRM contains all information that is collected about the customers, their contacts, wishes, demands and purchasing patterns.
- *Operational CRM*
  This CRM system supports the operational activities of the enterprise and the customers.

Result

The result of implementing this business strategy is an enterprise that is market-oriented, where a sustainable relationship is built up with its customers. Furthermore, the enterprise changes from a reactive enterprise to a pro-active one; the processes in the enterprise are attuned to each other and the personnel are results-oriented instead of task-oriented.

Focus areas

In many situations, CRM is implemented as an IT system, without the making the necessary adjustments within the organisation. The pitfall is that the system is deployed as a computerisation solution, instead of as corporate strategy, for which the software provides support. This pitfall is nurtured by many software companies.

Literature

* www.crm.com
* Greenberg, P. (2009). *CRM at the speed of light*. McGraw-Hill Education Europe.
* Goldenberg, B. (2008). *Empowering Customer Releationships*. CyberAge Books.

General management
Strategy
Marketing
Sales
Purchasing
Project & Planning
Production
Quality
Logistics & Distribution
Information management
Financial
HRM & HTM
Internationalisation

33
Customer Satisfaction

Authors	**Zeithaml and Bitner**
Year developed	**2000**
Also known as	**–**
Objective	**Establishing customer satisfaction**

Model

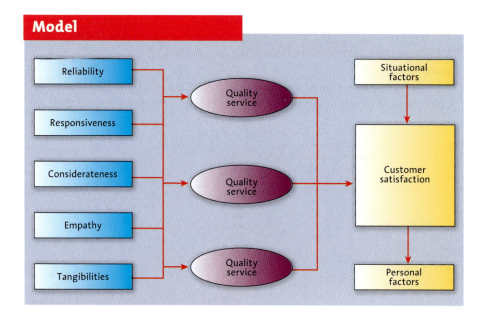

Background

The more enterprises work in a market- and service-oriented manner, the higher the importance of Customer Satisfaction for the enterprise. After all, the right to exist of the enterprise is based on the products and services the customer buys. If the question is asked, 'Do you wish to satisfy your customers?', the answer is invariably 'yes.' However, an unambiguous answer is never given to the question 'What is Customer Satisfaction?' The model of Zeithaml and Bitner gives an interpretation of this from different viewpoints.

Application

Customer Satisfaction is determined by factors that cannot be influenced by the enterprise and factors that can be influenced by the enterprise. The personal factors and the situational factors cannot (or hardly) be influenced by the enterprise but have a great influence on Customer Satisfaction. It is therefore extremely important that these factors are inventoried. The enterprise is able to influence the factors service quality, product quality and determine the price to influence Customer Satisfaction. To establish Customer Satisfaction, the enterprise must carry out the following steps:

1 **Determine the situational and personal factors**
These factors cannot or can hardly be influenced by the enterprise but should be established in relation to the impact they have on Customer Satisfaction. The customers after all assess the performance of the enterprise. When this is not as they expect, the assessment is negative. Apart from the fact of whether the enterprise can do something about it or not. This also applies to the personal factors. In the eyes of the customer these are very important, while for the company they perhaps mean nothing. If the enterprise does not take this into account, this immediately rebounds into lower Customer Satisfaction. To prevent this, it is necessary that these aspects are inventoried. Even if the enterprise cannot influence these factors, very often asking about them is sufficient to reassure the customer and not have a negative influence on Customer Satisfaction.

2 **Determine the service and product quality and the price**
Reliability: is a factor with which the enterprise does not score highly as long as it is good. However, when something goes wrong, this has a huge negative effect on Customer Satisfaction.
Responsiveness: is concerned with the aspects of time and speed. Depending on the product or service an enterprise supplies, this is an important factor. For the first-aid department in a hospital, time and speed have a totally different aspect than with a cosy dinner by candlelight.
Considerateness: is derived from the competences of the employees. If they are competent, mature in the task and polite, they know what they are doing. In short, this is the confidence that employees radiate to customers.
Empathy: is the ability of the employees to empathise with the customer. Does the employee understand what is at stake for the customer, apart from the service or product that is supplied?
Tangibilities: this factor relates to all aspects that can be touched. Is the equipment in use in order and up-to-date? Does everything, equipment, transport resources, offices and buildings, look attractive and neat and tidy?

These factors all have an impact on the price and quality of the product or service. Customer Satisfaction can be determined with the aid of the table.

Factor	Weighting	Score (0.1 to 1 incl.)	Result
Reliability	20	0.6	12
Responsiveness	10	0.4	4
Considerateness	15	0.1	1.5
Empathy	15	0.8	12.5
Tangibilities	10	0.9	9
Situational factors	10	0.7	7
Personal factors	20	0.8	16
	100		62

The highest result is 100 points. For a grade, this is then divided by 10. In the example, Customer Satisfaction is thus a 6.2.

Result

The result is a score on a scale from 1 to 10 for the degree of Customer Satisfaction. On the basis of the individual scores for the factors, it can subsequently be investigated on which factors efforts must be made to increase the Customer Satisfaction score.

Focus areas

The factors are generally described and it is recommended to do further research into what is understood by the enterprise and by the customers by the factors in question. This activity is performed once for each enterprise. Regular Customer Satisfaction surveys are subsequently carried out.

Literature

- Zeithaml, V., Bitner, J. & Gemler, D. (2008). *Services marketing: integrating customer focus across the firm.* McGraw-Hill Education.
- www.customersatisfaction.com
- http://managementhelp.org/customer/satisfy.htm

34
Customer-Value Profiles

Author	Treacy & Wiersema
Year developed	1995
Also known as	Value disciplines
Objective	Establishing core values on which the enterprise excels

Model

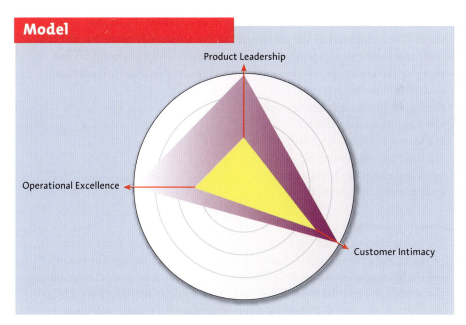

Background

Customers are not all the same and do not all have the same needs. Their need for a certain product or service can be the same; their choice is based on various factors. The one chooses solely based on price while the other opts for quality and a third, for example, the service of the enterprise. With the aid of the model from Treacy and Wiersema, this can be inventoried with the customer value:

- Operational excellence (total costs) cost leadership
- Product leadership (best product) product leadership
- Customer intimacy (best total solution) customer partnership

General management · Strategy · Marketing · Sales · Purchasing · Project & Planning · Production · Quality · Logistics & Distribution management · Information management · Financial · HRM & HTM · Internationalisation

Application

With this model there is no phased plan that leads to one of the three strategies, which subsequently becomes the strategy of the enterprise. In principle, customers always look at all three aspects but they will allow one to prevail. This says that the enterprise must score well on all three strategies and must excel in one of them if it wishes to achieve a competitive advantage.

Cost leadership (Operational excellence)

Cost leadership is the continuous capacity of an enterprise to deploy all operational processes, abilities and capacities as effectively and efficiently as possible, to produce the products and services (design, manufacture and deliver) where there is currently market demand.

Enterprises that opt for cost leadership must have a flat organisation and short lines of communication. These enterprises have excellent IT systems, which cover all the processes of the enterprise. All the employees have clear and concrete tasks and there is a cost-awareness culture in which organisation and planning are key concepts. Through this strategy, the enterprise can achieve customer benefits:

- the lowest (perceived) selling prices
- the shortest waiting times
- the lowest maintenance costs
- the least buying discomfort
- quick and easy sales transactions
- unambiguous communication

Product leadership

Product leadership is the capacity to continuously bring new 'state-of-the-art' products on to the market. These enterprises are always engaged in expanding their boundaries and seeking for new, bold products or services to put on the market and surprise their customers. These enterprises must have a huge amount of creativity available and a very short time-to-market. Moreover, they are always busy with new developments. They are continuously seeking to improve with respect to the competition and if the competition remains behind, they excel themselves.

With product leadership the enterprise has clearly defined objectives:

- the talents of some employees are stimulated (development of new products and services)
- making mistakes is allowed
- the organisation is extremely flexible
- the corporate culture is based on innovation and achieving results

By means of this strategy the enterprise can achieve customer benefits on their extensive product range and a short time-to-market due to controlled R&D,

with many successful market introductions and a great deal of knowledge about the market segments.

Customer partnership (Customer intimacy)

Customer partnership is the capacity of the enterprise to build up a long-term continuous relationship with customers, where the enterprise time after time capitalises on customer needs. The relationship here is more important than the transaction and the enterprise takes the problems out of the hands of the customer and ensures a total solution ('fit-for-purpose'). These enterprises have a high degree of flexibility. Moreover, they have employees with a great deal of knowledge of and experience in the sector in general and the customer in question in particular. The customer relations managers that they employ are the links between the enterprise and the customer. These enterprises select their customers on their need for expertise, search for niche markets, make long-term plans and offer a wide range of products or services. They are able to mobilise and combine the knowledge in the enterprise and the customer, know the customer in every detail and search for the right solutions to customers' problems. With customer partnership, the enterprise can achieve customer benefits through total solutions that are tailor-made and by acting as a partner to the customer in the development of products and services.

Distinctive power

After having chosen the strategy, the enterprise cannot stand still and hold on to this strategy year after year. The competition will naturally also be active in the market. Therefore, it is important to continually follow these rules:
- Excel in only one value discipline.
- Maintain the other value disciplines.
- Develop the chosen discipline every year.
- Organise the processes of the enterprise in line with the value discipline.

Result

On the basis of the model of Treacy & Wiersema, the enterprise opts for a strategy it is good at, in other words: the core competencies or core skills. From these core skills, all the processes of the enterprise are organised so that they are mutually well-attuned and lead to a well-oiled machine.

Focus areas

The question has been asked whether the model has any added value. Enterprises already naturally gravitate towards what they are good at. Through the application of the model, the enterprise will only have confirmed what it is good at. The model can then only be used for confirmation and a possible phased improvement to current methods.
Application of the model implies an almost fixed segmentation: cost leadership

is not or hardly segmented while customer partnership is maximally segmented. The model cannot apply to the whole enterprise if the operating companies are independent and service other market segments. Each operating company will then have its own interpretation of the model.

Literature

- Woodside, Gibbert, Golfetto (2008). *Creating and Managing Superior Customer Value*. Emerald Group Publishing.
- Mills, H., Mills, H.A. (2004). *The Rainmaker's Toolkit*. Amacom.
- http://www.themanager.org/pdf/Strategy_accelerator_article.pdf

35
Decision Table

Author	J. Roos
Year developed	1984
Also known as	—
Objective	Making a considered choice from various options

Model

Go/No-go		Weighting	Option 1	Option 2	Option 3
	Criterion 1				
	Criterion 2				
	Criterion 3				
Subscore					
Substantive					
	Criterion 1				
	Criterion 2				
	Criterion 3				
Subscore					
Total score					

(left vertical label: Criteria)

Background

As the overload in information increases, it becomes more and more difficult to choose from all the possibilities and considerations that exist.

Managers often make a decision based on their experience or their instincts. An easy aid to coming to a more considered choice is the Decision Table. Here, the different options are weighted against each other on the basis of a number of criteria.

Application

The Decision Table is filled in as follows:

Options

Prior to setting up a Decision Table, it must be clear which options are being considered. These options are simply described and included horizontally in the table.

General management

Strategy

Marketing

Sales

Purchasing

Project & Planning

Production

Quality

Logistics & Distribution

Information management

Financial

HRM & HTM

Internationalisation

The options that have been found via a confrontation matrix (see Confrontation Matrix), for example, can be considered via a Decision Table.

Criteria
In order to make these considerations, criteria will have to be established that can be assessed for each option. These criteria are divided into two groups: Go/No-go and substantive.

Go/No-go
For the Go/No-go criteria, conditions are established with which the criterion must comply. For example: the costs may not be above a certain amount. If the criterion does not fulfil these conditions, then the whole option is excluded. This is called a show-stopper.

Substantive
The substantive criteria go further into the considerations that must be made between the options in the Decision Table. For each option a consideration is made of each criterion with regard to the effect of the solution concerning this criterion. For example, if the turnover of an enterprise declines, there are various options to bring it back up to par. The enterprise can bring new products onto the market, take over other companies or fire personnel. The effect on the personnel is much less with the first two options than with the third one.

It is now important to find the right criteria on the basis of which the options are valued. A standard set of criteria is:
- suitability
  - aid to acquisition objectives
  - fulfils the objective
- feasibility
  - externally feasible
  - internally feasible
- acceptability
  - to the personnel
  - to the management
- financial
  - investment
  - revenues

The criteria must fit in with the objectives the enterprise has defined with regard to the project. Next to the selected criteria, weighting can be given so that one criterion weighs more heavily than another. This weighting could be a complex mathematical formula. It is preferable to keep the weighting as simple as possible, however. Too much complexity makes for lack of transparency and will have a negative effect on the support of the personnel with regard to the selected option.

Result

With the aid of the Decision Table, the enterprise gains insight into which choices should be made on the basis of the considered criteria.

Focus areas

With the selection of the criteria, it is important to be aware of the fact that they can be subjective, with the goal of influencing the total consideration. It is recommended to have the criteria established by more than one person.

Literature

None.

36
Deming Circle

Author	W. Deming
Year developed	± 1948
Also known as	Deming Wheel, Plan-Do-Check-Act (PDCA)
Objective	Rule circle for monitoring results

Model

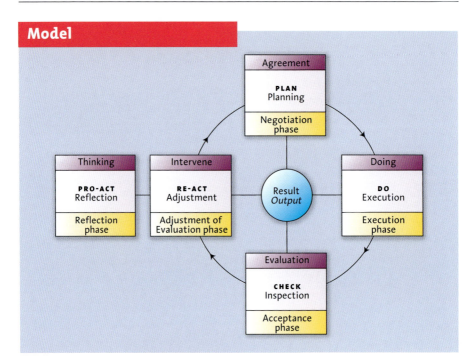

Background

Every process is composed of a number of aspects that must together deliver the result. These aspects are input, activities, output, checking standards and adjustment. The most important thing is that the output (the result) must comply with the standards that have been set. If this is not so, there must be adjustment or exceptionally, the standard has to be adapted. This is a rule-circle principle, which monitors that the results are actually achieved. One of the most used rule-circle principles is the Deming Circle or the PDCA cycle (Plan-Do-Check-Act).

The circle consists in four steps that must be followed. These steps are:

1 Plan

In the planning phase, agreements are made about the results to be achieved. The manner in which this takes place is included in a plan. Here it is important to take into account the pre-conditions and starting points. The results produced must be accurately and in any case measurably (SMART) formulated, to be able to establish afterwards whether the results have indeed been achieved compared to the standards. These objectives are the performance indicators on the basis of which the result is measured.

2 Do

The 'Do' step is achieving the output, or ensuring that the result is achieved. To this end, the activities included in the first phase of the project plan are carried out. During the performance of the activities, the results produced are measured constantly on the established performance indicators. It is however possible that the different performance indicators are divided among different (sub-) processes. It is important to establish in what manner measurement will take place in this case.

3 Check

The 'Check' step is the monitoring step. The measured results are compared with the predefined standards. It is possible that there is an upper or lower limit with the set standards, so that the result may deviate somewhat from the standard. This permitted deviation must be established in advance. It is naturally not so that in all situations a certain deviation from the standard is accepted. It is important that the deviations are analysed and the causes established. With checking, a check also takes place with regard to the completeness, reliability and timeliness of the information.

4 Act

The 'Act' step in fact consists in two moments. One moment as an actual adjustment to a check: the 'Re-act' step and another moment as the initiator of a PDCA: the 'Pro-act' step.

Re-act

In this step, the process is adjusted by the process owner. This is done on the basis of the results from the performance indicators of the 'Check' step. In cases where the result comes out below or above the standard, there must be adjustment. Such adjustment consists in thinking of activities that are directed towards achieving the original result as yet.

Pro-act

This step can be viewed as preparation for the PDCA and is thereby the initiator of the model. In this step it is established whether there are new results areas or intervention strategies that can be used in the 'Re-act' step or the 'Plan' step. This step is generally used only in complex controlling processes.

Result

The result of using this model is planned, continuous improvement for the enterprise in achieving the established targets in a shorter time and with a higher quality.

Focus areas

PDCA seems like a simple model. Many enterprises have tried to further develop this model in detail. The risk that is run, is losing sight of the objective of the model and still not producing any results. The model works exclusively when the performance indicators are defined in accordance with the SMART formula. This is sometimes regarded by enterprises as too simple, due to which no measurable results are created. In such a case, using the circle is no use at all.

Literature

- Deming, W. (2000). *Out of The Crisis*. The MITT Press.
- http://deming-network.org/14points.pdf

37
DESTEP

Author	Developed in practice
Year developed	–
Also known as	PEST, PESTEL, PESTLE, STEER, STEEP, STEEPLE, STEEPLED
Objective	Analysis of the sector at macro level

Model

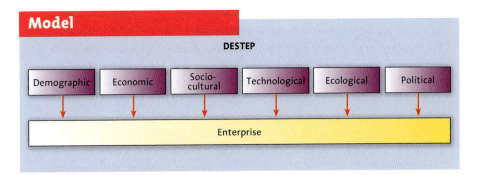

Background

Enterprises are able to exert influence on their suppliers and customers by making price-fixing agreements, for example. Enterprises have little to no influence however on the macro factors that are summarised in DESTEP model. DESTEP stands for Demographic, Economic, Socio-cultural, Technological, Ecological and Politico-legal. It is important to analyse these factors because from them, influence can be exerted on the enterprise or the whole sector in which the enterprise operates.
These influences are primarily related to:
- all enterprises active in this sector
- the attractiveness of the market in which the enterprise is active
- the enterprise itself, for example, environmental aspects with production, health & safety rules (arbo) in relation to personnel

These factors can also mutually influence each other. If a government allocates subsidies, different economic and technological changes occur. For the enterprise, this means that an analysis must be made for every factor, to establish what influence this factor can have on the strategy of the enterprise in the future (short- and long-term).

Application

Establishing the DESTEP factors proceeds as follows:

Demographic factors

The demographic factors are related to the development of the population in a certain region. Some examples being age structure, the proportion of adults to children, the proportion of men to women and the number and size of households. Information on demographics can be obtained from the CBS (Central Office for Statistics). It is immediately apparent that in the Netherlands, the population is currently ageing: an increasingly greater percentage of elderly and a lower percentage of young people. Companies can take advantage of this by producing special nutrition for the elderly next to baby food, for example.

Economic factors

The economic factors primarily influence the purchase of goods by consumers. In an economic recession, the sales of all luxury goods (sustainable consumer goods) will immediately decline, while the day-to-day goods such as food and drink sell as usual. Generally, however, a shift takes place from branded goods to the cheaper house brands. Examples of economic factors are Gross National Product, the spending power of the consumer, price level of consumption and unemployment. Information about economic developments in the past can be found at the CBS. A more interesting source of information can be the CPB (Central Planning Office), which gives predictions for economic developments. These are given annually and are called macro-economic prognoses.

Socio-cultural factors

The socio-cultural factors are related to the standards and values within a society. Examples of this are ideas in relation to the upbringing of children, living together or marriage, attention for a balance between work and free time, changes in the attention paid to environmental and health and safety matters. Following these developments is important for enterprises because from them new markets can arise or perhaps new target groups for advertising purposes. Information can be found at the SCP (Social and Cultural Planning Office). Moreover, there are various market bureaus that monitor the developments and trends via different forms of research. This information is generally exclusively available for payment.

Technological factors

In contrast to the other factors, the technological factor can be influenced by the enterprise itself, if the enterprise invests a great deal in an effective R&D department. Some companies see this as an important factor to keep the time-to-market (the time from development to market introduction) as short as possible and create the biggest market share as the first on the market.

Technological developments can have an enormous influence on the market and on the enterprise itself. The possibilities for consumers and companies to do business via the Internet have brought about a huge change in purchasing behaviour and supply. For one company, a development will mean an opportunity and for the another a threat. For an enterprise it means in any case that in all the areas of the enterprise, namely purchasing, sales, production, logistics and marketing, a reassessment must take place on the basis of the impact of technological developments. It is important that enterprises assure themselves that with new technological developments, a market must also be present to utilise this technology.

Information about technological developments will have to be collected by companies themselves. This is possible by joining a branch association. However, all enterprises that are members of this association have the same information available. Following periodicals in the sector and visiting exhibitions and seminars can also contribute. Collaboration with suppliers and customers provides possibilities to establish a joint R&D budget.

Ecological factors

The ecological factors are factors that belong to the physical environment of the market in which the enterprise is active or wishes to be. Examples are the climate, the weather, swine fever, BSE (mad-cow disease), environmental aspects, technical infrastructure and natural resources. Each of these subjects can influence sales of the product. For example, it is possible for a product to sell less when it is raining heavily that when there is little rain. For each of these subjects it is necessary to investigate what trends can be found or what to do when swine fever suddenly breaks out, for example. Information in this category will have to be collected by the enterprise itself.

Political and legal factors

The government regularly drafts policy on the different subjects. In it, various legislation and regulations are housed. Such legislation and regulations can have a limited or no influence at all on the enterprise, but can also have a very great influence. For example, when a product may no longer be manufactured due to stricter environmental requirements. Furthermore, government measures can also have a great influence on the outlets of an enterprise, for example, the years long campaign against smoking and drinking.

Information about government measures can be found in the *Staatscourant*. Obviously, the current news is also a source of information. If an enterprise is highly dependent on the decision making of the government, it will have to maintain multiple contacts with government officials or in the extreme case, appoint a separate functionary for this.

Result

The result of the DESTEP analysis provides the enterprise with insight into the opportunities and threats approaching the enterprise from the six determinative factors.

Focus areas

This macro-analysis is a snapshot and the enterprise should be aware that developments in the macro factors must be continuously updated, to be able to immediately take advantage of developing trends. This applies more to larger enterprises than smaller ones and trend followers. DESTEP is also sometimes extended with the L for Legal and the E for environment. The legal aspects are also included in the description of the political developments. Therefore, a separate statement of these factors is unnecessary. All aspects of DESTEP are concerned with the environment of the enterprise. A separate statement of this catchall is therefore superfluous.

Literature

- http://www.themanager.org/models/pest_analysis.htm
- http://www.renewal.eu.com/resources/Renewal_Pestle_Analysis.pdf

38
Diamond, Porter

Author	M. Porter
Year developed	1990
Also know as	Porters Diamond of Competitive Advantage, National Competitive Advantage
Objective	Determining the international competitive capacity of a nation or enterprise

Model

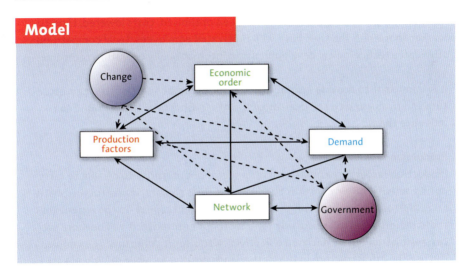

Background

The Diamond model is used when an enterprise wishes to establish whether there is a good starting point for internationalisation. The model comprises four aspects, on the basis of which the enterprise can determine its competitive position in its own country. These are the aspects Economic order, Production factors, Demand and Network. Next to these four aspects there are two variables that can influence the competitive position of the enterprise: Government and Chance

Application

The starting point of Porters Diamond is Economic order, which together with the other factors, has an influence on achieving the objectives of the enterprise.

General management
Strategy
Marketing
Sales
Purchasing
Project & Planning
Production
Quality
Logistics & Distribution management
Information
Financial
HRM & HTM
Internationalisation

The mutual relationships indicate that the factors influence this achievement in a positive or negative manner.

Economic order

The economic order is divided into three components: strategy, structure and rivalry.

The strategy goes into the manner in which the objectives of the sector or the enterprise can be achieved.

The structure indicates how the sector or enterprise is organised and contains its own production factors, people, capital, resources and information, and effort.

The competition indicates how strong the rivalry is between the branches or enterprises to fulfil the demand from the market. Porter has established that companies with strong competition in their home market can also handle strong competition on the world market. Furthermore, the products and services supplied by companies with strong competition are usually of good quality. Moreover, the business processes have been optimised, costs lowered, time-to-market shortened and they have well-motivated employees. Local competition stimulates technological developments in internationally operating companies.

It is important to provide insight into the three components of strategy, structure and rivalry and to see if and how the other aspects of the Diamond can influence them.

Production factors

Production factors are conditional for a sector or enterprise to be able to carry out its activities. This concerns conditions such as climate, infrastructure, natural resources (for example, oil), human resources and capital. To the extent that these factors work out positively for a sector or enterprise, it will be more successful in attaining its declared objectives. A transport company for example, can use the infrastructure in the Netherlands positively, while driving in east Europe demands a great deal from the trucks and more journey time. It must be investigated whether the necessary factors for the enterprise are present. Climate is a permanent factor and capital can be obtained elsewhere. Climate is therefore not mobile and capital is.

Demand

Enterprises prefer to service the market from one location geographically speaking, to produce more cost-efficiently due to the advantages of scale. The enterprise therefore selects a location where the demand from the customers is greatest and so saves on transport costs. Scale gives the enterprise a better competitive position on the international market.

Network

Clustering of companies offers advantages of scale in the areas of transport, marketing and R&D costs, for example. From this viewpoint, the enterprise can see if there are companies in the vicinity with which collaboration is possible in one or more areas. With collaboration, the international competitive position is stronger than without.

Government

The rules and laws promulgated by the government can provide advantages for sectors and companies or can be disadvantageous.
Subsidies can stimulate sectors and companies to develop specific products or services, while a nuisance act permit can make it difficult for a company to establish itself somewhere, for example.

Chance

A chance is an unexpected event that directly or indirectly influences the sector or an organisation. If these events are regularly repeated or become predictable, they are no longer chance factors but production factors.

Result

The result is insight into the situation in the home country, which serves as a basis for international activities. This situation should be stable and strong. On the basis of the model, the enterprise can establish whether there is sufficient basis for internationalisation with an acceptable risk.

Focus areas

The most important starting point of Porter is that enterprises can most successfully internationalise when the Diamond model is used for the home country. In many situations it turns out that a Diamond model can be made for the target country. Through the combination of the two countries, a better estimation can be made with regard to the international activities the enterprise wishes to commence in the target country.
The model assumes a free market. But this may not always be the case.

Literature

- Porter, M. (1998). *The competitive advantage of nations*. Basingstoke: Palgrave Macmillan, second revised edition.
- O'Connell, L. & Clancy, P. (2004). Business research as an educational problem – solving heuristic – the case of Porter's Diamond. *European Journal of Marketing*, 33,7 /8, p. 736.

General management

Strategy

Marketing

Sales

Purchasing

Project & Planning

Production

Quality

Logistics & Distribution

Information management

Financial

HRM & HTM

Internationalisation

39
Employability Scan

Author	Developed in practice
Year developed	–
Also known as	–
Objective	The correct deployment of personnel

Model

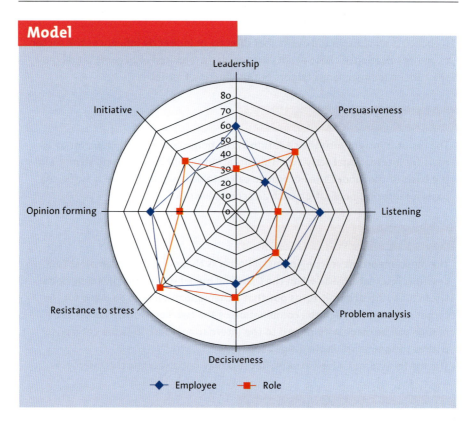

Background

Labour force participation and having sufficient and correct qualifications is not only of great importance for workers and employers, but also for society. Schooling, training and increased employability are instruments for the optimal deployment and the defences of individuals on the labour market. Policy in the area of employability is still too often narrowed down to agreements that are primarily related to schooling. Employability should, however, be understood as 'broad and sustainable availability'. Although schooling is an important component of employability policy, matters such as the stimulation of flexible availability, function changes, mobility, informal learning and recognition of competences acquired elsewhere are likewise components of employability. After all, schooling and expanding employability contribute towards strengthening the knowledge economy and, via productivity increases, to the capacity for growth of the Dutch economy. This is necessary to retain and improve its own competitive position in a globalising world.

Application

The Employability Scan inventories the usability of personnel. The scan is a list of questions filled in by the personnel, which can be used for study, choice of profession, selection and career development, for example. Furthermore this scan can serve as support for competence development.

The scan assumes a competence profile that comprises:
- training: all training followed for and during the career.
- experience: work experience acquired during training, career and projects.
- behaviour: personal skills and actions.
- attitude: beliefs with respect to general opinions and ideas.

In this way, employees obtain insight into their own personal qualities and subsequently, on the basis of the requirements (such as study and choice of profession), can make choices for further development. This concerns both personal development and career development within or outside the enterprise.

The enterprise will have to compile and make available a competence profile for every role within the organisation. This profile comprises what would be considered the theoretically most appropriate profile for this role.
By matching the profiles of the personnel with the profile of the role in question, it can be established to what extent the employee fits the theoretical profile. Depending on the degree of difference between these profiles and on which subjects they deviate, it can be established whether the employee concerned can fulfil this role in the future with the aid of training and/or coaching.
In this way, the profiles of all the personnel are established to obtain insight into their capabilities, so that they can be deployed where it is most suitable. It is important that this is not only viewed from the perspective of the enterprise, but also from that of the employees.
In the model, it can be seen on which aspects of the competence profile, in this case a number of personal characteristics, the profile of the employee corresponds with that of the desired profile (role). These aspects will have to be established first by the company for each role before the profiles can be compiled.

Result

With the aid of the Employability Scan, the personnel of an enterprise can be more broadly and productively deployed so that greater flexibility is created in the use of the personnel. The personnel feel they are taken more seriously and notice that the enterprise feels involved in their future development. This makes the personnel more motivated and they will do more for the company.

Focus areas

A risk in the use of the Employability Scan is that the enterprise will see this scan exclusively as a productivity-increasing device to improve the results of the enterprise. If the personnel cannot participate sufficiently and take part in deciding about their efforts, the scan will have a contrary effect.
Employability creates flexibility in the use of personnel. If flexibility is sought in solutions such as temporary contracts, this is incorrect policy with regard to employability.

Literature

None.

40
Entry Mode Decision

Author	Hollensen
Year developed	2003
Also known as	Factors affecting the foreign market entry mode decision, Entry Modes
Objective	Determining in which way the enterprise can best start up abroad

Model

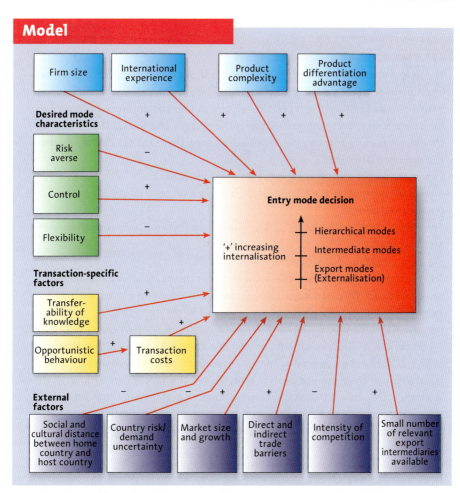

Explanation: with each of the sixteen factors, a question can be asked. For example, has the enterprise much international experience? If the answer is yes, the

+ or the − applies for this factor. The more plusses, the sooner the enterprise should opt for a hierarchical entry mode.

Background

Current developments in technology and the appurtenant world-wide provision of information enable companies to operate internationally more easily. After all, there is more and more information available about the market, the customers and the competition on the market in question. Furthermore, for a number of companies the home market is saturated or exactly because the one client on the other side of the border is closer by. This leads to more and more enterprises doing business with companies abroad. The foreign activities of a company usually start with export. Subsequently, the company sets up a sales office in the country concerned. Thereafter, the company possibly starts a production facility in the same country.

Application

The model assumes sixteen different factors that determine which entry mode (method of entry abroad) is important. The assessment of these factors occurs with a plus or a minus. The more plusses, the sooner the enterprise should opt for a hierarchical entry mode. The fewer the plusses, the sooner the enterprise should opt for an export mode. In between them, there is a third entry mode: the intermediate mode.

- Export mode concerns the exportation of goods abroad.
- Intermediate mode is the collaboration between several companies in one's own country and abroad.
- The hierarchical mode assumes own branches and/or own personnel that is active abroad.

To select the correct entry mode, each factor in the model above must be separately assessed. This assessment is best done in the form of a question. For example: is it a complex product? If the answer is 'yes' then this factor has a plus because there is a plus rating for this factor. A plus means that the enterprise will retain control of the investments to be made abroad. This means that the enterprise will itself retain control of the activities (internalisation). Another example is: intensity of the competition. If it is high, then this factor gets a minus. If there is a minus, this means that the enterprise forgoes performing these activities under its own management and leaves it to others (externalisation).
The model comprises the following sixteen factors (the scoring is explained for each factor):

- *Product differentiation advantage*: if the product clearly distinguishes itself from the products of the competition, the chance is greater that the enterprise will be successful abroad on the basis of the product differentiation. If this is the case, then a plus is scored.

- *Complexity of the product*: with complex products, proper explanation and support is needed on the spot to assist the users. With complex products, the enterprise will therefore opt to be present in the country. If this is the case, then a plus is filled in.
- *International experience*: if an enterprise has a lot of international experience, then it runs less risk that the foreign activities will fail. Due to this, the enterprise will sooner establish itself abroad. If this is the case, a plus is filled in.
- *Size of the enterprise*: large enterprises generally have more budget, resources and specialist personnel to shape the international activities. Hence, it is safer to start these foreign activities. But the enterprise is also able to perform the activities under its own management and need not outsource them. For large enterprises, a plus is therefore filled in.
- *Risk-avoiding behaviour*: if an enterprise demonstrates risk-avoiding behaviour, then it wishes to run little risk with the foreign activities. Hence, this enterprise will invest little abroad and leave the activities to others. If this is the case, then a minus is filled in.
- *Control*: if an enterprise wishes to control everything that occurs within the enterprise, then it will have to be able to control the foreign activities and thus carry them out under its own responsibility. Hence, a plus is filled in if this is so.
- *Flexibility*: flexibility concerns the possibility of the enterprise to withdraw quickly from a country if things go less well. This is easiest if there are no own sales or production locations abroad, but only contracts with external parties. These can be quickly dissolved. If an enterprise wishes to have this flexibility, then a minus is filled in.
- *Transferability of knowledge*: if a great deal of knowledge has to be transferred to the customers, then it is advisable to have the right people from one's own enterprise in the location in question. If this applies, a plus is filled in.
- *Opportunistic behaviour*: with opportunistic behaviour an agent/distributor or the production location can be too optimistic in their expectations and always give too high a forecast. To avoid this, the enterprise will have to be present on the spot because the agent/distributor/production location does not supply reliable figures. If this is the case, then a plus is filled in.
- *Transaction costs*: these are the costs that have to be incurred to obtain an order. If these costs are very high in a certain country, then it is better for the enterprise to establish itself in that country. If this is so, a plus is filled in.
- *Socio-cultural differences*: if there are great cultural differences, it is better not to establish oneself directly in a country. Therefore, a minus is filled in here.
- *Risk of the country*: in a risky country, it is not wise to invest too much. These investments are not safe after all. For this reason, a minus is filled in for risky countries.
- *Market scope and market growth*: with large markets with a great deal of growth, sales are almost certain. So investment by means of establishment is then the best option. Due to this, a plus is filled in.
- *Trade barriers*: in a country with trade barriers such as import levies, it is better to establish there because then the levies are not applicable. A plus is therefore filled in.

- *Intensity of the competition*: if there is fierce competition, the enterprise can better not directly establish because there is too great a risk in connection with the competition. So fill in a minus if this is so.
- *Small number of intermediaries*: if there are a limited number of intermediaries in a country, it is better to establish in the country. In this way, it is avoided that the enterprise is driven out by the intermediaries together and will therefore have to satisfy their demands. Due to this, fill in a plus for few intermediaries.

Result

The result is a clear pictured of the manner in which the enterprise can best go abroad. The plusses in the model are totalled and then, according to a graduated scale, it is determined which entry mode will be selected.

Score of the factors	Entry mode
0-5 plusses	export mode
6-11 plusses	intermediate mode
12-16 plusses	hierarchical mode

Focus areas

If some factors cannot be scored, a plus-minus or a zero may be filled in. This however means that the score changes into three divisions. There are then no longer sixteen plusses or minuses, but as many fewer as there are plus-minuses or zeros. It is best to seek further for the desired information. This is one of the most important choices an enterprise must make when it concerns international activities. The enterprise is going to invest in activities outside its own country. The higher the investment (the hierarchical mode is the highest) the more certain the enterprise must be about the choice of the manner in which it will enter a foreign country.

Literature

- Hollensen, S. (2007). *Global Marketing. A decision-oriented approach.* Harlow: Prentice Hall.

41
F-PEC scale

Authors	J.H. Astrachan et al.
Year developed	2002
Also known as	Family Power Experience Culture, F-PEC scale of Family Influence
Objective	Shows the extent and quality of the influence of the family

Model

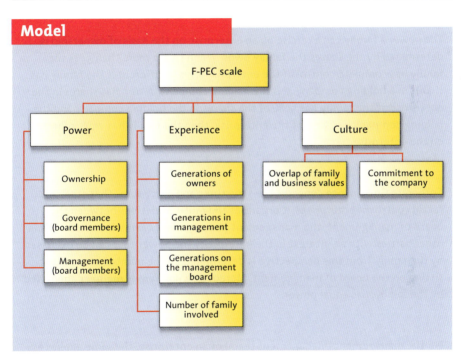

Background

Over the years it has become less and less clear when an enterprise is called a family business. There are family businesses employing a great many people and with many operating companies all over the world. Moreover, there are many smaller enterprises that are not family businesses. In his F-PEC model Astrachan et al. (2002) has given a structure with which companies, regardless of their size, can or cannot be called family businesses. In an empirical study by Vandekerkhof (2008), it was shown that family businesses perform better than non-family businesses. It must be possible thereby to establish whether an enterprise is a family business.

For family businesses it is no longer exclusively reviewed to what extent management and employees are family or not. But also to the influence that a family can exercise on an enterprise on the basis of experience and culture. This influence of the family on the enterprise can be divided into three elements: power, experience and culture.

Power

The element of power concerns the possibilities a family has to determine what happens within an enterprise and what strategy is implemented to achieve the vision and mission of the enterprise. The family exercises power by means of ownership of the shares, the extent of governance from the family and the extent to which the family is represented in the management of the enterprise.

Ownership

The power a family can exercise on an enterprise on the basis of ownership is determined by the shares the family owns. When this is more than 51% the family has complete control of the enterprise. This is different if the family has shares in a holding company and the holding company in turn has shares in the enterprise. If the family has 50% of the shares in the holding company and the holding company has 50% of the enterprise, then the family has 25% influence on the enterprise.

Governance

Corporate Governance concerns the structures and procedures that steer and retain control of enterprises. It organises the mutual relations between the board of management, the management (management team), shareholders and other parties with an interest in the enterprise. The power that can be exercised by the family from this perspective is determined by the number of members sitting on the board of management. Moreover, a non family member appointed by the family, has equal power.

Management

For the management (management team) of an enterprise, the same applies as to governance.

Experience

Experience is gained by working a great deal for a long time in a certain environment.

Generations of owners in management and the board of management

On the basis of the foregoing, it turns out that with the transfer from the first to the second generation of the family, the most experience is transmitted. The first generation is in the pioneering part of the enterprise and will therefore add a great many new developments. The second somewhat fewer and the third and following generations also slightly fewer.

Number of family members involved

The more family members involved in the enterprise the better the survival of experience will be. Within a family business, next to the owner partners, children and second-degree family members can be involved. Discussions in relation to the development of the enterprise give a substantial added value.

Culture

Every enterprise has a specific culture that is in principle separate from the managers, who come and go. Family businesses are run on the basis of the values and standards of the family. If these values and standards are in accordance with those of the sector, then the family has a better grip on the enterprise. If this is also reinforced by the attention and devotion the family gives to the company (commitment), then the family is able to exercise a great deal of influence on the enterprise.

Result

Enterprises can see how great the influence of the family is on the enterprise on the basis of this inventory. Especially enterprises that are growing and therefore can become bigger in this way deploy non-family members in management positions and ensure that the enterprise still remains a family business. It is important that family interests and company interests can be considered in appropriately, so that the results of the enterprise remain positive.

Focus areas

The model takes no account of the legal, economic and political situations that are present in certain countries. The strategy of an enterprise, in this case a family business, can hence be modified because these aspects are different than in one's own country. This is a much greater challenge for family businesses because these companies operate on the values and standards applicable within one family. The family will not easily relinquish these values and standards. The chance of doing business successfully in other environments consequently becomes smaller.

Literature

- Poutsiouris, P., Smyrnios, K., Klein, S. (2006). *Handbook of Research on Family Business*. Edward Elger Publishing Ltd.
- www.ffi.org

General management
Strategy
Marketing
Sales
Purchasing
Project & Planning
Production
Quality
Logistics & Distribution
Information management
Financial
HRM & HTM
Internationalisation

42

Functional and process management

Author	Developed in practice
Year developed	–
Also known as	–
Objective	Shortening logistics throughput time and improving communication between processes

Model

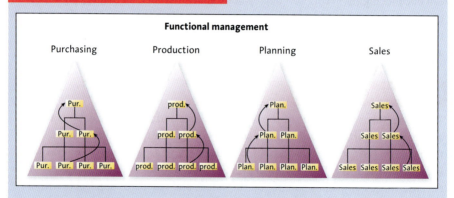

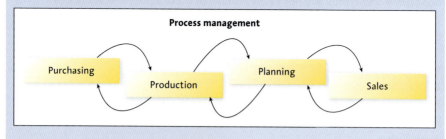

Background

Organisations are usually described via an organisational chart in which the departments and the responsibilities for the departments are included. The larger the enterprise, the greater the number of hierarchical levels. With product-oriented enterprises (mass production of consumer goods) such an organisational focus often occurs. The activities that must be undertaken are standard and do not or hardly change over a longer period. On the other hand, there are more and more companies that wish to respond quickly to market changes. Hence, it is necessary for the internal organisation of the enterprise to change from hierarchical or functional management to process-oriented management. By allowing the different departments in the enterprise to collaborate closely, changes can be picked up quickly. This is how a process-oriented enterprise is created. A much-used term for this is 'tilting the enterprise'.

Application

An enterprise can make the organisation functional or process-oriented.
The figure shows functional management and process management. Both forms are further explained.

Functional management: department, hierarchically oriented and product oriented

When there is a large, constant demand for a certain product, this product can be mass produced. The employees can directly be managed by the managers. This is a product-oriented and hierarchically-oriented enterprise. The activities that must be carried out are standard and repetitive. If enterprises exclusively produce to stock, then hierarchical orientation is also applicable. The departments can perform their activities independently from each other and are also managed independently. These enterprises are department oriented, hierarchically managed and produce on the basis of products.
Department oriented is to say that each department has its own tasks and objectives. It does not need to take account of the objectives of other departments. Every department has a manager who represents his department in the management team. In this way, the enterprise is hierarchically managed and communication always runs via the line. That is to say, from the employees of department A to the manager of department A to the management team and subsequently via the manager of department B to the employees in department B. The answer then goes back via the reverse route. The orientation of the enterprise is focused on the realisation of products that can be sold.

Process management: process-, team- and market-oriented

Due to demand from the market, many companies are obliged to adapt their organisation to the market's needs. The customers have high requirements for the quality, delivery times, reliability of delivery. Furthermore, there are also specific desires that customers have in relation to products, deliveries, packaging, etc. The development of the Internet has had a big influence on this because customers are now able to place their orders, indicate their specifications and follow their order status via the Internet and thus, exert more influence on suppliers. On the other hand, with their computerised systems the suppliers can better and more quickly adjust their production processes to the customer's specifications. To achieve this, companies 'tilt' their organisation. They attune the different departments closely to each other, so that when an order is placed, production immediately knows what is planned and has to be produced and purchasing can immediately place their order. The sales force can also immediately see when the order can be delivered. The processes, particularly the sales, production and purchasing processes, are closely attuned in this way. The employees of the different departments get together in teams to directly resolve any problems that occur with the processes. In this way, the enterprise is able to satisfy the requirements set by their customers.

Result

This model gives clarity about the manner in which the enterprise is organised and managed. Hierarchically and determined by the managers, with little freedom for the employees or team orientation. The responsibilities and authorisations are situated low down in the enterprise and a great deal of independence is created among the employees, as is the case with self-guided teams, empowerment and flat organisations.

Focus areas

Department orientation, hierarchical orientation and product orientation still fit only a few companies and are too rigid to meet the rapidly changing desires of the market. Process-, team- and market-orientation is an important structure for enterprises that produce on the basis of customer specifications. The change from the first orientation to the second is a complex process that takes a lot of time and energy to achieve. For successful implementation of the 'tilting' of the enterprise, the 'top-down' and 'bottom-up' approach is necessary. The management focuses on the main outlines and the teams themselves organise the activities to achieve the objectives they have established together with the management.

Literature

- Jeston, J., Nelis, J. (2006). *Business Process Management*. Elsevier Ltd.
- www.bpminsitute.org
- www.bpm.com

43
Gantt Chart

Author	Henry Lawrence Gantt
Year developed	1925
Also known as	Horizontal Bar Charts, Time Flow Charts, Work Breakdown Structure (WBS)
Objective	Giving an overview of activities to be performed

Model

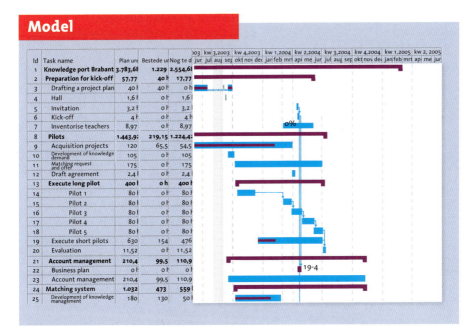

Background

The principle of the Gantt Chart was developed long ago and to this day, there is apparently no better means of planning activities than the famous Gantt Chart, which was used for the building of the Hoover Dam in 1931, among others. The Gantt Chart is the very insightful graphic representation of the activities that have to be carried out in a plan.

Application

The Gantt Chart consists in two parts. The first part is text and figures and the second part is graphics. In the textual part of the Gantt Chart, it is shown which activity it concerns, when this activity should begin, when the activity must be finished, how many hours will be worked on it and how many hours have been spent on it. The same in relation to the costs. In the graphical part of the Gantt Chart, it is shown what activities there are, what dependencies they have and to what degree the activities have been completed. These are the minimum aspects a project manager must know in relation to the status of the project. To realise a Gantt Chart, the following steps are necessary.

1 Determine the activities necessary

The employees in question determine in a brainstorming session what activities are necessary to realise the project. An activity is nominated and nothing further is said about it. Possible incorrect activities are taken out later.

2 Put the activities in sequence

Not all the activities can be carried out simultaneously because sometimes, an activity can only start when another is completed or because there are insufficient resources to do all the activities at once. The team, under the leadership of the project manager, establishes in what sequence the activities must be carried out from step one.

3 Select the dependencies

Many activities depend on other activities and as such, they have a relationship with each other. This relationship must be established so that with re-planning, the activities will not be carried out in the wrong order. When all the dependencies are known, the critical path is also known. The critical path consists of activities with a dependency: the following activity may only start when the previous one is completed. This is also the shortest throughput time of the project. The critical path is one of the most important aspects of planning and is clearly visible in the Gantt Chart.

4 Determine the number of hours

For each activity separately, the hours must be established for the performance of the activity by one employee. These hours concern the net time that must be spent on an activity before it is completed. In practice, the project manager can opt to have these hours worked by one or more people. However, unlimited resources cannot be added because people are in each other's way and more consultation is necessary.

The hours can be determined on the basis of a pessimistic estimate and an optimistic estimate The result is divided by two so that a more reliable estimate is created. When all the activities have been estimated in this fashion, the total number of hours that will be spent the project is known.

5 Determine who will perform the activities

Depending who will perform the activities, an adjustment can possibly be made in relation to the hours for the activities. If an activity is carried out by an inexperienced person it usually takes longer than if it was done by someone with more experience. In practice however, this averages out over all the activities. One activity may take a little longer, while another takes less time. In this way, the duration of the project remains the same. Along with the determination of the people who will carry out the activities, the responsibilities are also established.

6 Establish the throughput time

For every activity the number of hours that are necessary to perform it is determined. Moreover, it is established who will carry out which activities. These people will sometimes be employed on this activity for 100% of the time but sometimes also less. Moreover, it is important to know on which days the employees work. When an activity comprises many hours, the option can be taken to put several people to work on the activity at the same time. These components together constitute the throughput time of the project. The software assists in making these calculations, through which it is easy to see on the Gantt Chart how long the project will take. If the project has too long a throughput time, one can in this way look how the throughput time can be shortened (see Lead time / net time).

Result

The Gantt Chart gives a graphical overview of the activities in a project and provides direct insight into the status of a project in relation to the throughput time, dependencies and progress. The Gantt Chart is supported by project planning software and complex calculations and the dependencies are put together to make 'what-if' analyses.

Focus areas

The Gantt Chart does not indicate the actual efforts put into an activity and is therefore not effective when calculating for changes in the planning. Planning software is a godsend for this.

Literature

- www.ganttchart.com
- http://www.me.ua.edu/ME489/Gantt-Excel.pdf
- http://www.digitalparlor.org/pwenglish/ganntt

44
Global Sourcing

Author	Daan Kersten
Year developed	2006
Also known as	Offshoring, Outsourcing, Offshore Development
Objective	Purchasing and outsourcing on a world scale

Model

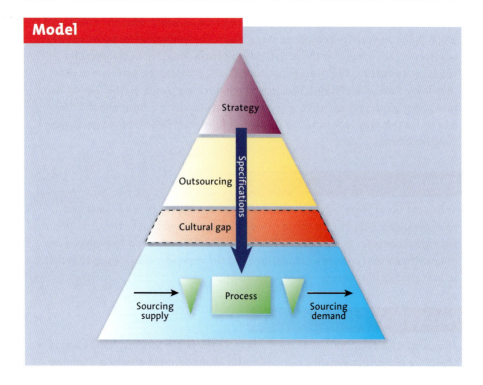

Background

Global Sourcing, outsourcing and off-shoring are themes that increasingly occur in the supply chain. The purchasing market has developed at a rapid pace from a regional to an international environment. Influenced by the provision of information via the Internet and very low-threshold transport, sources in other parts of the world are within reach. With thorough preparation, the chances of a successful Global Sourcing project are substantially increased.

Many buyers orientate themselves on outsourcing via the various media and by participating in business travel to make their first contacts with potential suppliers. Not seldom to wind up worse off later (an experience wiser), due to quality problems, breakdowns in communication and disappointing results. A structured and integrated approach and careful preparation can substantially increase the chances of success, however.

Application

With the aid of this method the Global Sourcing issue is systematically analysed by means of the following steps.

1 Evaluation of the strategy of the enterprise

With the evaluation of the strategy of the enterprise it is established what the corporate characteristics of the enterprise are. A look is taken at the position of the entrepreneur in the market, strategy in the short and medium-long term, and the distinctive competitive factors, for example. This evaluation is important to establish the aspects of whether a Global Sourcing programme fits within the strategy of the enterprise. For example, if the enterprise has innovation and speed as USPs, a transport time of two months does not fit in with the lead time of the chain.

2 Organisation of the communication

When doing business internationally, communication is one of the greatest failure factors. This is caused because people do not comprehend, let alone understand each other. Furthermore, cultural differences play an important role. The interpretation of items like quality, speed and precision plays a large role. To shape the organisation of the communication, the following elements are crucial:
- Limit the number of people involved in communications.
- Limit the contacts to one person, with a catcher for each process (purchasing, sales, engineering, finances, logistics, quality assurance, etc.)

3 Establishing the process to be outsourced

By establishing the process to be outsourced, it is determined which processes of the enterprise will be included in the outsourcing. This concerns the ingoing logistics, the process part done on site, and the outgoing logistics. The ingoing logistics covers the raw materials and materials or semi-manufactures. With local purchasing, the specifications must be strictly checked because the standards and deviations from them are differently interpreted than at home. The actual part of the process to be outsourced is explicitly described in detail, for example, in terms of technical operations, materials to be used, necessary knowledge and expertise and application experience. Possible partners can be assessed on the basis of these specifications. In this assessment should also be included whether the intended partner has the correct models and moulds to manufacture the products or possibly a specific testing rig for the benefit of quality control. The last phase of the process concerns the outgoing logistics. In this phase, it is established at what batch size and frequency the products will be supplied and what the delivery time will be. Furthermore, it is established what importance the products have in the whole, how much stock should be kept and how the products are transported, for example.

4 Setting up process control

The process control determines in what way the process will be controlled and directed. In this phase, it is in particular determined at what times checks will be carried out. These checks will have to be concretely defined in relation to when measurements must be taken, what must be measured and what must be done if there is a deviation from the standard. This step is very important in order to arrive at the correct and proper quality in connection with culture and language differences. It is particularly the cultural differences that produce deviations when establishing standards.

Result

The results of a Global Sourcing programme can primarily be seen in the areas of quality and control over the whole programme. In this manner, the pre-calculated costs will not quickly be exceeded and unexpected surprises are a thing of the past. Furthermore, this is a good basis for a request for quotations.

Focus areas

For western companies, a model is a basis for concluding a contract and making detailed agreements. In various other cultures people are not used to putting everything in detail in a contract and then actually fulfilling the contract. One should be aware that success is not guaranteed with the model alone.

Literature

- Kerkhoff, G. (2006). *Global Sourcing*. John Wiley and Sons Ltd.
- www.gscouncil.org
- http://www.purchasing.com/article/211497-The_9_hidden_costs_of_global_sourcing.php

45

GPS for Enterprises

Author	Flanders District of Creativity
Year developed	2006
Also known as	—
Objective	Generate ideas for innovation

Model

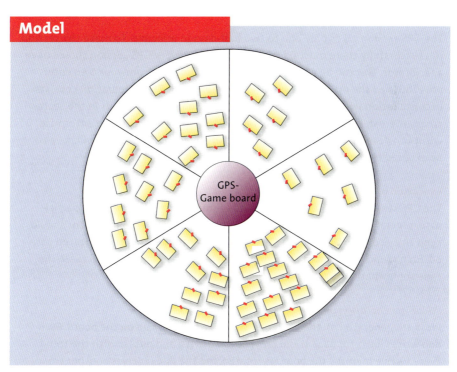

Background

Enterprises do not think up new products and services just like that. Solely if enterprises have large R&D departments can they make new products from scratch. For many companies, this is therefore not an option. If within the company however, a group of employees considers the current product portfolio and appurtenant new products or services in a structural manner, there is a possibility for small and medium (MKB) enterprises to introduce innovations. With the aid of GPS for Enterprises, this is now possible.

Application

GPS for Enterprises is a methodology where ideas with are shared mutually and further developed. The enterprise generates ideas, on the basis of the trends predominant in the sector, for how, via products, processes or procedures, these trends can be capitalised on. This is done in groups of twelve, at tables on which a round board is placed. The employees works in pairs per subject and after fifteen minutes the board is rotated, so that the ideas circulate among the participants. After all the subjects have been discussed, all the ideas the group wishes to develop are selected from them. In this way, renewal takes place via cross-fertilisation.

GPS for Enterprises is implemented according to the discussed steps.

1 Preparation for the session

The GPS session takes only one to two half-days in principle. To make the session run successfully there must be some preparation. Every GPS session should have a facilitator. This can be an external person or someone from your own enterprise, but he / she may not be involved substantively. The preparation consists in consultation with the enterprise and establishing which trends in the sector are of interest. Furthermore, it is established in what direction the enterprise wishes to develop further. The employees involved in the sessions will have to be excused from work, so they have time to spend on the session.

2 Execution of the session

The GPS session is played in three rounds. If more than twelve people participate, several tables can be set up with different subjects. The facilitator should keep an eye on the time, so that everything proceeds within the allocated period. Each round takes about an hour but the enterprise can opt to increase the time somewhat.

Round 1: generation of ideas

Ideas are generated on the basis of 5 trends, which are laid on the board. Each duo writes ideas for each trend on yellow 'Post-its' and puts it with the trend. Every twelve minutes the board is rotated and the duo receives another trend, for which ideas can again be generated. After six turns (one segment is empty), the board is back at the beginning and the first trend is again at the starting segment.

Round 2: selection of ideas

In the second round, the suggestions are divided into realisable ideas in the long and short term. This is done by attaching red stickers to creative ideas in the short term. Yellow stickers are thus for ideas in the long term. Each duo may put maximally two stickers on one idea. The participants in this round go round the table and vote on the ideas. The facilitator counts the votes for each idea and proposes the top three for the short term and the top three for the long term. Possibly, different ideas can be combined or there is an idea that was not selected but should nevertheless be included. To this end, the participants can issue one 'wild card'.

Round 3: development of ideas
For each idea, the plus and minus points are collected under the leadership of the facilitator. With every minus point the question is asked as to how this minus point can be restructured into a neutral point or plus point. From this, an action list is compiled for execution. When developing the ideas, it is more important to work out a few ideas fully than a large number of ideas only half way.

3 Implementation

The selected ideas can now be further developed for implementation in the enterprise. For each idea a plan is made, on the basis of which budgets and resources can be allocated.

Result

By rotating the board, all the participants are involved in the generation of the ideas for trends that are important to the enterprise. Because of this, cross-fertilisation occurs, which ensures that the application of the ideas is much more realistic. Use of the board and the facilitator provides structure, so that the session will yield results.

Focus areas

Quality goes above quantity in this model. It is better to work out a number of ideas fully than produce a whole range of ideas that are hardly or not feasible. Make sure therefore that there is enough time to develop the ideas.

Literature

- http://www.flandersdc.be/view/nl/2082234-GPS+for+Enterprises+.html

46
Growth Strategies, Ansoff

Author	I. Ansoff
Year developed	1987
Also known as	Ansoff Matrix, Growth Matrix, Product Market Grid
Objective	Determining growth strategy on the basis of market and product

Model

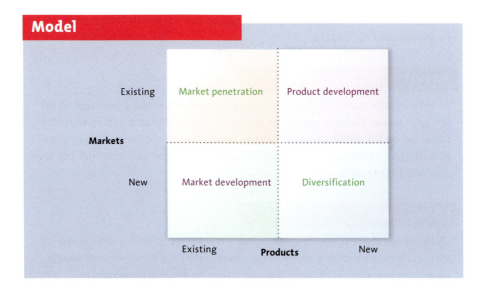

Background

Ansoff's growth model is frequently used, especially in economically favourable times. Due to the better economy, consumers will spend more and the productivity of businesses will increase. It is not always the case that the enterprise can just make the same products in larger quantities. It is advisable in such a growth situation to see in what way the enterprise can grow along with the market. The Ansoff growth model gives four growth situations in which the enterprise can end up. On the basis of two vectors, product and market, a matrix with four growth strategies is created: Market penetration, Market development, Product development and Diversification.

Companies can increase turnover and make more profit via the Growth Strategies of Ansoff. They can do this by:

- *Market penetration*: selling more products in the markets that are already serviced.
- *Market development*: start selling products in markets that have not been serviced up to now.
- *Product development*: sell new products or services in the already existing markets.
- *Diversification*: sell new products or services in markets that have not yet been serviced by the enterprise.

To apply the correct values to the model, the enterprise first establishes if it is market-oriented, or product-oriented. If the enterprise is product-oriented, that is to say, the enterprise makes products and is looking for markets, then it will look for new markets, market development or try to persuade more customers in the existing segment to buy its products (or services). If the enterprise is market-oriented, that is to say, the enterprise services a market and makes products or services, then the enterprise will always be looking for new products or services that are desired by its customers. The enterprise will therefore focus on product development. If the market changes quickly and the competition can quickly capitalise on this, a diversification strategy is applicable. The latter also brings the greatest risks with it. Risk-avoiding companies should not opt for diversification unless they have no choice.

Market penetration

Enterprises opt for market penetration when advantages of scale can be achieved. The market should then indeed offer these possibilities. On this point, market research is necessary. A risk with market penetration can be the reaction of the competition. It will naturally react to the further market penetration of the enterprise. This can possibly lead to a price war.

Market development

Market development is selected by enterprises when their own market is becoming saturated. With market development, new segments within the existing target group or perhaps a whole new target group is sought for the same product. Limited adaptations of the product or service are still classified as market development, as long as the function of the product does not change. The risk of new markets lies in unfamiliarity with these markets. This causes mistakes to be made. It is advisable to obtain some knowledge of the market and perhaps seek local support.

Product development

New products are developed because competitors bring new products onto the market or due to the introduction of new technologies. By new product is meant a product with a new function with regard to the existing products or services. Depending on whether the enterprise has a pro-active or a defensive attitude, product development will take place to stay ahead of the competition or avoid losing market share. With product development, the enterprise offers its existing customers new products and/or services. Risks with product development are among other things: products brought onto the market too early, time pressure and stress due to competition and teething troubles with products.

Diversification

This form of growth is generally used as risk spreading. To compensate for setbacks in its own market, enterprises sell products or services in several markets at the same time. Because diversification brings great risks, this form is not often chosen. To keep the risks as small as possible, the enterprise will have to slowly begin with diversification. The enterprise must have sufficient management capacity to service the new markets. Top management will also have to divide its attention over several operating companies, hence a deterioration in management can occur.

Result

The model provides the enterprise with a considered choice for a certain growth strategy. Risk-avoiding enterprises can better not apply diversification and perhaps exclusively stick with market penetration. Enterprises with a large R&D department will do a great deal of product development, while enterprises with an excellent marketing and sales staff will do more market development.

Focus areas

The model is easy to use but certainly not complete. Forward and backward integration are not included.
The model gives options for modelling growth but any further organisation of its development and the implementation of these options is lacking.

Literature

- Ansoff, I. (1988). *The new Corporate Strategy*. John Wiley & Sons Inc.
- http://claudiapiafidelis.org/cpf/videopedia/ansoffmatrix.aspx

47
Image and Identity

General management
Strategy
Marketing
Sales
Purchasing
Project & Planning
Production
Quality
Logistics & Distribution management
information
Financial
HRM & HTM
Internatio-nalisation

Authors	Birkigt and Stadler
Year developed	1986
Also known as	Communication-Identity Mix, Chain-Guard Model
Objective	Determining the personality of the enterprise

Model

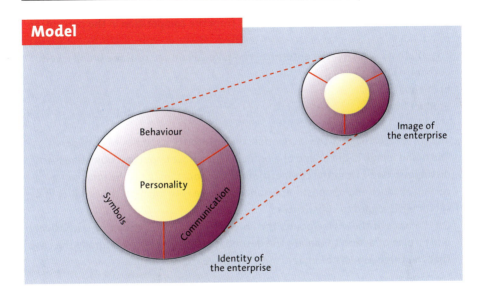

Background

Every enterprise maintains standards and values for the execution of its activities. If an enterprise has drafted a mission and a vision, the standards and values will be expressed in them. Everything that the enterprise does and particularly towards its stakeholders, is directed towards implementing the standards and values. Every enterprise has thus a clear picture of what it represents. This is called the *corporate identity* or *identity of the enterprise*.

An outsider looks at the enterprise on the basis of an own frame of reference of his or her values and standards. In this manner, an image is formed of the enterprise in question. The image that outsiders have of an enterprise is called the *corporate image* or the *image of an enterprise*.

When identity and image correspond, there is nothing wrong. But when it turns out that this is not so, then the enterprise has a problem. Evidently, outsiders then have a different image of the values and standards the enterprise strives for than the enterprise would like. On this basis, the enterprise will have to undertake action. With the aid of the model of Birkigt and Stadler, insight can be obtained into the Image and Identity of the enterprise.

Application

The construction of an image for an enterprise cannot take place in a short time frame. On the other hand, an image can be lost within two weeks. Because the image of an enterprise is determined by outsiders, the enterprise cannot itself create the image but can influence it. The enterprise can make use of various instruments to influence its image.

In relation to its image, the enterprise has the possibility to position the identity of a brand via branding. A brand means for outsiders identification, trust, quality and it has a symbolic function (shows who you are). The use of a brand has the objective of distinguishing itself from the competition in the perception of outsiders.

To radiate its identity, the enterprise can take advantage of three brand levels:

- corporate image
- brand image
- product image

The corporate image is the image that the enterprise itself has to outsiders. The brand image is the image of a brand and its most important objective is to distinguish itself from the competition. The product image is the image of a certain product and its most important objective is to position the product in a sector with regard to substitutes.

On the basis of these viewpoints the enterprise can better and more purposively draft a plan of action to radiate the desired identity. Here, it is naturally the case that the three aspects of image mutually influence each other.

To influence the image of an enterprise, use can be made of positioning. Positioning with respect to the image is putting an image in the heads of outsiders in general and the target group in particular. The complexity lies in the fact that this concerns perceptions and not the products or services themselves. With positioning, the values that should be perceived should be clearly communicated by the target group. To this end, the enterprise has four different positioning strategies available:

- informational positioning: communication of the benefits
- transformational positioning: communication of values
- bilateral positioning: communication of values and benefits
- operational positioning: communication linked to a unique symbol

With positioning, brand values are also important. Brand values are the properties of the brand, product or enterprise. The brand values must be selected on the basis of what outsiders think is important.

This can occur via various viewpoints. For example:
- end values according to Rokeach (what someone thinks is important in life)
- personality characteristics according to Rokeach (behaviour of people)
- needs hierarchy of Maslow
- marketing mix according to Kotler
- brand personality characteristics according to Aaker

Next to positioning, the enterprise can make use of names, logos, colours and designs, for example. The name of a product or enterprise is one of the most important instruments for the image. It is actually the main bearer of the identity. The enterprise can choose from the following types of brand name:
- functional name, for example, Daily Mail
- name with meaning, for example, Apple
- abstract name, for example, Avans
- abbreviation or number, for example, DSM

To arrive at a new name, the enterprise can opt to think one up itself, launching a competition or employing a branding agency.
The logo, colour and design are strongly linked to the brand and form the house style of an enterprise. A round logo for example, has a different association than a square logo. The same with colour: a green colour has a different association than a blue colour.

Outsiders have a certain attitude with respect to the enterprise and its products. This partly determines the image of the enterprise. The enterprise can try to influence this attitude for the benefit of the brand or the enterprise. To this end, the enterprise can make use of the *tri-component model*, which comprises the cognitive, affective and conative components.
- *The cognitive component*: is related to what the outsider knows or what knowledge the outsider has with regard to the brand, product or enterprise.
- *The affective component*: is related to the feelings or emotions an outsider has with regard to the brand, product or enterprise.
- *The conative component*: concerns the behavioural intensity or behavioural intention of the outsider with regard to the brand, product or enterprise. In other words: will the outsider also actually use the products of the enterprise and the brand?

Result

The result of the use of these instruments provides the enterprise with the possibility to prevent any mismatch between the identity and image of the enterprise, or attune them to each other.

Focus areas

This model does not take into account possible environmental factors that can influence the image of the brand, product or enterprise.

The model makes no distinction between the weighting of the three elements in the model, behaviour, communication and symbolism. Behaviour actually has the greatest influence on image.

Literature

- Birkigt, K., Stadler, M., Funck, H. (2002). *Corporate Identity*. Verlag Moderne Industrie.
- Ries & Trout (2001). *Positioning: The Battle for Your Mind*. McGraw-Hill.

48
Industrial column

Author	Van Goor
Year developed	1976
Also known as	Business chain
Objective	Selection of distribution channels

General management

Strategy

Marketing

Sales

Purchasing

Project & Planning

Production

Quality

Logistics & Distribution

Information management

Financial

HRM & HTM

Internationalisation

Model

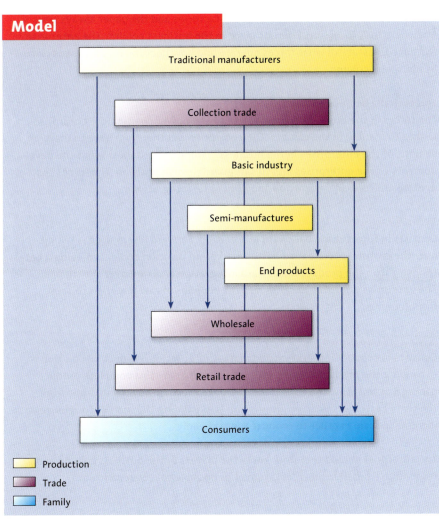

- Production
- Trade
- Family

Background

Products purchased by retailers are often composed of various semi-manufactures, which in turn are made from raw materials and auxiliary materials. It should be obvious that not everything is made and sold at the same location. This automatically means that manufacturers deliver their products to the retail shops via various intermediate links. The structure of the route of the manufacturer to the retailer is called the business column.

Application

An enterprise does not select a place in the business column but falls automatically into a certain place based on its activities. A paper manufacturer will always fall under basic industries for example, because the pulp – from which paper is made – is produced from trees by special factories and the paper always goes elsewhere for processing. From its place in the business column, the enterprise will have to establish what forces operate and how decision making takes place in a business column.

Forces in the business column

The forces in the business column relate to the power position the enterprise wishes to assume in the column. The enterprise will therefore have to make an analysis of the enterprises in the business column and establish what the developments of the enterprises are, to safeguard its own position. The forces that operate are vertical integration and horizontal integration.

Vertical integration

Consists in forward and backward integration. Forward integration is taking over the customer to create a better marketing position and/or achieving a better margin on the products. Backward integration is taking over the supplier. The enterprise does this to safeguard the supplies of raw materials or semi-manufactures.

Horizontal integration

Consists in product integration and market integration. Product integration is expanding the product range to provide customers with a complete product package. In this way, the enterprise can make more turnover and profit from the same customers. Market integration is expanding the market to achieve an increase in scale in order to produce more cheaply.

The enterprise should therefore know the players in the business column and respond to a possible (hostile) takeover or possible takeover candidate.

Decision making

Another aspect is the decision making that takes place in the business column when buying and selling products and services. This applies primarily to the business-to-business (B2B) market and not to the business-to-consumer (B2C) market. When several players are involved in the purchase of a financially strong product, for example business premises, there are several enterprises exerting influence on the ultimate purchasing of the end products or semi-manufactures. In many situations, it is not even the ultimate buyer who takes the decisions about the materials and services to be used, but one of the other the players that participates in the realisation of the total product.

As an example, we take business premises to be built. The enterprise that has the premises built often leaves it to the architect to decide which materials are used, while the architect leaves the purchase of wood, for example, to the contractor as long as it complies with the established requirements.

As a player in the business column, it is thus important to know how the decision making takes place, to attune the marketing and sales activities to the right parties and so achieve the highest turnover.

Result

From the vertical and horizontal integration, the enterprise can establish what opportunities and threats the companies and markets with which the enterprise will be directly involved, will pose. The opportunities and threats involve the takeover of another enterprise or being taken over. They also involve the expansion of markets on the basis of extra products or services or on the basis of market area expansion.

From the decision making, the enterprise has more insight into who, when and what has possibilities to decide about the purchase of products and services. With goal-oriented marketing and sales activities, the enterprise can then achieve more turnover.

Focus areas

Only insight into the structure can be obtained with the aid of the business column. A value judgement of the forces and the decision making in the business column cannot be given.

Literature

- Visser H. & Goor A. van (2006). *Logistics: Principles & Practice*. Groningen/Houten: Noordhoff Uitgevers.

General management

Strategy

Marketing

Sales

Purchasing

Project & Planning

Production

Quality ⊗

Logistics & Distribution

Information management

Financial

HRM & HTM

Internatio-nalisation

49

INK / EFQM

Author	European Foundation of Quality Management
Year developed	1992
Also known as	Institute for Dutch Quality Assurance (INK), EFQM Excellence Model, The European Model for Quality Management
Objective	Formulation of organisational objectives and organisational policy

Model

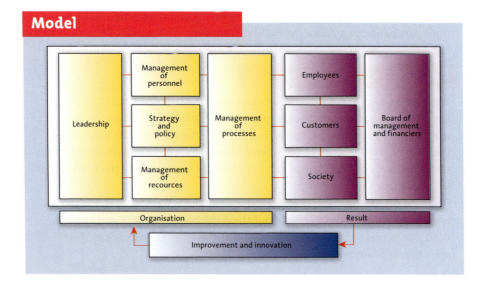

Background

The EFQM model is named for the organisation that developed it. The model was developed to be able to compete in Europe with enterprises from the Far East. The objective of the model is to create a complete quality system for an enterprise so that it is able to excel in any field and thereby resist the competition. The model is built up out of nine focus areas; five organisational areas (enablers) and four results areas (results).

The INK model is a translation from the EFQM model to a Dutch model and used to be more comprehensive than the EFQM model. To excel, a company has to go through five development phases. These five development phases have been integrated into the original model.

Application

The model assumes that if a company wishes to excel, it must be strong in all the *organisational areas* in the model and score highly in the *results areas*. For each enterprise, these areas will be specifically filled in. The areas are described and the critical success factors are nominated.

Leadership

The leadership should satisfy the critical success factors below:
- determining the mission, vision, objectives, goals and strategy
- being a role model in a culture that strives for excellence
- being personally involved with the improvement of the operating system
- being involved with customers and partners and being representative of the society
- motivation, support and (re)cognition of staff in the enterprise

Strategy and Policy

The critical success factors of enterprises that wish to excel are:
- based on the wishes and expectations of all the interested parties (stakeholders)
- based on information on results measurements, research, learning and creativity
- continuously developed, evaluated and kept up to date
- backed by a set of key processes
- communicated and implemented

Employees

The employees of the enterprise play a crucial role in achieving an excellent enterprise. The critical success factors are:
- planning, managing and improving human resources
- establishing, developing and retaining the competences of the employees
- giving authority to employees and involving them
- ensuring there is dialogue between employees and the enterprise
- rewarding, (re)cognition of and caring for employees

Resources

To excel in the area of resources, the management must take care of:
- partnerships
- financing
- buildings, equipment and materials
- technology
- information and knowledge

Processes

Within the processes, the activities are carried out by the employees with the aid of the resources allocated by the management. To excel in these, the processes should be:

- systematically designed and controlled
- continuously improved to increase their added value
- producing quality products and services on the basis of what the customers want.

Furthermore, it is important to maintain relationships with customers and if necessary, improve them.

The enterprise will have to score highly in the results areas. Perceptions in the areas of customers and suppliers, employees and society must be measurable. All this will ultimately result in the critical success factors that must be drafted by the enterprise from the vision and mission strategy.

Result

Although in the first instance the model was intended to achieve and implement improvements, the model is primarily used as a reference model and to analyse the current situation. The status of an excellent enterprise can be established with this model and insight is provided into the critical designs.

Focus areas

The model provides no support with the actual implementation of a change process to make the enterprise genuinely excellent. A new strategic direction does not emerge on the basis of the model from the analysis of the enterprise. The model gives a static and rigid summary of success factors that must be gone through. There is no room for flexible and innovative processes.

Literature

- WWW.EFQM.ORG
- www.ink.nl
- www.mavim.nl/ink-model
- http://www.proveandimprove.org/new/tools/efqm.php

50
Intelligence Pyramid

Author	J. Rodenberg
Year developed	2004
Also known as	Marketing intelligence, Competitive intelligence
Objective	The translation of raw data into action-focused strategic decision making

Model

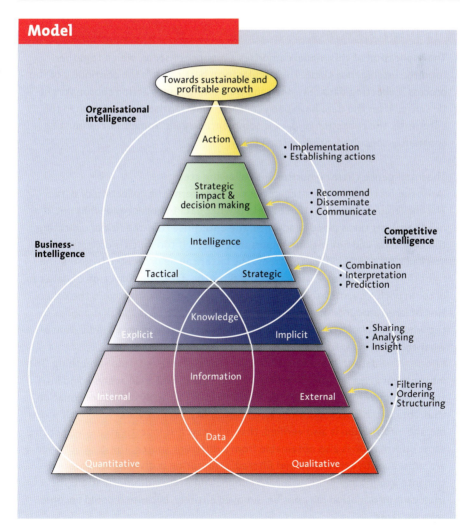

Towards sustainable and profitable growth

Organisational intelligence

Action
• Implementation
• Establishing actions

Strategic impact & decision making
• Recommend
• Disseminate
• Communicate

Competitive intelligence

Intelligence
Tactical — Strategic
• Combination
• Interpretation
• Prediction

Business-intelligence

Knowledge
Explicit — Implicit
• Sharing
• Analysing
• Insight

Information
Internal — External
• Filtering
• Ordering
• Structuring

Data
Quantitative — Qualitative

Background

The collection of information from the market has been done for a long time. It is becoming more difficult, however, to collect exactly those data that will produce more growth and profit than the competition in time. The translation of these data into information, knowledge, intelligence, a strategy and actions for the enterprise is consequently becoming increasingly important. Next to business intelligence, which focuses on internal quantitative data, and competitive intelligence, which focuses on external qualitative data, we also see the upsurge of organisational intelligence. Organisational intelligence translates the knowledge found into intelligence for the enterprise such that it can determine impacts on strategy and can thereby take the right decisions and plan actions. The combination of these three intelligences is represented in the 'Intelligence Pyramid'.

Application

The application of this model comprises a number of steps, which together form the intelligence circle. The circular form best reflects the continuity of the process. Collecting data only once and translating it into action thus makes little sense. After the data have been collected and translated into action in the enterprise, the collection of data is commenced again. Some sources must be constantly consulted, others occasionally.

The intelligence circle comprises the following steps:

1 *Data*: the first step in the intelligence circle concerns the collection of data. The challenge in the collection of data is what data to collect and what not. If a needs analysis takes place in advance, the enterprise runs the risk of collecting too little data and not making important choices. If too much is collected, then you can't see the wood for the trees. The latter can be prevented by using the right IT systems to order, structure and filter the data. The collection of data can occur in both a quantitative and qualitative manner. Quantitative is the collection of large amounts of data so that a statement can be made that applies to the whole population investigated. Qualitative research gives an indication of what the thinking is of the population investigated.

2 *Information*: data that are new to the enterprise; these data add something. This information gives insight into the enterprise via the internal analysis and into the environment of the enterprise from the external analysis. The information thus obtained is checked for relevance, reliability, accuracy and validity. If possible, the information is also verified, that is to say, it is investigated whether the same information is also obtainable from a different source. The data obtained are subsequently structured and filtered. Structuring is dividing the information into groups and filtering means eliminating irrelevant information. The irrelevant information may not be removed entirely, because it could become relevant later.

3 *Knowledge*: after this step, the information can be shared with others. Together with these others, analysis of the information is performed. This analysis leads to more insight into the enterprise and its environment. The information produced leads to knowledge within the enterprise, which becomes available at different levels: operational, tactical and strategic. At the operational level in great detail, at the tactical level combined into performance indicators and at the strategic level combined into the success factors established for the enterprise. Explicit knowledge can be stored in IT systems and made accessible to others. Implicit knowledge is usually present in the minds of the personnel. This knowledge must also be made accessible in order to make the right choices for the future. Choices are also based on the competences the enterprise possesses after all.

4 *Intelligence*: through the combination and interpretation of the knowledge, a degree of intelligence arises within the enterprise at the three indicated levels. This intelligence is used to make pro-active analyses and predict what will happen in the market. Due to this, the enterprise is able to anticipate the developments in the market earlier than the competition. Precisely due to this intelligence, an alert and rapidly responsive enterprise is created.

5 *Strategic impact and decision making*: for the management now arises the possibility to make choices for the enterprise based on the predictions. At the operational level, they can be made immediately (in the short term), while on the tactical and strategic levels, consultations are necessary. The dissemination, communication and recommendation of the intelligence is a condition to coming to a proper insight with regard to all the processes in the enterprise.

6 *Action*: as the last step, the necessary actions are compiled and carried out, to arrive at a sustainable and profitable enterprise.

Result

By making use of the Intelligence Pyramid, the enterprise can change from an enterprise that approaches the market reactively to one that approaches the market pro-actively. An enterprise that approaches the market pro-actively is able to have an action plan ready as soon as market changes become apparent.

Focus areas

The collection of data is often an IT matter. The Intelligence Pyramid is clearly not an IT matter, but has the objective of guiding the strategy of the enterprise. Recording the knowledge in the minds of the personnel is often a complex problem, because the personnel soon feel superfluous if their knowledge has been recorded.

Literature

- Josèph, H., Rodenberg, R. (2007). *Competitive Intelligence and Senior Management*. Eburon Academic Publishers.
- www.globalintelligence.com

51

International Market Research

Author	S. Hollensen
Year developed	2006
Also known as	−
Objective	Consideration of potential in countries

Model

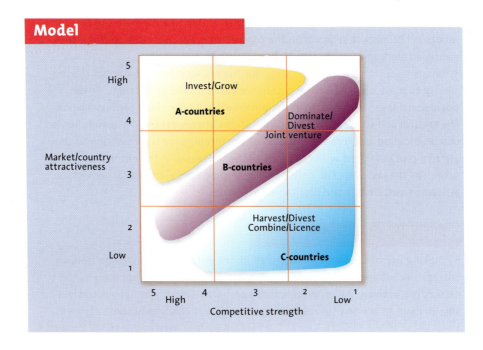

Background

In the current era of worldwide information exchange and further globalisation, in which more and more enterprises operate internationally, it is becoming increasingly important for enterprises to make well-founded choices with regard to the countries or regions in which the products and/or services will be sold. Formerly, internationalisation was primarily started in neighbouring countries, while due to developments such as the Internet, interactive ordering can now be done worldwide. Against this background it is important for enterprises to be able to make the right choices when it comes to the question of which countries can or cannot be supplied.

With the International Market Research model, an enterprise can select the most interesting regions from a group of countries or regions that are of interest for doing business. The risks of doing business internationally are thereby strongly reduced.

Application

The model is based on a number of components that were developed by Hollensen and combined, they give an overview of the risks and possible market opportunities in the selected regions or countries. The research extends over three subjects: A-, B- and C-countries, the BERI index and the competition.

A, B, C Countries					BERI index		
Country	Market	Own relative competitive strength	ABC Countries		BERI index		Risk level

Competition			
Competitor	Country	Strength	Competitive strength country

These three subjects are further elucidated.

A-, B- and C-countries
This concerns a selection into A-, B- or C-countries where A-countries are the most interesting, B-countries need to be carefully considered and C-countries are not of interest for further investment.

The research into the countries of the regions with which the enterprise wishes to do business is in two parts. Firstly, there are countries established with which the enterprise thinks it may wish to do business in the future. These countries are inventoried on a number of subjects. The minimum subjects are:
- market size
- market growth
- commercial activities
- government investment
- intensity of the competition
- positioning of the enterprise

- substitutes on the market
- infrastructure of country

For each situation, this list can be supplemented with subjects of interest. For each subject, a weighting is indicated, for which the total score should be 100%. For each country or region, a grade is give on a five-point scale, where a low number is a high grade. Next to the grading of the countries, for the actual determination of A-, B- or C-countries, an evaluation of the strength of the competition should be represented. See the evaluation of competition for this. The combination of market attractiveness and the intensity of the competition determines whether an enterprise falls in the category of A-, B- or C-country.

BERI index
The Business Evaluation Risk Index (BERI) is a risk analysis on a number of subjects that indicates the size of the risk of doing business with enterprises in the country in question. The subjects in the index are fixed and are evaluated on a five-point scale. The weighting between the subjects is also fixed.

Competition
Thirdly, the competition doing business in the same market or country is reviewed. This should involve both local and international competitors. Here too, a weighting is established for each subject, of which the total is 100%. In this category it is possible to add more subjects or leave them out if they are not of interest. Examples of subjects are: market share, product fit on the market, price, technology, quality and service.

Result

On the basis of the inventory of the risks, the intensity and power of the competition and the attractiveness of a country or region, the enterprise can estimate whether doing business with enterprises there will lead to successful internationalisation. The conclusion could also be that the circumstances are so risky that it is not wise at this time to do business with enterprises from the country or region in question.

Focus areas

The use of this model is to support the policy of the enterprise and it may not be over-simplified.

Literature

- Hollensen, S. (2007). *Global Marketing*. Harlow: Pearson Education Limited, fourth edition.
- Graham, J., Cateora, P. (2007). *International Marketing*. McGraw-Hill Education.
- www.export.gov

52
International Pricing Strategy

Author	S. Hollensen
Year developed	1998
Also known as	–
Objective	Determining prices internationally

Model

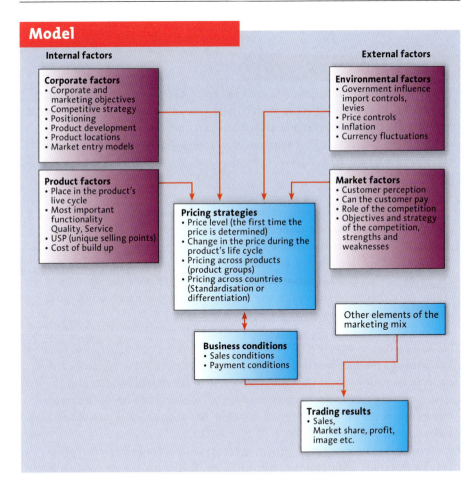

Internal factors

Corporate factors
- Corporate and marketing objectives
- Competitive strategy
- Positioning
- Product development
- Product locations
- Market entry models

Product factors
- Place in the product's live cycle
- Most important functionality Quality, Service
- USP (unique selling points)
- Cost of build up

Pricing strategies
- Price level (the first time the price is determined)
- Change in the price during the product's life cycle
- Pricing across products (product groups)
- Pricing across countries (Standardisation or differentiation)

Business conditions
- Sales conditions
- Payment conditions

External factors

Environmental factors
- Government influence import controls, levies
- Price controls
- Inflation
- Currency fluctuations

Market factors
- Customer perception
- Can the customer pay
- Role of the competition
- Objectives and strategy of the competition, strengths and weaknesses

Other elements of the marketing mix

Trading results
- Sales, Market share, profit, image etc.

Background

Price is the most important component of the marketing mix. All the other components in the marketing mix lead to cost increases. Only the price provides the profit. The price for a product or service is in many cases determined by adding up the costs of production, sales, management, marketing and service and multiplying this total by a profit margin.

In an international environment, pricing is much more complex because more factors play a role in the determination of the price. Extra factors in an international environment are for example, currency differences, different inflation and alternative payment methods like leasing and barter. The enterprise will further have to choose whether pricing policy will be centrally established or that there will be possibilities that different prices can be established on local markets. Determining an International Pricing Strategy should therefore be done carefully.

Application

The decision making about the International Pricing Strategy can occur with the aid of the factors included in the model. These factors are sub-divided into two main groups, internal factors and external factors and four sub-groups, corporate factors, product factors, environmental factors and market factors. The four sub-groups are further elucidated.

Corporate factors

The pricing strategy of the enterprise is based on its corporate and marketing policy, in which positioning, competitive strategy, product development and production location are included. In its own country, the enterprise can establish the prices entirely unilaterally. Abroad, the enterprise must take into account distributors or partners in a joint venture, who may determine the ultimate selling price themselves. Only if the enterprise has its own branch office can it determine the price itself.

Product factors

The price of a product or service is influenced by its place in the product's life cycle, the functionality of the product, the USP of the product and its cost structure. In an international environment, the following additional factors are important for the ultimate price the customer has to pay for the product or service.

- If a product has to be adapted, this brings costs with it. For example: for different raw materials, adaptations to the machinery inventory, training of employees, adaptations to the product itself and development costs.
- Depending on the number of links there are between the exporting enterprise and the ultimate selling enterprise, the price will be higher.
- The length of the distribution channel brings extra costs with it.

In this way, a price calculation can be created and the product could become too expensive for the customer. Measures to avoid price escalation are:

- reduce the number of links in the distribution process
- lower the price ex-factory
- have the product produced in the object country
- put pressure on intermediaries to accept lower margins

Environmental factors

The environmental factors abroad cannot be influenced. They can have a great influence on the price, however. It can concern the following factors:

- government regulations such as import levies, safety requirements and quotas (lower stock levels thus more frequent distribution movements)
- currency fluctuations
- inflation (has a negative effect on the profits and forces prices up)

Market factors

Market factors that influence the price are:

- purchasing power of the customers (can produce big differences for each country)
- negotiating power of the customers
- intensity and pricing of the competition
- threats from substitutes and newcomers in the market

Pricing strategies

The determination of a price for a product on a new market can be done in three ways:

- Skimming: a high price is demanded to 'skim off' the top of the market
- Market price: price in line with the market on the basis of equivalent products
- Penetration price: low price to gain market share and stimulate market growth

Other pricing strategies are:

- Experience-oriented pricing: because more experience is being gained with production, the costs per unit will decline.
- Product pricing: by including several versions of a product, cheap, medium and expensive, a better competitive position can be captured.
- Product-service combination: a low price for the product and a good price for the service thereafter.
- Prices across countries: standardisation or differentiation. Standardisation is one price established at head office for all countries. Differentiation takes into account local deviations.
- Settlement prices: these are prices maintained between daughter companies of the same mother concern.

Corporate conditions

A very important aspect in international sales is the moment that the products change ownership. This actually also changes who is at risk if things go wrong. International agreements have been made to this end, which are established in the Incoterms or international delivery conditions. These delivery conditions can easily be obtained via the Internet.

The Letter-of-Credit is used a great deal for international money transfers. Here, a bank agrees to pay an agreed amount on production of the documents named in the Letter-of-Credit.

Result

By taking account of the extra factors in pricing strategies in an international environment, the enterprise is able to prevent that the product or service becomes too expensive abroad and the risks are covered. For example, in the event of currency fluctuations or if products are transported at the risk of the enterprise itself.

Focus areas

The price is a component of the marketing mix and must thus be integrated in the total marketing mix. The price is easy to influence and adjust without high costs. Developing and filling in the model requires time.

Literature

- Hollensen, S. (2007). *Global Marketing*. Harlow: Pearson Education Limited, fourth edition.
- Boone. E., Kurtz. D., Snow. K. (2010). *Contemporary Marketing*. Nelson Education Ltd.
- www.iccwbo.org/incoterms

53
ITIL V3

Author	**The Stationary Office (TSO)**
Year developed	**2007**
Also known as	**IT Infrastructure Library**
Objective	**Managing information systems**

Model

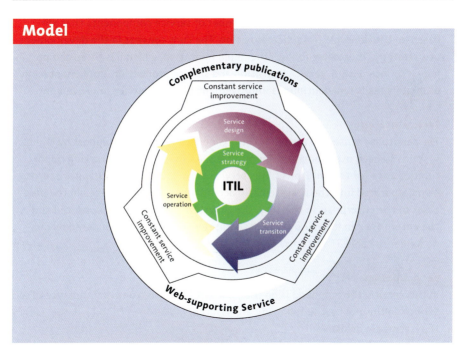

Background

The development and management of information systems has been a problem for a long time. Information systems became too expensive and management activity could hardly be controlled in a structured fashion. The Central Computer and Telecommunications Agency (CCTA) has developed a set with which a grip can be obtained on the development and management of computerised information systems. This set comprises procedures and documentation. When it was first started, ITIL comprised five parts (sets) for the development and management of IT. These sets were:

General management
Strategy
Marketing
Sales
Purchasing
Project & Planning
Production
Quality
Logistics & Distribution
Information management
Financial
HRM & HTM
Internationalisation

- Service Support
- Service Delivery
- Managers
- Software Support
- Computer Operations

The latter three sets were developed to support the first two. Later, the Office of Government Commerce (OGC) in England took over the management and development of ITIL. In 2007, a new version was released in which the sets have been replaced by services (service components), where the provision of service is the starting point.

Application

The structure of ITIL V3 consists in a number of service components that are based on the life cycle of service provision. The core consists in the development of a strategy. Thereafter follows the implementation, which has three components: service design, service transition and service production. Implementation ultimately leads to a continuous improvement process: service improvement.

Service strategy

The service is focused on attuning the business processes and support by IT systems to each other on a continuous basis. As soon as new marketing opportunities arise for the enterprise, this service ensures that these changes can also be incorporated into the IT systems, in accordance with the changes in the processes of the enterprise. In this way, the IT systems will not grow outdated and the enterprise can further develop its strategy without being hindered by old, no longer suitable, IT systems.

Service design

In this service, the emphasis is on the policy of the design and maintenance of a service. In this policy, the following are assured:
- IT systems are available
- there are sufficient resources for design
- continuity is provided
- a security design will come

Furthermore, this service makes sure of the correct documentation with regard to the IT systems designed.

Service transition

This service ensures that once designed, systems become available for the final user in the enterprise. Aspects of this service lie in the field of change management, release management, configuration management and service knowledge management. All this is related to the implementation and management of changes in the information systems. It is important that the right changes are implemented at the right times and in combination with each other, to guarantee the correct functioning of the IT systems.

Service operation

With the users of the IT systems, it is agreed how the functioning of these systems must be organised. This is established in a document: the Service Level Agreement (SLA). The service production must ensure that the systems remain 'on the air' and that in the event of breakdowns, a solution is quickly found for the problem. Under this service falls the help desk for example, as first-line support.

Service improvement

Once the services have been initiated, there is then a continuous quest for improvement. On the basis of the different reports, the performance of the services within ITIL is measured and compared with the standards agreed in the SLA.

The five services embrace complete support of the business processes of the enterprise through IT systems. They will have to be gone through step-by-step to be able to successfully organise them. Every service comprises a number of processes that have to be organised. For each service and its processes, books are available that exhaustively define in what way the service must be organised and which processes and activities the service includes.

Result

With the aid of ITIL, the support of business processes through IT can be set up in a controlled fashion. The results of a controllable IT environment are:
- cost savings on IT resources, time spent by users and IT employees
- higher quality of the results of the value chain of the enterprise
- fewer malfunctions in production
- faster solutions for problems and standstills
- satisfied customers due to higher delivery reliability

Focus areas

Larger organisations make a great deal of use of ITIL because this model is so comprehensive and detailed. Herein is an immediate pitfall for smaller enterprises. Blindly filling in everything in the ITIL will not lead to success for smaller enterprises. These enterprises must properly select what they will and will not use from ITIL. Furthermore, they must conform with the rules that are contained within ITIL to successfully implement the services. ITIL does not take any account of corporate culture. Due to this, implementation will be more difficult for informal organisational cultures, for example. Employees of an enterprise where ITIL is implemented, have to realise that holding on to existing rules and procedures can severely delay implementation.

Literature

- www.itil.org
- www.itil-officialsite.com
- www.itilv3.net

54

Karasek's Job Strain Model

Authors	R. Karasek/R. Karasek and Theorell
Year developed	1979/1990
Also known as	Job-demand job-control model, JDC Model
Objective	Preventing work-related stress

Model

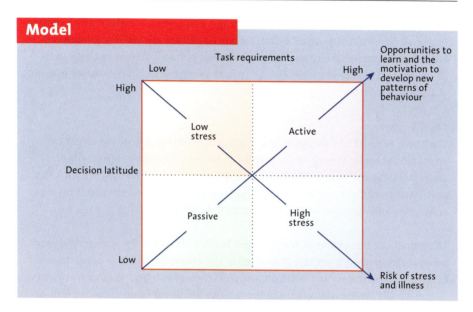

Background

Work stress is often seen as the consequence of too much work. But there are other factors that influence work stress, for example, physical loading, environmental factors, styling of the function and the social relationships. Work stress has consequences for society, organisations and individuals. The employees constitute one of the most important production factors. Therefore, it is important that they are treated in the right way. Motivation and pleasure in one's work lead to better results for the enterprise, society and individuals. The possible causes of stress are obtained with Karasek's model.

Application

The model comprises two aspects: decision latitude and task requirements. In 1990, social support was added.

Task requirements

The task requirements are concerned with, among other things, the heaviness of the work, the amount of work, the physical loading involved with the work, the work pace, the necessary skills and concentration. An important item with the task requirements is the intensity with which the stressors (causers of stress) appear.

Decision latitude

The decision latitude is the possibility the employee has to take independent decisions when carrying out the task package. Employees are often given bigger responsibilities but the appurtenant authorities to act are lacking. Employees are, however, addressed when things go wrong, but an instrument to do something about it is often lacking. Due to this, the employees almost always end up in a stress situation.

Social support

The social support of colleagues and managers often has a positive effect on an employee under stress. This support can be with regard to appreciation, understanding and emotional. But it can also consist in actual support with the performance of the tasks of the employee. An employee who can count on his colleagues and manager will be less susceptible to stress.

The model can be used at different levels in the enterprise. For each employee on an individual level, per role (function) in the enterprise and per department. On the basis of the survey 'Job Content Questionnaire 1985', roles/departments or individuals can be utilised in the model. The following figure includes four roles that can occur in an enterprise.

Role 1, for example, is a porter who can organise his work himself but the tasks he must carry out are rated low. In this case, this role means an easy position where stress will not easily arise.

Role 2, for example, is a director of an enterprise. He has extensive authority to take decisions but has to report to the board of management. His task requirements are relatively high, for example, the concentration that he must produce on a certain subject. Because this director is able to decide himself how situations will be handled, this role offers latitude for further development without becoming stressed.

Role 3, for example, is an employee on the shop floor who gets his orders from the foreman. For this, the employee needs little decision latitude because the foreman largely takes all the decisions. The task requirements are also low for the employee because he has carried out the actions concerned for quite some

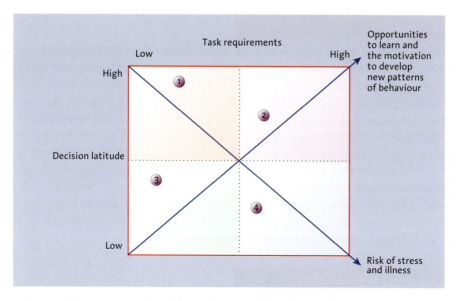

time and the amount of work is well attuned. The chance of experiencing stress or illness is present.

Role 4, for example, is a teacher in education. The task requirements are high because more and more is being demanded of teachers next to their primary activities. The decision latitude for teachers is low because the structure of schools is organised on the basis of schedules and the headmasters take all the decisions, except for the content of the lessons of the teacher. Overpressure on teachers is then possible.

Result

The model gives insight into which people, roles or departments in the enterprise can end up in a risk situation. The roles with high stress must be tackled immediately but the roles in the passive quadrant may not be forgotten. Employees with boring roles can also be or become unhappy in their work.

Focus areas

There are employees who say they perform well under pressure. This can exclusively occur if there is sufficient decision latitude for these employees. If there is not, then the chance that these employees will nevertheless perform poorly is certainly present. Later, the social support component was added. This can partly ensure less stress with high task requirements and low decision latitude because the employee knows that colleagues and managers will help and support him if necessary (Van Yperen and Hagedoorn, 2003). The role of the manager is extremely important here.

Expansion

Nowadays, a great deal of use is made of the Welfare at Work (WEBA) method. With the WEBA (qualitative) and the NOVA-WEBA (quantitative) methods a number of aspects of the work situation can be mapped out. With the WEBA method, the quality of the work is mapped out and data are collected on the functional composition, the control possibilities and the control problems. The WEBA method was developed for the labour inspectorate. This agency thereby has an objective instrument for establishing compliance with labour standards. With the NOVA-WEBA questionnaire, which was developed by the TNO, it can be established if and where there is work stress in the organisation. The questionnaire gives information on work-related causes of pressure at work or stress. Because this method is based is on the Karasek (1979) model and Karasek and Theorell (1990), Karasek's model is explained here.

Literature

- Karasek, R. (1979). Job demands, job decision latitude and mental strain: Implications for job redesign. *Administrative Science Quarterly*, 24, 285-306.
- Karasek, R. & Theorell, T. (1990). *Healthy work: Stress, productivity and the reconstruction of working life*. New York: Basic Books.
- Hosie, P., Sevastos, P., Cooper, C. (2006). *Happy Performing Managers*. Edward Elger Publishing Ltd.

55
Knowledge management

Author	M. Weggeman
Year developed	1997
Also known as	Knowledge value chain
Objective	Managing production factor knowledge

Model

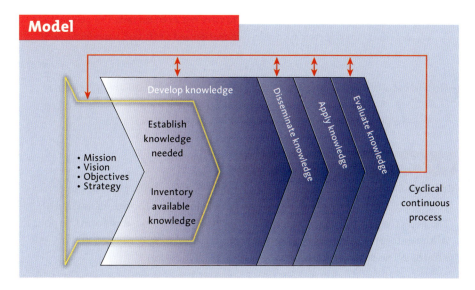

- Mission
- Vision
- Objectives
- Strategy

Develop knowledge

Establish knowledge needed

Inventory available knowledge

Disseminate knowledge

Apply knowledge

Evaluate knowledge

Cyclical continuous process

Background

Every enterprise has four production factors to achieve the desired results of the enterprise. These desired results are established in the vision, mission and objectives. The four production factors are:

- labour
- resources
- capital
- information

Meanwhile, the collection of data is no longer a problem. The opposite is even true, there is an overload of data. From this overload it is now important to extract the right data, which can lead to knowledge. By making use of Weggeman's knowledge value chain, this knowledge can be disseminated

General management
Strategy
Marketing
Sales
Purchasing
Project & Planning
Production
Quality
Logistics & Distribution
Information management
Financial
HRM & HTM
Internationalisation

so that it has meaning for everyone and can be handled in the right way. Knowledge management can be viewed from different angles. These are:

- *Business angle*: the improvement of business processes in enterprises as a task of the management.
- *Policy angle*: the achievement of optimal conditions under which knowledge workers can function.
- *Strategic angle*: the organisation of knowledge acquisition as a strategy of the enterprise.
- *Administrative angle*: tackling bureaucratic structures to collaborate more flexibly together through knowledge.

Weggeman's knowledge value chain starts from the business angle. Weggeman defines knowledge as:

'A personal ability that enables someone to carry out a certain task. This personal ability comprises two aspects, a hard side, information and a soft side, experience, skills and attitudes.'

On the basis of these two aspects, Weggeman derives the following formula:

Knowledge = Information × Experience + Skills + Attitudes (K = I * ESA).

Application

The knowledge value chain comprises a number of processes that are gone through in succession to deploy the available knowledge for the realisation of the objectives of the enterprise. These objectives are formulated from the policy of the enterprise. This policy is established in the mission, vision, objectives and strategy. The successive processes are:

1 Establish
The first step in the value chain is establishing the presently available knowledge. In other words, that which the enterprise or the employees have at their disposal. Especially establishing the experience, skills and attitudes in competence profiles is an important component.

2 Inventory
Step two is an inventory of the knowledge the organisation needs to achieve its objectives. This knowledge is established in the same way (competence profiles) as in step 1, so that it can be established whether all knowledge is present or knowledge is lacking.

3 Develop or acquire the knowledge
When it is known what knowledge is not yet present, the enterprise must make a choice about what way the knowledge will be acquired by the enterprise. The

enterprise can choose to further train its own employees or recruit new people who already have the knowledge concerned.

4 Disseminate the knowledge
With the dissemination of the knowledge, the enterprise trains employees or recruits new employees for those places where the knowledge is lacking. These employees will communicate the knowledge they have to their colleagues, so that they will ultimately have access to the knowledge that is necessary to perform their activities.

5 Apply the knowledge
If employees have the necessary knowledge for the correct execution of the process for which they are responsible, they will then use that knowledge to make this process run as smoothly and as optimally as possible.

6 Evaluate the knowledge
Each process produces a certain result. This is established in advance but deviations can arise in the performance of the activities in a process. Therefore, the enterprise must evaluate whether there is sufficient knowledge present to adjust for any deviations that may occur during the execution of the process.

With each step in the knowledge value chain, new knowledge can arise. Therefore, it is important to continuously feed back the knowledge that has arisen from every process to the available knowledge and so keep it up-to-date. The result of the knowledge value chain is then the realisation of the vision, mission and objectives of the enterprise.

Result

Because all the employees have the correct knowledge available, the production process can proceed more efficiently and effectively. Be aware that here by knowledge is meant that next to experience and skills, the employees also have the right attitude to allow the processes of the enterprise to run smoothly.

Focus areas

With the implementation of knowledge management, sometimes too much is done and there is too little thought. Just beginning to establish the knowledge has little added value. It is important that the thinking of the employees in the enterprise must change. The creed 'Knowledge is power' must be transformed into the creed 'Sharing knowledge is power'. Knowledge management affects the whole enterprise. It is therefore wise to first think carefully about which way this knowledge management can successfully be implemented in the enterprise.

Literature

- Leistner, F. (2010). *Mastering Organizational Knowledge Flow.* John Wiley and Sons Ltd.
- Lennex, M. (2010). *Ubiquitous Developments in Knowledge management: Integrations and Trends.* Information Science Publishers.

56
Kraljic Matrix

Author	P. Kraljic
Year developed	1983
Also known as	–
Objective	Portfolio analysis for purchasing

Model

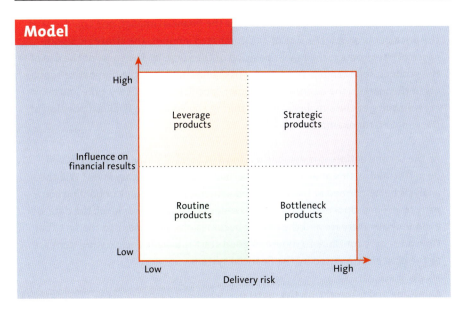

Background

With starting enterprises, the focus is on its customers because that is where turnover can be achieved. Purchasing is a process to which beginning enterprises pay little attention. As the enterprise grows, the numbers of suppliers and products and services that must be bought in increase. With a less flourishing economy or with Supply Chain Integration, the necessity to save costs and review the purchasing portfolio arises. Kraljic's model puts the portfolio in a matrix according to two different viewpoints, financial and risk. He defines four different product groups: leverage products, strategic products, routine products and bottleneck products. An improved purchasing strategy can be established for each product group in this way.

The development of the model is explained in a number of steps.

1 Starting up portfolio analysis

Although the model excels in simplicity, in practice this situation is certainly more recalcitrant than is first assumed. A lot of unforeseen choices will have to be made during the project. Due to this, in the start-up phase it must be carefully considered which people and resources will be deployed. The objective of the analysis should be clearly defined and measurable. The management of the enterprise will have to stand squarely behind the purchasing project.

2 Establishing and filling in the matrix

As the first action in this step, it is established what criteria will be used to measure the financial impact and risk. For the financial impact, one could look at the price per product, the size of the purchased amount, the strategic significance of the product, the power position of the supplier, the costs of the use of the product, for example. For delivery risks one could look the number of suppliers in the market, the degree of customer specification, delivery time and delivery reliability of the supplier, damage during transport, the financial position of the supplier, for example.

As the second action, it is established to what level of detail the analysis will be performed. Is this at article, article group or article category level? Will the analysis be performed at individual, department, business unit or holding company level? In proportion as the detail comes down to a lower level, the data will exponentially increase and the matrix becomes obscured, next to the fact that time and costs continue to mount. A good start is usually the existing item list or the classification used by the financial system.

3 Analysing and interpreting the matrix

When analysing and interpreting the matrix, it is wise to allow latitude and time for thorough discussions and a critical review of the placing of products in a quadrant. The enterprise thereby achieves a thorough strategic discussion of purchasing. To what extent does the matrix correspond with the policy starting points of the enterprise with regard to purchasing? Are there no products in the strategic quadrant, though the enterprise should have them? Are there too many products in the bottlenecks quadrant? Is the enterprise as a whole too far to the bottom-right in the matrix? When consensus is achieved about the position of the products in the matrix, one can move on to establishing the actions needed to obtain correct positioning in the matrix.

4 Setting up purchasing strategy

Setting up the purchasing strategy is performed for each quadrant. For each quadrant it is established for each product what improvements must take place or are desired. These improvements must fit in with corporate policy in a general sense and with purchasing policy specifically. For each product, it is applicable that with improvements, either the product stays in the same quadrant or the product must go to another quadrant. For the latter, radical improvements usually have to be accomplished.

Bottleneck products must be removed from the quadrant or converted into another quadrant. If this is not possible, improvements will also have to be established to limit the detrimental effects as much as possible.
Routine products can best be standardised and combined. Framework contracts can also be concluded with suppliers.
Leverage products can perhaps be promoted to the strategic quadrant, but then exclusively where the performance of the supplier is continuously excellent. The leverage products provide the purchaser with latitude to negotiate, compare suppliers with each other, assess them and regularly change suppliers due to better offers. The suppliers of leverage products are in general small companies that provide the enterprise with flexibility, low prices, short delivery times and delivery reliability.
Strategic products belong to the core business of the enterprise.

Between the supplier and the enterprise there exists a mutual dependency, which can continue to exist for as long as this collaboration functions well. Sometimes, the enterprise is trapped in this strategic quadrant because there is only one supplier who can deliver the product in question, for example. Adapting one's own products so that this particular product is no longer necessary, can then be a solution.

5 Implementation and aftercare

Lastly, the strategy has to be implemented. The most simple *quick-wins* approach lies in the quadrant for routine products. Usually, these products are simply ordered on the basis of demand. Combining and setting up framework contracts can save a great deal of time and money. For the second approach, it is best to tackle the biggest purchasing risks and cover them. Thirdly, a look can be taken at the bottleneck quadrant. In the context of aftercare and future developments, it is wise to do this analysis once a year, to follow developments. Do the activities performed lead to the right result?

Result

Critically studying the products and suppliers produces cost and time savings for the enterprise. Particularly standardisation of the purchasing package, lowering the number of suppliers, simplifying the ordering procedures and the better negotiating position of the enterprise produce the greatest profits. Because the enterprise has performed this analysis, the purchasing department often knows more about the products (such as under what conditions the products are purchased) than the suppliers themselves. This advantage in information should not be underestimated and gives the enterprise a strong negotiating position.

Focus areas

Filling in the model for the first time requires a prodigious effort from the enterprise. Particularly the definition of the criteria on the axes and the amount of detail to which data are obtained can lead to much discussion. Furthermore, the model becomes cluttered with too much detail.

The model offers the possibility for the personnel of the enterprise to opt for a certain supplier, based on subjective observation.

Literature

- Kraljic, P. (1983). Purchasing must become supply management. *Harvard Business Review*. 61, 5, 109-117.
- Bohlin L. ea, (2008), Purchasing Transformation, IBX Group AB.
- http://www.impgroup.org/uploads/papers/4413.pdf

57

Lead time/net time

Author	M. Mulders
Year developed	2006
Also know as	–
Objective	A planned approach to working

Model

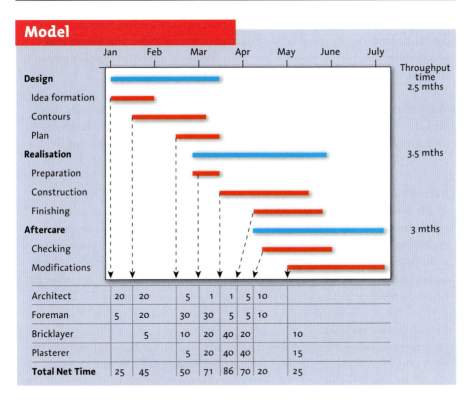

	Jan	Feb	Mar	Apr	May	June	July	
Architect	20	20	5	1	1	5	10	
Foreman	5	20	30	30	5	5	10	
Bricklayer		5	10	20	40	20		10
Plasterer			5	20	40	40		15
Total Net Time	25	45	50	71	86	70	20	25

Background

Enterprises are continuously evaluating and adapting their strategy and planning because of stronger or new competition, technological and economic developments and changes in the needs of the customers. The management of the enterprise wishes to realise the activities that arise as a result of these adaptations as quickly as possible. This is also logical because the speed of society is ever increasing and the customers expect the enterprise to keep up with

General management
Strategy
Marketing
Sales
Purchasing
Project & Planning
Production
Quality
Logistics & Distribution management
Information management
Financial
HRM & HTM
Internationalisation

this speed. It is therefore becoming increasingly important to make the planning that is produced more reliable. In many cases there exists a lack of clarity between the throughput time and the net time of a set of activities. Many activities are also always done besides existing work, without looking at the impact on the personnel of the enterprise. By providing insight into the lead time and the net disposable time, enterprises can produce and execute more reliable planning.

Application

The lead time of a set of activities (project) is the calendar time the project needs from the starting date up to and including the finishing date.
The net time of a set of activities (project) is all the hours worked by the project staff added together.
The lead time of a project is determined on the basis of the net time and the available resources. By resources in this situation is intended: the people that will perform the work, the activities. These personnel use hours that are planned for the activities and are booked on the project.

The lead time/net time is determined via a number of steps. It is assumed here that the objectives and processes involved are known, so that it can be established which people should be involved in this project. Should an extra process be added later, then a person from that process will then participate.

1 Determine the activities
As the first step of this model, all the activities that are necessary to achieve the desired objective of the project are established. These activities can be established in one or more brainstorming sessions. When all the activities have been inventoried, it is important to arrange them in chronological order. Which activities are carried out first and which ones later? Moreover, it is important to establish which activities can be performed simultaneously with other activities.

2 Determine the net time
To determine the number of hours for each activity, an estimate will have to be made. The most reliable estimates are based on experience. The more often a similar activity is performed, the better the estimate that can be made.
In the second place, it is important to establish if the activity will be performed by an experienced or an inexperienced person. Taking this into account saves problems in the execution of the project. If it is not (yet) possible to establish whether an experienced or an inexperienced person will perform the activities, it is important to take the average of the estimates for an experienced and an inexperienced person. Over the whole project this will cancel itself out, so that the planning for the number hours remains reliable. This estimation is performed for all activities. The number of hours so obtained is the net time of the project.

3 Determine the mutual dependencies among the activities

As the third step, the mutual dependencies of the different activities must be established. Activities in a project have the following dependencies:

- The following activity may not start if the previous one is not yet completed.
- The following activity must start before the previous activity is completed.
- The following activity may not be completed if the previous one has not yet been completed.

In most planning, exclusively first-order dependencies appear. This is also the most important dependency.

4 Determine the lead time of the project

The lead time is the calendar time that is necessary to execute the project. In the project calendar is included on which days there can be worked on the project. For each activity, the number of hours that must be worked is planned. When one person (resource) works on this activity, the lead time is the total number of hours for the activity divided by the number of workable hours per day.

If the employee has eight working hours per day, it could be that he or she may only spend half of their time, four hours, on this activity. In this way, the lead time of an activity comprising a hundred hours with an input of four hours a day for five days per week, is five weeks (if there are no holidays or free days).

If the lead time for the activity is too long, multiple resources can be put on the activity.

5 Determine the critical path

When all the dependencies of the activities have been established, the critical path of the project is established. The critical path is to say: the activities that are determinative for the total lead time of a project because they follow each other. Often, a project has several paths that run parallel. The critical path is thus the longest path of the project. The critical path is defined by the activities in which, with regard to the hours, there is no *slack*. Delays in these activities therefore lead by definition to delays in the whole project.

6 Establish the play (slack)

The play or slack in an activity is the extent to which the activity can run out without endangering the total duration of the project. The play is calculated on the basis of the starting and finishing dates of the activities. The play is the difference between the last possible starting date and the earliest possible starting date or the difference between the last possible finishing date and the earliest possible finishing date.

Result

By making use of the difference in net time and lead time, insight is obtained into the work load of employees and bottlenecks can be signalled on time, in order to achieve the established finishing date.

Focus areas

When determining the lead time, if someone else puts in four extra hours per day on an activity, the lead time is halved. Here account should be taken of the fact that this calculation holds true to be sure, but in practice unlimited numbers of extra personnel cannot be employed on an activity. There is clearly an optimisation point.

Furthermore, the model indicates no limits with regard to controllability. The bigger the project, the more difficult it is to retain an overview. It is advisable to divide such a large project into smaller sub-projects. Never allow a (sub) project to take more than nine months to a year.

Literature

- Grit, R. (2008). *Project Management, English edition*. Groningen: Noordhoff Uitgevers.

58
Levers of Control

Author	Robert Simons
Year developed	1995
Also known as	Belief and Boundary Systems
Objective	Finding a balance between the empowerment of employees and steering towards the objectives of the enterprise

Model

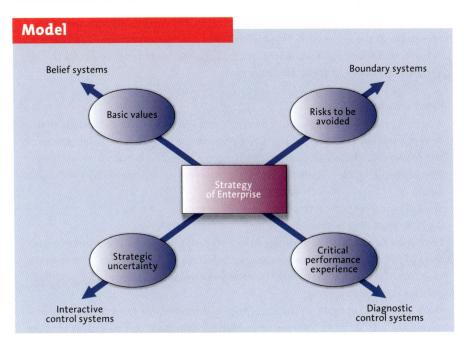

Background

In flat organisations, hierarchical levels have been reduced to a minimum. Middle managers that gave direction to subordinates and were accountable to their managers have also disappeared. This also means that part of the control that enterprises need, to establish whether the desired objective is being pursued, has disappeared. Employees receive more responsibilities and authorities (empowerment), while the managers are less directive but more coaching and facilitating. These enterprises are confronted with the question in what way the employees remain working on the objectives and still use their creativity to

General management | Strategy | Marketing | Sales | Purchasing | Project & Planning | Production | Quality | Logistics & Distribution | Information management | Financial | HRM & HTM | Internationalisation

achieve innovations. To be able to manage this issue, Simons' model provides possibilities.

Application

Central to the model is the strategy of the enterprise: in what way will the enterprise achieve its objectives and what are these objectives. The second level comprises four key factors: basic values, risks to be avoided, strategic uncertainties and critical performance variables. These key factors are important for the management of an enterprise. Each of these key factors is controlled and managed by a different system or lever. These systems are: belief systems, boundary systems, interactive control systems and diagnostic control systems.
The four key factors create the opposing force fields – Yin and Yang – to be able to implement a strategy successfully. The belief and the interactive control systems create positive and inspiring forces. The other two forces boundary and diagnostic control systems handle demarcation and correspondence with the objectives of the enterprise. This means that the enterprise must keep these systems in balance and constantly adapt to changes over time. To set up these systems, a number of steps are important.

Belief systems

A belief system is the explicit set of organisational values and definitions that bear out the basic values, the right to exist and the direction of development of the enterprise. These values and definitions are reflected in the vision and mission of an enterprise. A belief system is supported and reinforced by the management.
The following steps help to set up a belief system:
- Draft an appealing mission and vision.
- Draft a list of the articles of faith of the enterprise. What are the primary objectives of the enterprise, to earn money or provide a fine work place? For example, collaboration is more important than competition. Be clear about this. And bear out this conviction clearly.
- Make sure that everyone in the enterprise is informed, for example, by disseminating the articles of faith in posters or having printed it on small cards that are given to every employee.

Boundary systems

These systems indicate what is desirable in the enterprise (allowed) and what is not. They determine the behaviour of employees. Furthermore, they indicate to what extent these employees are free to make individual choices. With these boundary systems the limits are established within which employees can further experiment. This prevents time being spent on topics that are not in the interests of the enterprise. The boundaries can be handled as follows:
- Delineate the boundaries clearly.
- Publicise the boundaries in the same way as the belief systems.
- Include the boundaries in manuals and procedures, so that everyone knows them.

- Include the boundaries in quotes.
- Pay close attention above all to the boundaries where the reputation of the enterprise could be at stake.

Diagnostic control systems

By exactly measuring predetermined results, it can be established if the enterprise is still on course. These objectives can be established for each employee, department and enterprise. Furthermore, it can be measured to what degree the objectives have been achieved. Employees are responsible for these objectives and can also influence them. This motivates them to actually achieve the objectives. The management can then concentrate on the objectives that have not been achieved and so focus on the correct areas.

When setting up diagnostic control systems, the art is to include a limited number of critical success factors for the employees or departments. There are usually only a few that are genuinely critical. An overload of success factors engenders bureaucracy. A good system for this is the Balanced Scorecard (see Balanced Scorecard).

Interactive control systems

These systems are not only to recognise, motivate and coach employees, but also for their further development. This can be implemented formally and informally. The formal side is the functioning and remuneration system that every organisation must have. The informal side is that the manager also shows himself on the work floor and thus supports, shows interest in and motivates the employees. For small enterprises, an informal manner can already be sufficient. As the enterprise grows, a formal system will have to be implemented, whereby the informal character may not be lost.

Result

The Levers of Control provide the enterprise with strategic and operational control. Employees are motivated because it is clear what is expected of them and the management supports the achievement of the objectives. The momentum that this creates has a positive effect on the performances of the enterprise. The individual needs of the employees are brought into line with the objectives the enterprise has established. Due to this, the personnel of the enterprise remain 'employees' and do not become 'counter-workers'.

Focus areas

The implementation of the four levers is a complex and drawn out task, which must be controlled by the top management and supported by the employees. A pitfall of this model is that managers too easily use it as a checklist and want to have all the levers filled in too quickly. The risk hereby arises that strategic priorities have not been discussed and thus an operational bureaucratic system is created that does not help with the results of the enterprise.

Expansion

The Levers of Control do not directly contain a set of tools for a manager to use. This is why later, in America, *The Guidance on Monitoring Internal Control Systems* was developed. This comprehensive questionnaire was compiled by the Committee of the Sponsoring Organisations of the Treadway Commission (COSO) and later adapted for the Dutch situation by the Peters Committee. The objective was twofold:

- Setting up a codification for the design of or improving control systems in organisations.
- Formulating guidelines that can be followed for the assessment of the effectiveness of such systems.

On the basis of this questionnaire, the manager can see if the enterprise is 'in control' or not. In the COSO report, eight components of the internal control process are distinguished:

- control environment
- objective setting
- event identification
- risk assessment
- risk response
- internal control activities
- information and communication
- monitoring

Literature

- Simons, R. (1995). *Levers of Control*. Harvard Business School Publishing.
- www.executiveforum.net/pdfs/simons.pdf
- http://alumni.actonmba.org/ or in the list of PDFs under the tab ACTON NOTES. www.coso.org

59
MaBa Analysis

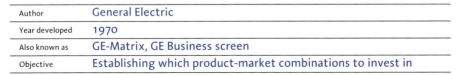

Author	General Electric
Year developed	1970
Also known as	GE-Matrix, GE Business screen
Objective	Establishing which product-market combinations to invest in

Model

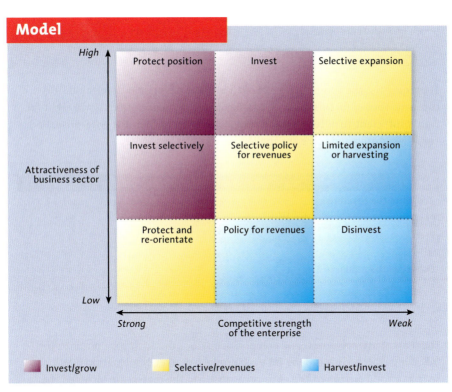

Background

MaBa Analysis stands for Market Attractiveness and Business Attractiveness. With the aid of this analysis, it can be established in which product-market combinations can be invested and which not. To make this choice, the market attractiveness of the sector and the competitive strength of the enterprise are established. These are the two factors that have the greatest influence on this choice. With an attractive market, a great deal of turnover and profit can be achieved. If the enterprise is in a strong competitive position, the chances of success are greatest.

Application

First of all, the *market attractiveness* is established. The criteria for market attractiveness are first determined. These are different for every sector. There are, however, a number of main factors that apply to every sector. These factors are scored on a scale of 0 to 1 where 0 means low attractiveness, 0.5 is average and 1 is high. For each factor a weighting is allocated, of which the total should be 100. In this way, the following table is created, where weighting and score are examples.

Factor	Weighting	Score	Total
Size and growth	20	0.7	14
Degree of homogeneity	10	0.2	2
Competition intensity	25	0.5	12.5
Competition strategies	20	0.3	6
Product differentiation	10	0.6	6
Phase in product life cycle	15	0.1	1.5
Total	*100*		*42*

Subsequently, the competitive strength of the enterprise is determined. Here too, a number of factors must be established. A number of from six to eight factors is sufficient to determine the competitive strength of the enterprise. Here too, a weighting and score are applied.

Factor	Weighting	Score	Total
Budget of the enterprise	40	1.0	40
Production capacity	10	1.8	8
Production possibilities	15	0.2	3
USPs	10	0.6	6
Quality of the product	10	0.3	3
Selling power	15	0.6	9
Total	*100*		*69*

The market attractiveness and competitive strength can now be put into the following matrix. This is done for each product-market combination (PMC), so that a total picture of the enterprise arises. In the matrix are included the PMCs from the E-learning training (ET), the Customisation training (CT) and the Standard training (ST). Next to the place where the PMCs are in the matrix, more items can be derived. The size of the circle reflects the overall turnover of the product concerned on the market. The starting point reflects the market share of the enterprise. The three boxes at the top-left indicate that the market is interesting for these PMCs and that the enterprise has a good competitive position there. The three boxes running diagonally from bottom-left to top-right indicate that large investment in these PMCs is not wise because their ROI (Return On Investment) is too low. The three boxes on the bottom-right indicate that the market is no longer attractive and the enterprise has lost its competi-

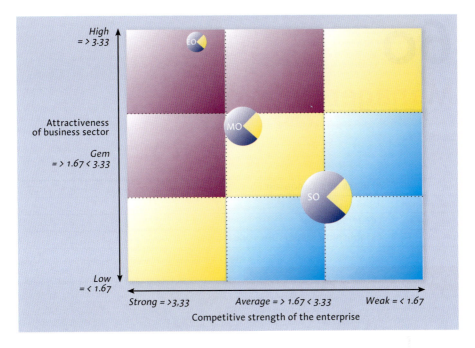

High
= > 3.33

Attractiveness
of business sector

Gem
= > 1.67 < 3.33

Low
= < 1.67

Strong = >3,33   Average = > 1.67 < 3.33   Weak = < 1.67

Competitive strength of the enterprise

EO

MO

SO

tive strength. It is wise to harvest these PMCs as much as possible and invest as little as possible to nothing, or completely disinvest to avoid future losses.

Result

With the aid of the MaBa Analysis, the enterprise can establish in which product-market combinations to invest and in which to disinvest. It can also be seen whether the PMCs with the biggest turnover are still in the most attractive areas.

Focus areas

Because the model makes use of factors and weightings that must be selected and determined by the personnel, a certain subjectivity occurs, which can lead to incorrect interpretation.

It takes quite a lot of time to collect all the relevant information to fill in the model fully. Mutual relationships and connections between the different PMCs that can provide a synergetic effect, are not included in the model.

In a saturated market, a replacement issue can arise where a good competitive position is possible, while the market growth is almost zero. With sophisticated marketing strategies, it is then nevertheless possible to achieve a good turnover for a PMC.

Literature

- Kotler, Ph. (2009). *Marketing Management*. Prentice Hall International.

60
Managerial Grid

Author	R. Blake and J. Mouton
Year developed	1964
Also known as	Leadership Grid
Objective	Establishing leadership style

Model

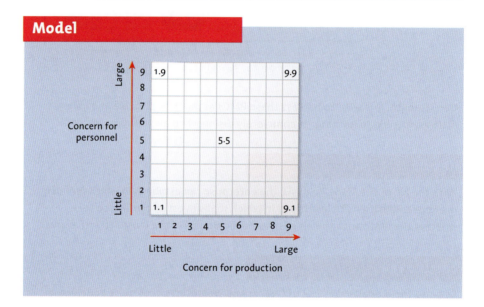

Background

The Managerial Grid is one of the best-known models for leadership behaviour. Leadership is primarily described as 'the process of influencing group activities to determine and achieve objectives'. On the other hand, managing is often described as 'achieving set objectives in a structured manner'. Managers direct and control, while leaders inspire, motivate and instruct. The model of Blake and Mouton is a behavioural model, which later changed its name to leadership model. The model assumes different attitudes in the behaviour of managers. These attitudes are schematically represented in two lines:

- concern for people
- concern for production

To each of these, a nine-step refinement has been applied. Due to this, there are 81 leadership styles. The designers indicate that the 5 styles indicated in the model are the most important to look at carefully and critically.

Application

The five styles in the model are pure behavioural styles. These behavioural styles are determined by the nature of the leader: the manner of decision making, the manner of persuasion and motivation, how conflicts are resolved, humour and so forth.

False leadership (1.1)
This leader is neither concerned about the people nor the production. His/her efforts are as low as the involvement. Working is not the complaint of this leader and he or she also avoids this. This person is often indifferent, disinterested, acquiescent and not devoted.

Authoritarian leadership (9.1)
This leader is exclusively interested in people's performances. Objectives must be achieved and the personal aspects of the personnel may not delay achieving them. The focus is on efficiency. This style is therefore a hard leadership style with authoritarian features. This person is often demanding, controlling and clearly demonsttates his power as the boss.

Country-club leadership (1.9)
This leader is only interested in a good relationship between himself and the personnel. This is therefore a soft leadership style, which has less regard for the results that have to be achieved. This person is understanding towards the personnel and gives them all the space to feel comfortable.

Status quo leadership (5.5)
This leader seeks the optimum between paying attention to the personnel and to the results. This person is always seeking intermediate solutions with opposing interests between people and production. Due to this, sometimes one side must concede and sometimes the other. The results are good but remain mediocre.

Team leadership (9.9)
This leader motivates the personnel to achieve the desired results by integrating them into the personal needs of the personnel. This leader stimulates participation, makes matters discussible in a group, sets priorities and is broad minded. Due to this, a good corporate climate and high production are created. This style

is the most effective one. Blake and Mouton have set up a phased plan for further growth into this style. This phased plan comprises six phases: laboratory-seminary training, team development, inter-group development, organisational objectives, achieving objectives and stabilisation. (Blake & Mouton, 1975, 35-37.)

There is, however, a third dimension to the model. This is called the thickness of the model by Blake and Mouton. A third axis thus. This is connected with the tenacity of someone to a certain style. Someone with a score of 1.9.1 will quickly change when encountering difficulties, while someone with 1.9.9 will not quickly change and thus persevere with the style. In this way, a type of cube is created consisting of all the styles.

Result

Once it has been established what leadership style someone has (there are tests for this), it is possible to set up a phased plan on the basis of which the leader can grow further in the direction of team leadership (9.9). For every style, the developers have produced an overview of the anxieties and desires that belong to them.

Leadership style	Desires	Anxieties
1.1	desire to cope	anxiety for hopelessness
9.1	desire to dominate	anxiety for failure
1.9	desire for approval	anxiety for rejection
5.5	desire to be popular	anxiety for critisism
9.9	desire to develop	anxiety for failure

Focus areas

Although it is a wonderful theoretical model, Blake and Mouton have also noticed that changing the character of a person is hardly possible and this therefore means lifelong learning. Behaviour can be influenced, however, by the said training.
Blake and Mouton indicate that team leadership (9.9) is the best style. This is correct in most cases. It can however occur that due to certain circumstances a different style is desired; for example, with someone from a different culture, who only works under direct supervision.

Literature

• Blake, R. & Mouton, J. (1964). *The Managerial Grid: The Key to Leadership Excellence.* Houston: Gulf Publishing Co.

- Blake, R. & Mouton, J. (1975). An overview of the grid, *Training & Development Journal*, May 1975, vol 29, issues, p. 29-38.
- www.academicrepublic.com (links via the menu: select Dissertation Downloads and select 'Analysis of the influence of different leadership styles on the enterprise's results').
- Gebhardt, A., Heinrici, F. & Pavan, A. (2003). *Important Theories of Leadership and Management in Organisations*. home.hio.no/~ araki/arabase/emne/frncangel.pdf

61

Mergers and Takeovers

Authors	P. Haspeslagh and D. Jemison
Year developed	1998
Also known as	Mergers and Acquisitions, Takeovers, Buy-out
Objective	Determining the form of collaboration with companies

Model

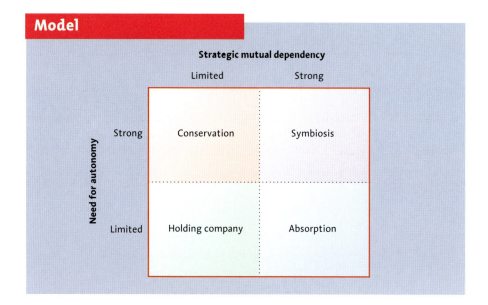

Background

Companies are constantly merging and taking over others or being taken over. The difference between a merger and takeover is clear. With a merger, two or more companies (but usually two) combine to form a new, third enterprise. In takeovers, one player is taken over by the other, where the first one is completely absorbed by the party taking over. No new enterprise is then created. With the further development of this model, it concerns both Mergers and Takeovers.

As soon as two (or more) companies merge, the question immediately arises as to what will be used from each company and what not. Every enterprise has good and less good aspects and the good aspects are used to achieve synergy. Two factors are important in this:

- *Need for autonomy*: to what extent will the enterprises continue to operate independently? Need for autonomy arises when there are large differences in culture or if the synergy will be lost by far-reaching integration. Too radical changes within a corporate culture often lead to a negative effect on the merger or takeover.
- *Strategic independence*: to what degree are the processes of the enterprises integrated to achieve synergy effects? Strategic independence (what is intended with the merger or takeover) determines the degree of integration of the enterprises. This is always ranked above the need for autonomy.

Application

On the basis of the two starting points of the model, strategic independence and the need for autonomy, the possible integration models are created: conservation, symbiosis, absorption and holding company.

Conservation

With conservation there exists a strong need for autonomy and a limited need for strategic independence. The enterprises thereby function more or less independently but both belong to a larger enterprise. In this way, the corporate culture and added value of each enterprise are retained. The task of the management is guiding these enterprises towards added value and the knowledge within these enterprises. Control is retained remotely.

Symbiosis

Symbiosis consists in a strong need for autonomy and a strong need for mutual independence. This means that companies wish to remain autonomous but also wish to integrate, to achieve the synergy effects. This is the most difficult form but also the one that can ultimately produce the most for the enterprises. With this form, the management seeks a balance between autonomy and the exchange of the strategic capacities of both enterprises. In the first instance, it is ensured that the enterprises operate alongside each other. Thereafter, the actual transfer of the strategic capacities of the enterprise is accomplished.

Absorption

Absorption consists in a limited need for autonomy and a strong need for mutual dependence. With this form, one party is completely absorbed by the other. When only part of the absorbed enterprise can be added as knowledge, the other components will be incorporated into the party taking it over and will no longer be recognised as such. Often, the personnel of the party taken over sees this as a loss of added value from their viewpoint. The effect of this is to produce opponents of the merger and/or the mass departure of employees. If the cultures of the two companies are the same however, then there are greater possibilities for the success of the collaboration than with the idea of 'us' against 'them'.

Holding company

The holding company consists in a limited need for autonomy and a limited need for mutual independence. In this situation there is little added value in relation to the exchange of strategic capacities. The companies have equivalent processes. Integration will not occur. The companies remain intact and function under a holding company. Depending on the management model, the holding company there is only reporting on a financial basis or the holding company controls it very tightly. In the latter case, this can lead to the loss of the independence of the personnel for the enterprise taken over. The effect of this is diminished motivation and declining involvement of the employees.

Integration with Mergers and Takeovers

Integration can be determined and implemented in the following steps:

1. Compare the functionality of the processes of the enterprises to establish possible areas of synergy. For each process it is investigated whether there is a similar process in the other enterprise or if the functionality is the same, or if there is some way that synergy can be derived from the process.
2. In any area where synergy has been established, the effectiveness of that area is determined. This is done on operational, commercial, strategic- and cost-effectiveness.
3. Determine the synergy on the basis of the functionality and the effectiveness of the processes:
   a. The same functionality and both are effective, then an equivalent integration of the processes is created.
   b. The same functionality and both not are effective, then the effective process is selected.
   c. Unequal functionality and both are effective, then look for the best combination (as defined by conservation or symbiosis).
   d. Unequal functionality and not both effective, then both processes continue to exist.

Result

Mergers and Takeovers often lead to uncertainty in the enterprises concerned. Due to this, too little attention is paid to the market and this in turn leads to fewer customers and loss of turnover. A clear and promptly implemented policy helps to connect the enterprises to each other and to act as soon as possible with regard to the market on the basis of the new added value. A careful selection on the basis of the model can help with this.

Focus areas

With Mergers and Takeovers, there are often changes in the enterprises. This can cause employees to leave. Usually, these are employees with knowledge and experience because it is easier for them to get another job. The big risk with this is losing the knowledge.

Literature

- Gaughan, P. (2007). *Mergers, Acquisitions, and Corporate Restructurings*. John Wiley & Sons Inc.
- Machiraju, H. (2004). *Mergers*. Acquisitions and Takeovers.
- www.bus.ucf.edu/barringer/SLIDES/carpenter_ppt_ch10.ppt (or search on 'Studying Mergers and Acquisitions').

General management

Strategy

Marketing

Sales

Purchasing

Project & Planning

Production

Quality

Logistics & Distribution

Information management

Financial

HRM & HTM

Internationalisation

62

Multichannel Marketing

Author	Unknown
Year developed	–
Also known as	Multichannel E-commerce
Objective	The balanced use of marketing channels

Model

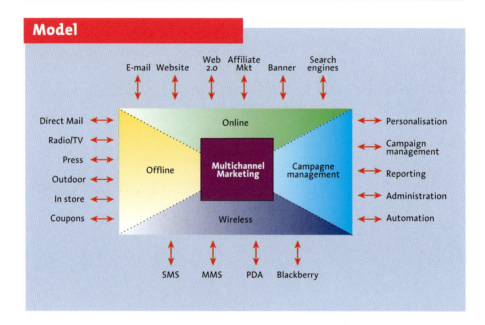

Background

Multichannel marketing is not entirely new. In the past there was often investigation into what way a certain segment could best be approached. This was then from the thinking that products or services were 'pushed' onto the market. It needed to be investigated exclusively via what channels which customers could be reached. Nowadays, customers are more mature and look more at their own wishes and actively look for products and services. Subsequently, enterprises will have to realise products and services more from the needs of the customer: 'pull' strategies. Furthermore, due to the technological possibilities, several contact moments occur, at which customers request information about products and/or services or purchase them. The total amount of possibilities now available is very large. Enterprises will therefore have to develop a policy to reach the right channels, the right segments and *vice versa*. With the right channels, the customers in the segments will also have to be able to approach the enterprise to request information or purchase the products and/or services.

Application

To allocate the available budgets in the correct way for the benefit of the various marketing channels, the enterprise will have to formulate a policy. This can be done on the basis of the following steps.

1 Setting up a multichannel strategy

There is a big difference between multichannel and multiple channel. With multiple channels, there are simply several buying channels. With multichannel, the different channels are mutually connected so that they can be used in various ways. If, for example, someone wants to buy a product in a shop, they can first look on the internet in which branches it is in stock. For instance, the selection of a coffee maker. The selection can first be made via the internet. Subsequently, the consumer looks in which shops (close by of course) the device is for sale. The choice for such a comprehensive concept is based on two factors: the size and potential profit of the segment in question.

Customers who opt for multichannel purchasing, constitute an increasingly large proportion of consumers. They are primarily looking for two benefits: more ease and more detailed information. The greater ease consists for some in the ability to purchase via the internet and not having to buy via a salesman, for others in the ready access to information about products or services and for yet others in the more personal attention in the shop. More detailed information and an aid on the web site to give more personally attuned advice, will stimulate the choices of customers. Moreover, it is important that the different channels are integrated, in other words, via all the channels the customers must be able to both obtain information and buy products, as well as look up the status of the order.

2 Developing a multichannel network

Allowing several channels to grow organically can lead to a diffuse system of channels in which the customer loses his way. Therefore, a good design is needed to establish the significance of the channels and determine their mutual relationships. The following questions are thereby important: What is the primary objective of a certain channel? What functionalities does the channel have? What are the physical possibilities of the channel? How does the channel communicate with other channels?

For this, the use of the channels in question by the customers must be monitored and compared with the costs of designing these channels. This can, for example, mean that some channels will disappear and be replaced by other channels.

3 Managing the channels

Whether someone becomes a regular customer is dependent on the experience the customer has with the enterprise. This means that the expectations of the customer must be included in the organisation of the different channels. Can the promise the enterprise makes for each channel be lived up to? Do the channels also provide the promised added value? The following factors play a key role in this:

- *Cooperation of management and personnel*: not only the managers must feel responsible for customers in relation to the different channels. The personnel who are directly involved with the channels must also radiate this.
- *Use of personnel and budgets*: the use of personnel and allocation of budgets must be clearly attuned and communicated for each channel. Furthermore, the performance indicators will have to be re-attuned.
- *Marketing*: the marketing activities must be organised on the changed methods of the customer, the marketing mix for each segment and the brand value across the whole enterprise.
- *Measurement of performances*: the enterprise will have to make a distinction between the performances of customers who are not susceptible to the different channels and the performances of customers who are. For the first group of customers, matrices have been set up to measure the performances on, for example, customer value, share of portfolio, repeat purchases, use of the channel, service costs and quality. These must be attuned to the measures that the managers of the channels monitor to clearly indicate what the effects are with regard to the experience of the customers.
- *Contribution per channel*: it is important to define a system on the basis of which the success of a channel can be included in the profit and loss account of an enterprise.

The marketing of a multichannel enterprise

Multichannel marketing adds a multiplicity of areas for attention to the enterprise. It is important to focus on three elements:

- Attune the promise the enterprise makes with the brand with what is promoted via the various channels. If a contradictory promise is made, customers will immediately pull out.
- Because multichannel customers often buy more than non-multichannel customers, it is important to have an information system that can register this, for example, a CRM system.
- Make use of learning in practice. Because certainly not everything has yet been crystallised and because multichannel marketing can expect a great deal more in the field of technological developments, experimenting with channels is advisable.

Result

With a well-considered policy in the field of multichannel marketing, the enterprise provides its customers with the right ways to request information, buy products and follow the status of the order. This satisfies the ease that more and more customers expect from the new technologies on offer.

Focus areas

Cannibalisation (the sales of one product at the cost of another one) is a much heard problem with multichannel marketing. In fact, this is not true. The customers use several channels to come to the decision to buy a product from a certain enterprise. Exactly because the different needs of the customer can be covered via the different channels, the opposite will even be true.

Literature

- Arikan, A. (2008). *Multichannel marketing*. John Wiley & Sons Ltd.
- Wilson, H., Street, R., Bruce, L. (2008). *The Multichannel Challenge*. Elsevier Ltd.
- www.tridion.com (click on 'download free info' and then on 'white papers'. It concerns the white paper 'Multi Channel marketing').

63
Organisation Chart

Author	Developed in practice
Year developed	–
Also known as	Organogram(me), Organisation structure
Objective	Drawing out formal direction and accountability of the enterprise

Model

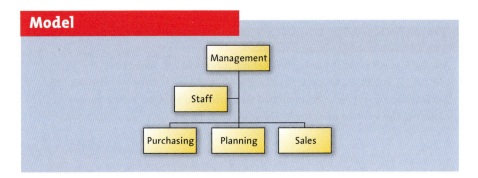

Background

In the Organisation Chart, the formal authority relationships with respect to people and departments in an enterprise are schematically represented. The tasks, responsibilities and authorities of the personnel are established in procedures and decision trees. The objective of the Organisation Chart is establishing control and final responsibilities to render the enterprise manageable. The larger the enterprise, the more important the Organisation Chart and accountability with regard to decision making.

Application

Every enterprise has an Organisation Chart, regardless of the size of the company in numbers of personnel. In an Organisation Chart, the following structures are graphically represented:
- Line organisation
- Line-staff organisation
- Matrix organisation
- Network organisation

Line organisation

The line organisation consists only in hierarchical authority relationships along which the control and accountability runs via the vertical route between manager and subordinate. The manager determines what must happen and the subordinate has to do it. This form of organisation is usually encountered in small enterprises.

Line-staff organisation

If an enterprise has developed a specialisation in a certain field, then the personnel involved must be put together to further develop this specialisation. It is then illogical to put these personnel between the other employees on the work floor. They are, after all, specialists in a certain field and support the management, the production process or the R&D department with their knowledge. These specialists are called staff employees and have a specific place in the organisation as a staff body. The tasks of staff bodies is to provide both requested and unrequested advice to the management level above them, in this example, the manager. The ultimate decision making always follows the line and the manager can follow the advice or ignore it. Staff employees can be addressed by their line manager about the quality of their advice.

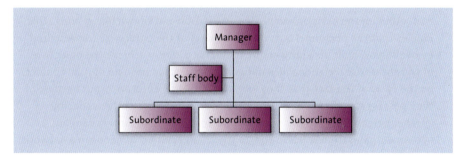

Line-staff organisation

Matrix organisation

The matrix organisation is a combination of a line and a staff organisation, where personnel from different departments are placed in one project together. The personnel formally remain working for their department and account to their direct line manager. These personnel are placed in one or more projects, where they work under a project manager and account to this project manager with regard to their tasks in the project. The challenge for the personnel that both participate in projects and work in their departments, is that they serve two bosses with opposing interests. The matrix organisation is the most prevalent organisational form. This form arises when a specific topic is not related to only one department but across several departments.

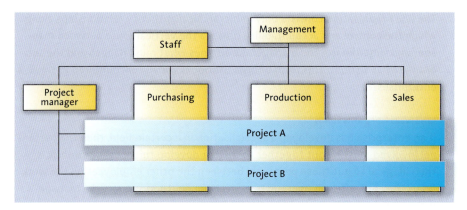

Matrix organisation

Network organisation

The network organisation has become more prevalent in recent years, particularly with enterprises that have organised their primary process on the basis of knowledge acquisition and knowledge sharing. The network organisation consists in individuals (represented by circles) who maintain contacts with each other on the basis of knowledge acquisition and knowledge sharing. This implies that the personnel outside the borders of the enterprise (represented by ovals) have built up a network of contacts to jointly achieve the objectives of the enterprise. Personnel in a network organisation have no mutual contacts on the basis of the fact that they work for a specific enterprise, but because they possess specific knowledge and skills, which are currently needed by another person. Because the need for information is constantly changing, a network organisation will also constantly change. When someone in a network seeks knowledge, this person asks advice from someone in the network who is expected to have that knowledge. If this is not the case, the person asked can look further in his own network and refer them on. In this way, new contacts are constantly made between knowledge workers.

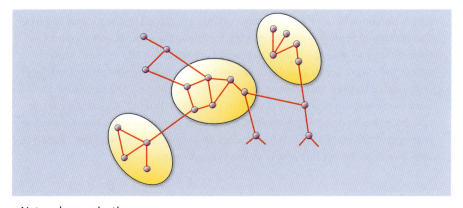

Network organisation

Result

The Organisation Chart of an enterprise gives insight into the manner in which and by whom, enterprises are managed. Furthermore, it is established to whom personnel are accountable for the realisation of their activities.

Focus areas

An Organisation Chart is a very static aid to describing enterprises. Enterprises work in general, with the exception of the network organisation, highly hierarchically and on the basis of tasks, responsibilities and authorities. The larger the hierarchy, the less flexible the enterprise and the longer decision making takes. Furthermore, the Organisation Chart provides insufficient insight into the informal decision making and power positions within an enterprise.

Literature

- Daft, R. (2008). *Organization Theory and Design*. Cengage Learning.
- Tyson, E., Schell, J. (2008). *Small Business for Dummies*. Wiley Publishing Inc.
- www.orgchart.net

64
Organisational Climate Index

Author	Prof. Dr G. de Cock
Year developed	1986
Also known as	VOKIPO, Business and Organisation Climate Index (BOCI)
Objective	Mapping out the culture of the enterprise

Model

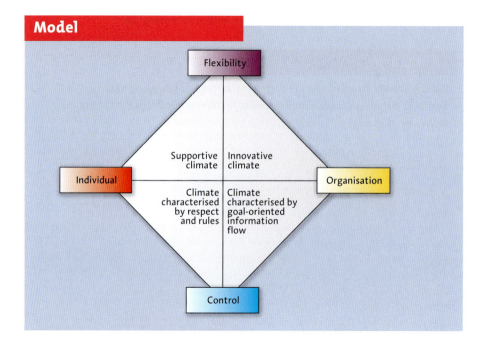

Background

Organisational climate is not the same as organisational culture. Organisational climate is related to the perception and experience of characteristics of the organisation, such as the organisation and work environment. The organisational climate gives a description of the extent to which organisational characteristics are experienced. The culture relates to the collective suppositions, values and standards of a group (the team, for example). Organisational climate is important for the working experience of the personnel in an enterprise. If this is not in one line, a feeling of not belonging arises, 'the chemistry isn't right'. This is caused because the organisational characteristics do not correspond with the characteristics of the employees in that organisation.

The organisational climate is described on the basis of two dimensions. Both dimensions are typified by two competing values:

- The first dimension can be characterised by a focus on the individuals in the organisation versus a focus on the organisation.
- The second dimension has the extremes: focus on flexibility versus focus on control.

The combination of these two dimensions produces four types of organisational climate:

Supportiveness

The scale for supportiveness is at the top-left in the figure. The opinions that members of the organisation have with regard to each other and with regard to the management are discussed there. The result indicates to what extent people trust, help and respect each other and feel comfortable within the organisation.

Respect for the rules

At the bottom-left in the figure is the scale for respect for rules. The result on this scale indicates to what extent the members of the organisation experience that there is a strict functional definition, a check on the quality and quantity of their work and there is sustainability in the situation.

Goal orientation and information flow

At the bottom-right is the scale for the goal orientation of the information flow. This concerns the appropriateness of the information flow in the organisation. It encompasses the extent to which people experience clarity with regard to their task and the coordination between the different tasks they perform.

Innovation

At the top-right in the model is the scale for innovation. Essential here is to what extent a tendency towards improvement is observed in the organisation. This is expressed in extra training, demonstrating broad interests and creativity, taking account of scientific findings and capitalising on the changing demands of the environment as an organisation.

Filling in the model takes place based on forty questions, which are converted into the axes of the model via a conversion table.

In this way, it can be seen where the value focus of the enterprise lies. The management and personnel can subsequently steer towards this type of climate.

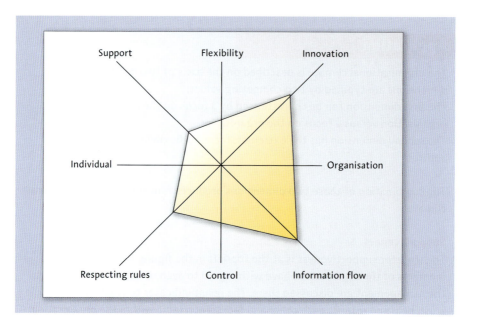

Result

The result of this analysis is a model in which it is established what organisational characteristics the enterprise maintains in its organisational climate. The enterprise obtains insight into which aspects they emphasise and, as a result, which processes in the enterprise should receive the most attention (budget).

Focus areas

When determining the culture or climate of the enterprise, there can never be an assumption of right or wrong. The added value of this model is the fact that it indicates on which organisational characteristics the enterprise puts an emphasis. The knowledge of this is often sufficient to learn how the organisation can be handled. A change in these characteristics means a demanding change programme of several years.

Literature

- Shane, S. (2010). *Born Entrepeneurs*. Born leaders, Oxford University Press Inc.
- cep.lse.ac.uk/pubs/download/dp0626.pdf

65
Organisational growth, Greiner

Author	L.E. Greiner
Year developed	1972
Also known as	Growth model Greiner
Objective	Surmounting an internal crisis situation with the growth of the enterprise

General management
Strategy
Marketing
Sales
Purchasing
Project & Planning
Production
Quality
Logistics & Distribution management
Information management
Financial
HRM & HTM
Internationalisation

Model

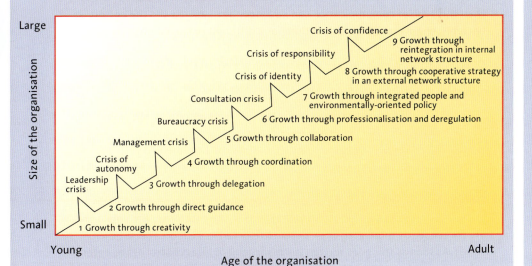

Background

Just about every enterprise grows or is focused on growth. This growth is subdivided by Greiner into five phases (1 to 5). Keuring (2004) added four more phases (6 to 9). This is how the model with nine phases that are gradually gone through during the growth of an enterprise arose. Although going through them is gradual, the transition from one phase to the following one will not proceed gradually. Even stronger, with each change of phase the need arises for a different management style. Due to this, the enterprise gets into an internal crisis, which it must get out of again as soon as possible. Acknowledging these changes and quickly anticipating them can keep the disquiet in an enterprise within limits. Due to this, the focus can very quickly be back on the market, without losing too many customers or much turnover.

Application

Every enterprise finds itself in a certain phase. At the end of a phase the enterprise has a time of revolution and change. Recognising and subsequently choosing the correct management approach helps the enterprise to evolve to the following phase.

The growth model has the following nine phases:

1 *Creativity*: in the start-up or pioneering phase of the enterprise, its growth lies in the creativity of the employees in the organisation. Nothing in the enterprise is yet developed, there is little structure, the market is still insufficiently charted. The creativity of the employees ensures that the development of products/services and the market take shape. As long as it concerns a small enterprise, communication is on an informal basis. If the enterprise becomes larger, then this type of communication can no longer be managed and the enterprise becomes ungovernable. It is then time for a different management style.

2 *Direction*: to shape the further development of the enterprise, the personnel will have to be clearly directed and communication must be structured. In proportion as the enterprise exists for longer, due to this style of management (direction), with further growth there is a greater need for autonomy because the employees have for too long been restricted from working independently by the management. The crisis of autonomy that arises can be remedied with a different management style.

3 *Delegation*: to satisfy the need for more responsibility, tasks, responsibilities and authorisations are also assigned to lower levels in the enterprise. The employees are consequently motivated anew because they can make more choices themselves. As soon as this goes too far, the management loses control of the enterprise. The employees then make too many autonomous choices that are no longer attuned to the other processes in the enterprise. This causes a management crisis.

4 *Coordination*: to regain control of the management of the enterprise, employees at the lower levels will have to account for what they have and have not done. To this end, procedures and management reporting are implemented. The effect is much more communication and information exchange. When this becomes too big, a bureaucratic crisis arises.

5 *Collaboration*: to try to stop the bureaucracy, more mutual attuning will have to take place between departments, managers, working groups, project groups and so forth. Closer collaboration is set up, which leads to more and more meetings and finally, to a consultation crisis.

6 *Professionalisation and deregulation*: due to the large amount of consultation, the means has become the objective; consultation. The results that the enterprise must achieve remain lacking because no-one is focused on them any longer. To resolve this, a great many consultation structures and procedures will have to disappear: deregulation. Furthermore, there must be more results-oriented operation. To achieve results quickly, an efficiency round is implemented by means of reduction in personnel and so forth. Due to this, a crisis of legitimacy arises.

7 *Integrated human and environmental policy*: in this phase the management focuses attention on corporate social responsibility (CSR), an effective organisational culture, the identity and image of the enterprise. Moreover, the cohesion between the people in the enterprise and the quality and efficiency of the production process is investigated.

8 *Growth through cooperative strategy in an external network structure*: this phase is characterised by increasingly flatter organisations, where the accountability and authorities lie lower down the enterprise (empowerment). Furthermore, efforts are made to ensure further collaboration with external organisations, to arrive at a network of organisations that satisfies the needs of the customer. What was formerly an opponent is now seen as part of a collaborative network to collectively create a win-win situation.

9 *Reintegration into an internal network structure*: after the collaboration from the previous phase, which is based on mutual trust, it can only be logical that the trust will be broken at a given moment. A crisis of confidence therefore constitutes the end of the cooperation-based development of enterprises. Enterprises will then focus more on their own interests because during the collaboration, little can be enforced and risk-avoiding behaviour occurs with a lack of hierarchy.

Result

By closely watching the symptoms of the different phases, it can be recognised when a crisis is threatening and action must be undertaken. If no action is undertaken, then managers will function insufficiently. Employees will become dissatisfied and the chance that they will leave is then very great. Customers notice the internal problems of the enterprise and place fewer and fewer orders.

Focus areas

It is difficult to determine how much time there is between the different phases. The management will therefore clearly have to recognise the symptoms itself and take the appropriate action.
Larger enterprises comprise several branches. From the holding company, it must be seen that not every branch is in the same growth phase and must thus be differently managed.
The transitions between the phases are not black and white. They will manifest

themselves gradually. This is one more reason for the management to monitor what is happening in the enterprise.

Literature

- Greiner, L.E. (1972, 1998). *Evolution and Revolution as Organizations Grow.* Harvard Business School Press.
- www.organizationalgrowth.org
- www.ils.unc.edu/daniel/131/cc04/Greiner.pdf

66
Organisational Management

Authors	Kaplan & Norton
Year developed	2000
Also known as	Strategy focus
Objective	Managing the enterprise in the short-, medium- and long-term

Model

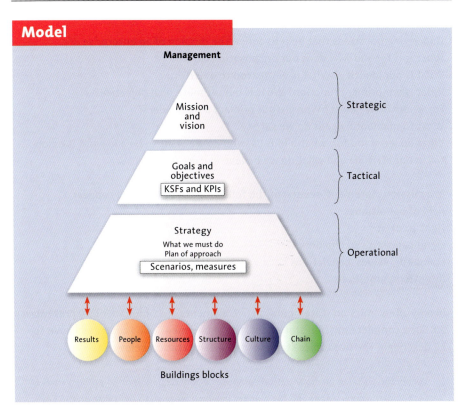

Background

Everything that takes place in an enterprise has the objective of allowing the primary process to function correctly. To this end, building blocks such as people, resources and structure are deployed. To attune the building blocks to each other, not only is mutual consultation necessary, but also guidance from the management. This guidance takes place at three different levels in the enterprise: strategic, tactical and operational.

General management

Strategy

Marketing

Sales

Purchasing

Project & Planning

Production

Quality

Logistics & Distribution

Information management

Financial

HRM & HTM

Internationalisation

The three management levels in an enterprise are necessary because at each level of management, a different time interval on the basis of which decisions have to be made is applicable.

Mission and vision

The top management, the management board, is responsible for planning over the long term. They have an horizon from three to maximally five years. They determine the policy of the enterprise and establish this in the vision and mission statements of the enterprise. This is called management at the strategic level.

> Mission: a mission is a representation of the added value an enterprise can have for its environment.

Underlying questions that help to define the mission of an enterprise are:
- What is it for and why does our organisation exist?
- What is our identity? What is our reason to exist?
- What is our primary function? What is our ultimate final objective?
- For whom do we exist? Who are our primary stakeholders?
- What fundamental needs do we satisfy?
- What do we stand for, what blinds us, who do we want to be and what is essential in our attitude and what do we believe in (core values)?

In a mission statement, several of the following topics generally appear:
- field of operations
- right to exist
- significance to stakeholders
- standards, values, convictions
- intentions, ambitions

In only a few 'mission statements' all five elements are simultaneously presented. For a complete mission statement, the above-mentioned topics will have to be described. The five topics stand for the interpretation below.

> Vision: the vision of an organisation comprises a general definition of product-market-technology combinations and the manner in which we wish to capitalise on the environment of the organisation.

Underlying questions that help to define the vision of an enterprise are:
- What is our image of the future?
- What are our ambitions in the long term?
- What do we wish to accomplish?
- What is our collective image of a desirable and feasible future situation and the change programme that is necessary to get there?

Goals and objectives[11]

The goals and objectives must be established very concretely because they must be measurable (SMART defined). This is important to be able to steer the enterprise in time if the expectations are not being fulfilled. Moreover, in this way it can be seen afterwards whether the measures taken have led to the required objective. If this is not the case, the enterprise is able to steer towards the goals and objectives or activities.

Goals: goals are the results that people wish to attain with the enterprise.

Vision and mission are starting points for defining the goals or critical success factors (CSFs).
Mission and vision are focused on the longer term and goals and objectives on the shorter term. Furthermore, the mission and vision are usually phrased in general terms and the goals and objectives in concrete, measurable units. These terms are dependent on the turbulence of the environment in which the enterprise is situated.
Underlying questions that help to define the goals of an enterprise are:
- When will we consider our enterprise is a success?
- What factors make us unique?
- What is decisive for the success of our organisation?
- Which factors in the vision are essential for the viability of our organisation?

Objectives: the objectives are the measurable concrete topics for achieving an objective.

Underlying questions that help to define the objectives or the performance indicators of an enterprise are:
- What are the measurable results that we wish to achieve?
- Over what term do we wish to achieve these results?
- On what scale are we going to measure?
- What instruments will we use for measurement?
- With what frequency will we measure?

The objective 'an 8 for customer satisfaction' cannot be established just like that. Customer satisfaction can comprise a number of measurable aspects, such as the number of seconds before the telephone is answered, how many minutes has to be waited at the service desk or how many complaints there are. The aggregation of these three aspects constitutes a figure on a scale from 1 to 10. The management (team) of the enterprise reviews the developments of the enterprise over a period of one to three years on the tactical level and provides the personnel with the facilities to achieve the objectives.

Strategy

The strategy indicates in what way goals and objectives will be achieved and comprises a number of activities to be undertaken. These activities take place on the operational level of the enterprise, where the planning horizon is limited to a maximum of one year. On the operational level, the day-to-day activities of the enterprise are performed and the building blocks the enterprise has available are deployed. Although the planning horizon is up to a year in advance, the personnel will also have to produce the daily, weekly, monthly, quarterly and semi-annual planning. In this way, an account manager must every month, quarter and six months, remain in step with the annual objective.

> Strategy: the strategy of the enterprise comprises the actions that will actually be performed, which the enterprise will plan to achieve its goals and objectives.

Underlying questions that help to define the strategy of an enterprise are:
- What are we good at?
- How do we wish to achieve the results?
- How can we achieve the goals?
- What measures are we going to take?
- What improvement actions are we going to perform?
- How do we create support for the strategies developed?
- How are we going to communicate this to people?
- How do we ensure that we are constantly learning?

This strategy is subsequently established in the various plans, such as:
- business plan
- marketing plan
- financial plan
- operational plan
- human talent management plan
- IT plan
- R&D plan

To define a mission and vision and the translation thereof into goals and objectives, the following phased plan can be followed:
1 desk research
2 workshop to establish elements of vision and mission
3 grouping elements
4 group discussion about rudimentary sentences
5 draft mission and vision
6 dissemination within the enterprise and feedback
7 definitive mission and vision
8 result

The results are agreed and supported goals are set with concrete, measurable objectives with which the enterprise wishes to achieve its mission and vision. On the basis of progress, the enterprise is able to give guidance in a timely fashion and achieve the planned goals in the set time.

Result

The result is that all the personnel, from high to low, are informed about the values and standards maintained in the enterprise. Furthermore, all the personnel must support these values and standards. The activities on the three management levels are attuned to each other so that the goals of the enterprise can be achieved within the established term.

Focus areas

When the vision and mission have been established, they will have to be translated to the two lower management levels. A translation round that is all too often overlooked. Due to this, the situation arises that the personnel no longer understand why the management has made certain choices. The contribution that the personnel will make to the enterprise is then unclear. This has a negative effect on motivation. This will negatively affect the results of the enterprise.

Literature

- Kaplan, R.S. & Norton, R. (2001). *The Strategy-focused organization*. Harvard Business School.
- Elsbach, K. (2006). *Organizational Perception management*. Lawrence Erlbaum Associates Inc.
- http://managementhelp.org/

[11] Goals and objectives can be translated one to one into critical success factors (CSF) and performance indicators (Key Performance Indicators, KPI).

67

OSO model

Author	J. Bunt
Year developed	1994
Also known as	–
Objective	Strategic planning

Model

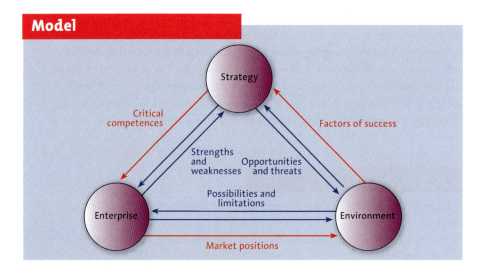

Background

Strategic management is occupied with the analysis, planning, execution and evaluation of the strategy of an enterprise. To determine the strategy of an enterprise, a consideration will have to be made between what the enterprise wants (strategy), what the enterprise can do (competences) and what the environment offers (market potential). These aspects influence each other and will have to be considered mutually, if the enterprise wants to operate successfully on the market. The enterprise has its strong and weak sides, while the environment offers opportunities and threats to realising the strategy of the enterprise. The result is the possibilities and limitations for actually implementing the strategy. Via the OSO model, the enterprise has the possibility to attune these mutually cohesive components to each other.

Application

Because developments in the world follow each other at an increasingly rapid rate, it is becoming increasingly important to closely examine the strategy of the enterprise more frequently. Formerly, a strategic horizon was five years, nowadays it is only three years because one cannot oversee what will happen thereafter. It is therefore highly recommended every year, via the OSO model for example, to reconsider corporate strategy and possibly adapt it.

For the application of the model, the enterprise goes through the following steps:

1 **Researching the environment and establish the opportunities and threats**

The environment is the sum total of markets in which the enterprise wishes to implement its strategy. The most important aspect that the enterprise has to take into account is its customers. After all, the enterprise derives its right to exist from them. Not all customers will be the same and so the enterprise must take account of several markets in which its products and services can be sold. To service these markets, the enterprise will have to organise its activities around them. This means that capital will have to be procured from the financial market (or the enterprise is itself a provider of capital to others) and the activities to be performed will require the input of raw and auxiliary materials. In this way, the enterprise will also operate in the purchasing market. To carry out the planned activities, the enterprise needs personnel and will seek them on the personnel market. When offering products and services on a market, the enterprise will soon not be the only one. There will be several suppliers that wish to capitalise on the demand from the market. The enterprise is then concerned with the competition, which is also active in other markets, such as purchasing, personnel and finances. Furthermore, the enterprise is involved with macro developments and developments in the sector, which have a positive or a negative effect on realising the strategy of the enterprise.

The result of this research is establishing the threats from these markets that can influence the strategy of the enterprise.

2 **Researching the organisation and establishing its strengths and weaknesses**

The organisation comprises processes in which activities are performed to realise the strategy of the enterprise. These processes are:
- purchasing
- sales
- marketing
- R&D
- production
- logistics
- planning
- preparations
- administration
- finance

On the basis of these processes, it can be determined at what the enterprise is very good (strengths) and at what the enterprise is less good (weaknesses). The core competences or critical competences are the competences in which the enterprise is good. It is also important on the basis of these critical competences to seek the competitive advantage and, in this way, determine the 'Unique Selling Point': USP. The critical competences can be established by the personnel of the enterprise itself.

But then, a rose-coloured image of reality will possibly arise. Next to one's own assessment, it will have to be seen by means of a survey of the customers (customer-satisfaction survey), what they think of the enterprise. On the basis of this, the strong and weak sides of the enterprise are established.

3 Determine the possibilities and the limitations of the strategy

Now it is established what the enterprise is good at and what opportunities there are on the market besides the weaknesses and threats. The enterprise can determine what possibilities and limitations it has to capture a certain market position. These market positions are compared with the competences of the enterprise for each market in the environment, for example, according to the table below.

Market / competences	Marketing / sales	Personnel	R&D	Purchasing	Production	Finances
Sales market						
Labour market						
Technology market						
Purchasing market						
Financial market						

On the basis of the possibilities and limitations of each market-competence combination, an action plan can subsequently be drafted to secure these market positions or capture them. In this manner, the strategy of the enterprise is transformed into a strategic plan.

Result

The result of the model is an overview of the actions to be performed to deploy the strategy of the enterprise in the market. Moreover, the enterprise can determine what resources must be linked to which activities.

Focus areas

Establishing the possibilities and limitations is done by making a combination of the selling markets and the competences of the enterprise. Because the estimation of people is determinative for the result, this method is not entirely objective and the enterprise runs the risk that personal preferences are expressed in the strategy.

Literature

None.

68
Pareto Analysis

Author	**J. Juran**
Year developed	**1937**
Also known as	**ABC analysis, Pareto's principle, 80-20 rule**
Objective	**Examination of articles range**

Model

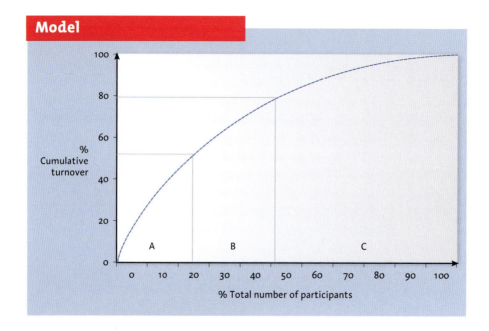

Background

The best-known method for examining one's whole range of articles is the Pareto Analysis, also called ABC analysis. With it the performance of individual articles (or article groups) is established based on various criteria. The objective of ABC analysis is having those articles in stock that contain the greatest potential for improvement. Articles belong to group A if the total of the articles with the highest turnover is 50% of total turnover. Articles belong to group B if it is 30% and group C if it is 20%. The above percentages are indications and can be adjusted for each situation. The point of ABC analysis is to establish what is the most important group of articles, which produces the largest contribution to turnover. This can be at the cost of another article group. The risk arises here that C articles that are needed in combination with a A articles cannot be replaced just like that. It is important to consciously select the criterion for the ABC analysis. In the above example, turnover has been chosen. Other possibilities are: the average stock value, the number of stock transactions per period, the number of times that an out-of-stock situation occurs, and so forth. The criterion must always be selected in line with the objective of the analysis. Furthermore, it is important to consciously choose the frequency of the analysis because articles can change classes over the course of time.

Application

The analysis takes place in six steps. For this it is advantageous to be able to download the data from a purchasing system or a financial system. The purchasing data are generally analysed on three subjects: suppliers, departments or business units (cost centre) and materials or service (cost type). Analysis on these subjects takes place according to the steps below:

1 Sort and group the data
The data are sorted on the subject in question and subsequently grouped in the desired groups within the subjects. The groupings should correspond with the departments or business units on which the analysis will be performed. In some situations, it can occur that people are sorted and grouped.

2 Clean up the data produced
The data produced are not always up-to-date; data could be lacking and erroneous data has possibly been input. Furthermore, subjects have possibly been included doubly, because input errors have been made (for example, Jansen and Jansse). These have to be checked and rectified to produce a correct analysis.

3 Repair contamination
In the data there will doubtless be materials or services booked under the wrong department or under the wrong material or service or perhaps, on a code where there was still budget available but for another project. Invoices booked to the wrong departments also need to be decoded. This is a collective action by the financial, purchasing and processing departments.
If the enterprise wishes to perform an analysis of which departments or business units carry out what purchasing, the cost centres will have to be involved in the analysis. Combine the cost centres per department or per business unit for analysis.
If an analysis is also made of the suppliers, these data must be checked and sorted on supplier.
What this is ultimately about is the analysis of the materials and services used. These are booked on the cost types and the data will thus have to be sorted and grouped on cost type.

4 Make the data suitable

Ensure that the data to be analysed is accessible such that it can be sorted and grouped in different ways and interim totals can be produced. This can possibly be done with an Excel spreadsheet or a small database (MS Access). Larger files with information and a comprehensive analysis from several viewpoints are best analysed with the aid of a data warehouse system.

5 Perform the ABC analysis

Now perform the analysis with the selected system, where articles belong to the group of A articles when their turnover totals 50% of total turnover, to the group of B articles when this is 30% and to group C when it is 20%.

Result

The result of this analysis is that insight is obtained into the materials or services that are purchased. With it, the enterprise can save costs by making far-reaching agreements with a limited group of selected suppliers from whom the A products are purchased. After all, 80% of the purchasing budget goes to 20% of the materials or services purchased. On the basis of the agreements made, delivery reliability will also increase.

Focus areas

A risk in using this model is that a supplier gladly delivers because next to an article from group A, articles from group C are also supplied, for example. If the article from group C is replaced by a cheaper article, it could be that for the supplier it is no longer of interest to continue to supply article A because too little profit is made on it.

Literature

- Koch, R. (1999). *The 80/20 Principle: The Secret to Success by Achieving More with Less*. Doubleday & Co. USA.
- http://www.80-20rule.net/
- http://www.lifehack.org/articles/lifehack/how-useful-is-the-pareto-principle.html

69
Performance matrix for family businesses

Author	P. Sharma
Year developed	2004
Also known as	Performance of family firms
Objective	Determining the performances of family businesses

Model

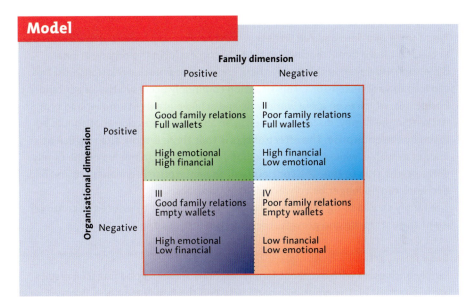

Background

Just like every other company, family businesses want healthy turnovers and to make profits. There are two dimensions in the family business: the organisational and family dimensions. Here, it is of interest to know what influences both dimensions have on the success of these family businesses. What the family understands by success, does not immediately say that it has exclusively to do with turnover and profit objectives. Family businesses often have a combination of financial and non-financial objectives. It turns out that in the eyes of the stakeholders in family businesses, there are wide variations in the perception even of the most basic subjects (Sharma, 1997). Family businesses can therefore be successful in one dimension but not in another. With the aid of Sharma's matrix, insight can be obtained into the total results of the family business.

Application

I   Good family relations and full wallets

Family businesses in quadrant I are the most successful family businesses. Companies in this quadrant have the best combination between the family and organisational dimensions. In the family there is good harmony, so that collaboration can be done in the right way to achieve the family's objectives. Furthermore, these companies operate in a market where good turnovers and profits are achieved. This means that these family businesses have sufficient capital. Furthermore, the family members have a good emotional bond with each other. Due to this, the enterprise can survive, even when there is an economic downturn or when emotional moments occur in the family. Lingering in this quadrant is the best thing that a family business can do.

II   Poor family relations and full wallets

In quadrant II are family businesses that are successful in the organisational dimension. However, in the family there are less good mutual relationships. This can lead to various tensions. This situation commonly occurs in the larger family businesses, which even grow worldwide and achieve greater turnover and profits. Within the family, discord can then arise about the direction that should be taken by the enterprise. The effect of this is that there is more than sufficient budget available, while the emotional bond between the members of the family deteriorates. Due to this, the continuity of the enterprise is endangered and bad decisions can no longer be converted into good ones.
The family should bring the mutual relationships in order to assure the continuity of the enterprise and grow further into the first quadrant.

III   Good family relations and empty wallets

Family businesses with excellent family relations and less good financial results are in quadrant III. The emotional bond between the family members is very good. The results of the business however, are disappointing. This is not a problem for a short period. The good mutual relations between the family can take a few knocks and somewhat poorer business results. If this situation perseveres however, the available resources will dry up. The latter will put heavy pressure on family relationships.
A renewed strategy towards the company and market is necessary to improve the business results of the enterprise. To this end, an enterprise will have to be able to move from quadrant III to quadrant I.

IV   Poor family relations and empty wallets

Family businesses in quadrant IV have quite simply failed, because both the business results and the family relations are poor. If good results are not achieved in the organisational dimension, a family can better start up another enterprise, with which good results can possibly be achieved in the future. But to come to good relations within the family, a much longer time is needed. And perhaps this will not succeed at all.

Although for family businesses quadrant I is the best situation, it is difficult for companies in quadrant IV to realise this directly. Usually, a path via quadrant II or III follows. First make improvements in one dimension and thereafter in the other, in order to grow into quadrant I.

Result

On the basis of this matrix, family businesses can set up the correct strategy to go from quadrant II, III or IV to quadrant I. It is important that this strategy is carefully set up and implemented. For example, a company that is in quadrant III and exclusively focuses on the business results can become entangled in family relationships and therefore not end up in quadrant I but in quadrant IV.

Focus areas

Sharma's model comprises two overall dimensions and gives a general strategy on which family businesses can focus. The strategy that is ultimately established will have to take place based on more and further detailed aspects. These aspects are, among others:
- the total shareholding of the family in the enterprise
- the background of the director (someone from the family or outside the family)
- what power positions there are
- the culture of the enterprise
- the number of family members in the management of the enterprise
- the number of generations of the family participating in the company

Literature

- Sharma, P. (1997). *Determinants of the satisfaction of the primary stakeholders with the succession process in family firms.* Doctoral dissertation, University of Calgary.
- Poutziouris, P., Smyrnios, K., Klein, S. (2006). *Handbook of Research on Family Business.* Edward Elgar Publishing Inc.
- Phan. P., Butler. J. (2008). *Theoretical Developments and Future Research in Family Business.* IAP-Information Age Publishing Inc.

70
Physical Distribution

Author	**Developed in practice**
Year developed	**–**
Also known as	**Logistics**
Objective	**Establishing transport movements**

Model

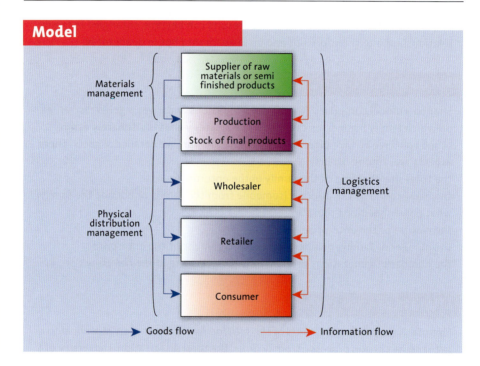

Background

Physical Distribution embraces the process from the warehouse-ready product to delivery to the customer. Although the diagram looks simple, it is a lot more complex in practice. For example, a supermarket. It has products on the shelves and a limited stock in its own stockroom. Most products come from other suppliers. Due to this, the provisioning of all the shops belonging to such a concern becomes a very sophisticated distribution network. The stocks of the end products from all the suppliers are transported via various distribution centres (DC) in the country. The DC will place all goods received in the warehouse, after which the orders are delivered to the shops. Products from one supplier go to different shops. Physical Distribution is a very important process for many companies and comprises three sub-processes, namely warehouse management, stock management and transport.

Application

Physical Distribution is applied as follows:

1 Distribution structures

As a first step, the enterprise will have to choose from the different distribution structures. The distribution network of an enterprise is formed by a system of distribution channels, transport companies and warehouses, among which the goods of an enterprise are moved to bring them closer to the customers. First of all, the organisation should make choices in relation to the performance indicators at distribution level. For example, these involve the logistics service degree, the product characteristics (such as density value, packaging stability, shelf life and appearance), the market structure, the distribution costs and the size of the goods flow. The distribution structures from which the enterprise can choose are direct distribution and distribution via consolidation. With direct distribution, the goods go directly to the customers and with consolidation they first go to a distribution centre, where the goods from different suppliers are combined before being shipped further.

2 Choice of places of business

The choice of one or more places of business is strategic in nature because the enterprise will have to remain there at least five to ten years. Factors that can play a role in the selection of a place of business are:
- delivery time: the time needed to deliver the goods from the DC to the customer
- reliability of delivery: does the enterprise deliver to the customer according to agreements
- the flexibility to service new markets
- the distance between the most important customers and suppliers
- improving cost effectiveness by the new place of business
- government regulations
- availability of personnel
- presence of infrastructure

3 Management of the distribution network

Management is necessary to prevent the *slingshot effect* in the chain. This is the effect that every link in the chain takes extra stock to avoid risk. This can even lead to 40% too much unsaleable production remaining with the manufacturer. It is thus important to establish the responsibilities properly and to have an information system in which the management of the distribution can be handled. Such a system is called Distribution Requirements Planning or DRP. This system makes it possible to attune the different decisions in the distribution network to each other.

4 Physical processing of the orders

Here we are concerned with a convergent and a divergent flow. In the DC (warehouse) the goods from the suppliers are stored and orders from customers are delivered. The steps in the DC are order entry, reception and storage of goods, order-picking, packing and delivery.

Order entry

With order entry, it is important that as much as possible is done via the information systems, to save time and errors with the use of documents.

Reception and storage of goods

With the reception and storage of goods, as little as possible handling should be involved and account must also be taken of the later removal of the goods. The organisation of the warehouse is thus also an important aspect in the minimisation of handling. A fully-automatic warehouse with computer-driven cranes is perhaps a large investment, but will soon pay dividends. With the storage of goods, account should be taken of aspects such as the rate of turnover, physical properties of the goods, articles that belong together or article groups, bulk stocks and operational stocks, free locations or fixed locations.

Order-picking

For order-picking, the enterprise has to make choices in relation to the number of employees involved with one order.

Packing and delivery

Packing takes place due to the lower handling costs and for protection during transport. This repackaging will be on the basis of the packaging module (agreed standards for packaging) because better efficiency in the handling and transport is achieved.

5 Transport

Transport is the biggest cost item for Physical Distribution. The most important choice is the method of transport: by road, over water, by rail, by air or through a pipeline. Container transport provides the possibility to transport items with different modes of transport without transhipping the goods. The enterprise can make considerations in relation to speed, accessibility, variability in time, the application of a mode of transport, frequency of the transport method, damage to goods and costs per ton per kilometre.

6 Costs

The costs of Physical Distribution are categorised in logistics viewpoints: transport, storage, interest, handling and administrative processing. The value density (value per m³) and packing density (the number of packages per m³) play a role in the choice of distribution. If they are both low, the costs of warehousing and transport prevail.

With a high value density, the cost of interest is high and with a high packing density, the handling costs are high.

Result

Well-organised Physical Distribution provides the enterprise with benefits in the area of the logistics of service to the customers in relation to delivery times and reliability of delivery. The total logistics costs are to a large extent controlled by the Physical Distribution costs. The enterprise has control of the stocks, so that no excesses or shortages occur. The management of the Physical Distribution contributes towards the integrated goods flow within the chain and connects both to the goods flow of the enterprise and that of the customer.

Focus areas

The model indicates neither the complexity of convergent and divergent goods flows nor the organisation of the DC.

Literature

- Leeman, J. (2010). *Supply Chain management*. Institute for Business Process Management.
- Kapoor, S., Kansal, P. (2004). *Basics of Distribution management*. Prentice Hall.

71

PMT, Abell & Hammond

Authors	**Abell & Hammond**
Year developed	**1979**
Also known as	**Product-Market technology, Business Definition Model**
Objective	**Determining the growth markets of an enterprise**

Model

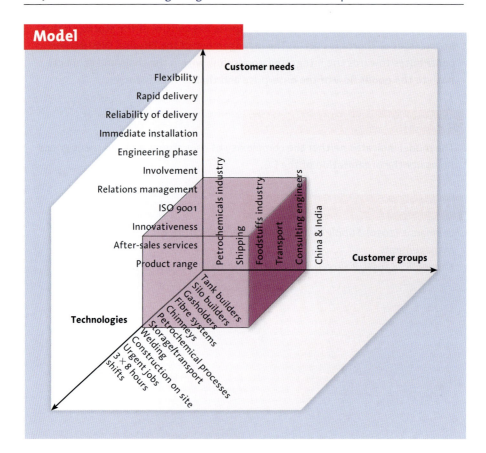

Background

Next to establishing the products put on the market by enterprise, it is important to know in which markets the enterprise is active. Three important components in this model are: customer needs, customer groups and technologies.

The concrete question that can be asked is: with the aid of which technologies does the enterprise serve what customer needs of which customer groups? This question leads to the demarcation of the market within which the enterprise is active.

Furthermore, the model indicates on which of the three axes expansion can be achieved. This is also the direct objective of Abell's model: determining growth.

Application

The demarcation is formed by the three axes:
- Customer needs: what needs do the customers have, what do the customers expect from suppliers?
- Customer groups: which segments are important for the enterprise and which segments ultimately constitute the target group of the enterprise?
- Technologies: with the aid of what resources and products are the needs of the customers satisfied?

For each axis, all the existing possibilities are scored, where the possibilities already covered by the enterprise are closest to the intersection of the axes. The cube is created by scoring the three axes. It can then be immediately established in which areas the enterprise has development potential. The example shows the Abell model of a company, of which the primary activity consists in the engineering, manufacture and delivery of storage tanks, gasholders and equipment in stainless steel, carbon steel and other materials, such as duplex. These are produced at the behest of companies in the foodstuffs, (petro)chemicals and related industries.

To place the correct subjects at the axes, the following questions are asked:
- Customer groups: who are the customers we wish to sell our services/products to?
- Customer need: what do these customers wish to achieve with this product or service?
- Technologies: how does the enterprise satisfy the needs of the customer groups?

The model is filled in at two different times. First of all with the analysis of the current situation and secondly, with the newly formed strategy. After all, based on the research, factors will probably change, including the axes of the model. This also indicates in what direction the enterprise will develop. By the second time the model is filled in, the cube of the first time can be visualised so that it can clearly be seen in which areas the enterprise will develop.

To deploy the model effectively, the following questions are posed:
- Which extra new customer groups with the same needs can we service also?
- What needs are we not yet servicing for the existing customer groups?

- What technologies are available to satisfy the existing needs of the current customer groups?

After these questions have been answered, a further look can be taken at:
- new customer groups with existing needs and existing technologies
- new customer groups with new needs and existing technologies
- new customer groups with existing needs and new technologies
- new customer groups with new needs and new technologies

Result

With the model, the enterprise can in the first place demarcate its activities. Moreover, the model also provides the possibility to discover the possibility for expansion of its activities on one or more axes.

Focus areas

Expansion of the activities of the enterprise via the model gives the temptation to simultaneously expand several axes, to book the quickest and most success. This however entails great risks because it is very risky to radically adjust three subjects in the enterprise. The advice is therefore: always limit expansion to one of the three axes.

The model is very rigid and takes no account of other influencing factors, such as interest groups and governments.

There is no structure in the axes, except that the already covered possibilities are closest to the intersection of the axes. How and what possibilities for growth can be selected and tackled is not shown by the model. Furthermore, the model provides no insight into the potential of the possibilities that exist. Therefore, it is also important to perform a portfolio analysis in combination with this model.

Literature

- Abell, D.F. & Hammond, J.S. (1979). *Strategic Marketing Planning: Problems and Analytic Approaches*. Prentice-Hall.
- Abell, D.F. (1980). *Defining the Business. The Starting Point of Strategic Planning*. Prentice-Hall.

72
Positioning

Authors	**Ries & Trout**
Year developed	**1981**
Also known as	**–**
Objective	**Obtaining a place in the mind of the customer**

Model

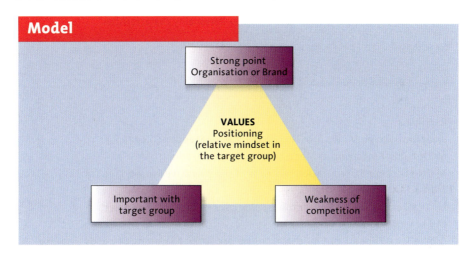

Background

Positioning concerns the perceptions of the customers with regard to the product or service of the enterprise. It is thus not about the actual product or service, but the image of this product or service the customer has. The image that the customer has of the product or service is the image of the enterprise. When an enterprise wishes to position itself, it is important to select values (properties, consequences, final values and benefits for the customer) to which apply:

- the target group must consider them important
- the enterprise is strong in them
- the competition is less strong in them

Positioning is therefore intended to get into the mindset of the customer and be distinguished therein with regard to the competition.
Positioning comprises three levels:

- corporate level
- product group level
- product level

General management

Strategy

Marketing

Sales

Purchasing

Project & Planning

Production

Quality

Logistics & Distribution management

Information management

Financial

HRM & HTM

Internationalisation

These levels should be attuned to each other. If at corporate level it is radiated that there is no R&D but new products are constantly coming onto the market, then these positioning levels are not in line with each other.

Application

To obtain the correct positioning, the following steps are undertaken:

1 Determine the positioning characteristics

For positioning, first of all a number of characteristics are selected. These characteristics should match what the target group considers important. In the table are included the characteristics of each researcher.

Rokeach	• Final values • Personality characteristics
Maslow	• Needs pyramid
Kotler	• Market instruments
Aaker	• Brand personality characteristics

Examples:
- Ikea: *Desining your own life*: Terminal Values – Freedom (Rokeach)
- McDonalds: *I'm Loving it*: Market instrument – Product
- Martin Lockheet Corporation: *We never forget who we are working for*: Market instrument – Image
- Lucent Technologies: *Deliver more value over IP (Internet Protocol)*: Market Instrument – Price
- Global Jet Airlines: *Light is Faster, but we are Safer*: Hierarchy of needs – safety

2 Inventory the needs of customers and own strengths and weaknesses

On the basis of the positioning characteristics, the target group is asked how one's own enterprise scores, how the competition scores and what the most ideal product range would be. Subsequently, the strengths and weaknesses of one's own enterprise are mapped out via an internal and an external survey. The results of this step can be visualised in a positioning matrix or a benchmark (see Benchmarking).

3 Determine points for improvement

On the basis of the inventory, it is established on which points the enterprise already has a competitive advantage and on which points the product or service must be adapted to cover the needs of the customers and become better than the competition. These are the Unique Selling Points (USP) of the enterprise with regard to that product or service. The points on which competitive advantage can be achieved are:

- price
- service
- complaints handling
- maintenance of a relations network
- quality
- added value
- technology used
- reliability

4 Select position
The enterprise has a choice from 4 strategies to select position:
- *Informational positioning*: communication of concrete benefits for customers.
- *Transformational positioning*: communication of values in life that customers consider important.
- *Bilateral positioning*: combination of the first and second strategies.
- *Implementation positioning*: positioning with the aid of an advertising characteristic.

5 Attune the marketing instruments to the selected positioning
As the last step, the enterprise will have to deploy the marketing instruments on the basis of the selected positioning. In this way, it is attempted to create the perceptions of the customers.

Result

The enterprise is able to bring the products and services and the enterprise itself to the attention of customers in a clear and structured manner, with regard to the offer of the competition.

Focus areas

If the positioning according to this model is carried through too far, a huge difference can arise between the image from the model and what is produced in reality.

Literature

- Ries, A. & Trout, J.O. (2001). *Positioning, The battle for your mind*. McGraw-Hill Companies.
- Trout, R., Rivkin, S. (2009). *Repositioning*. McGraw-Hill.
- Hooley, G., Oiercy, N., Nicoulaud, B. (2008). *Marketing Strategy and Competitive positioning*. Prentice Hall.

73
PRINCE2

Author	CCTA
Year developed	1979 (4th edition 2005)
Also known as	Projects IN Controlled Environments
Objective	Managing complex projects

Model

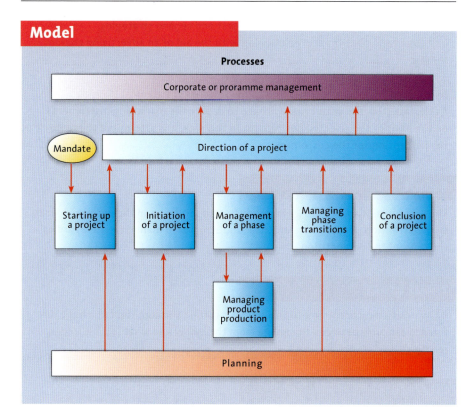

Background

Every activity carried out in the form of a project will have to be managed in some way or another. With small projects, probably by one person with a simple approach. The larger the project the more complex it is to oversee and keep up with everything. A method for managing more complex projects is PRINCE2. This method consists of components and processes. The components provide a con-

General management

Strategy

Marketing

Sales

Purchasing

Project & Planning

Production

Quality

Logistics & Distribution

Information management

Financial

HRM & HTM

Internationalisation

trolled and manageable project environment. The processes describe what activities must be performed to achieve a predetermined objective. Furthermore, PRINCE2 has the following characteristics:

- *Management*: managing projects.
- *Business case*: the added value of the project for the enterprise must be demonstrated.
- *Product-based planning*: products that deliver the project constitute the added value for the enterprise and not the activities that are carried out.
- *Project organisation*: the project organisation is set up according to the 'BUS' principle (business, users, suppliers).
- *Documentation*: for PRINCE2 extensive documentation is available for all the facets of the execution of the project.

Application

When implementing projects with PRINCE2, two aspects are important: the components that create a controllable environment and the processes that ensure a manageable execution.

Components

With the aid of the components, a controlled and thus manageable project environment is created. Due to this, the objectives of the project can be achieved. This concerns the following components:

- *Organisation*: this component describes the project organisation consisting in the Project Board, Project Manager and Teams.
- *Plans*: this component shows not only activities to be carried out in time, but also who performs these activities, to deliver the established products.
- *Controls*: this component monitors the progress and the budget of the project. Moreover, this component ensures the timely delivery of the products within the planned time and budget, in accordance with the quality requirements set for the products.
- *Business case*: this component justifies the project. As long as there is an added value for the enterprise on the basis of the relationship between the costs and benefits, the project can be further executed. The benefits can also be expressed in other aspects besides money, for example, service to customers.
- *Management of Risk*: this component comprises risk analysis and risk management and examines business risks (business benefits) and project risks (time and budget).
- *Quality in a project environment*: this component examines the process quality (execution of the project) and product quality (quality of the products produced).
- *Change control*: this component controls the changes that occur in the project.
- *Configuration management*: this component ensures that the products produced are identified, registered, followed and secured during the project.

Processes

PRINCE2 approaches project management in the form of processes. Each of the eight processes comprises an objective and activities to ensure the objective is achieved. This concerns the following processes:

- *Directing a project (DP)*: the project board (steering group) follows the project and gives authorisation for the following steps and products to be produced.
- *Starting up a project (SU)*: preparations before the actual project is started.
- *Initiation of a project (IP)*: describing the whole project in detail, including planning.
- *Controlling a stage (CS)*: description of the day-to-day activities of the project manager.
- *Managing product delivery (MP)*: the production and delivery of the business products.
- *Managing Stage Boundaries/phase transitions (SB)*: checking all the boundaries within the project.
- *Closing a project (CP)*: the official handover of the results to the organisation.
- *Planning (PL)*: is used by other processes to draft the Project Plan, Stage plans and possibly Team Plans.

Result

With the aid of a structured and planned method, the enterprise is better able to bring in projects at the planned time, within the established budget and to achieve other preconditions.

Focus areas

This method is very extensive and this means that experienced people must be present to implement PRINCE2 in the correct manner when using it. Due to its size, a bureaucratic whole can be created at the cost of time and budget.
A second focus area is that this method does not take account of is the skills of the people themselves. The skills of the project manager play a huge role in the successful achievement of a project, for example.

Literature

- The Stationary Office. (2009). *Managing Successful Projects with Prince2*. The Stationary Office.
- http://www.jiscinfonet.ac.uk/ (PRINCE2 in the search field)
- www.ogc.gov.uk/

74
Product Life Cycle

Author	Levitt
Year developed	1993
Also known as	PLC
Objective	Insight into the sales prognosis of a product or service

Model

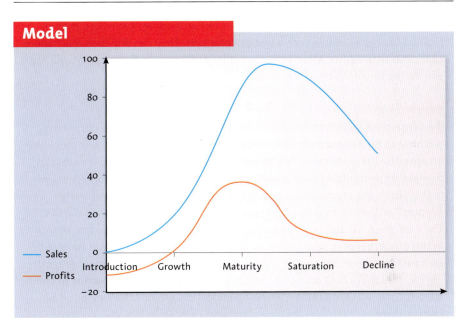

Background

A product that is introduced onto the market will sell very little in the beginning. When the product becomes better known, the number of products sold
will rise and turnover will increase. At a given moment, the market will be saturated and turnover will decline.

Every product or service will go through this development, this is certain. It is
therefore important for the enterprise to be able to estimate in which phase
of the product life cycle a product or service is placed, to obtain an impression
of the possible turnover and profits. In this manner, new products can be introduced before sales of the old product are expected to decline.

The Product Life Cycle (PLC) has five phases:

1 Introduction
2 Growth
3 Maturity
4 Saturation
5 Decline

The costs incurred for a product already begin in the design phase, before the product comes onto the market. These costs can increase enormously and it is therefore important that the enterprise cancels any non-viable products in time. The actual PLC begins by the introduction of the product onto the market.

Application

Although the graphic representation looks like an S-curve, it is not so that all product life cycles follow such a smooth progress. They can also look much more capricious or irregular. After all, it cannot be predicted in advance what will happen during the life cycle of a product.

1 Introduction

If an enterprise wishes to introduce a product or service, then the customers will have to be informed about it. Furthermore, the product or service must be accepted by the customers. To this end, a great deal of promotion is necessary to make its possibilities for the user and the benefits for the customers known. In this phase, the promotion is primarily focused on the segment of 'early-adopters' who must be persuaded to buy with campaigns and personal visits. The enterprise will still not make a profit on the sales of the product or service in this phase, because sales are rising slowly and the initial expenses have to be paid back. Furthermore, the enterprise should take into account possible teething troubles that could occur with the product or service. The objective of the introduction phase is a certain market penetration and/or achieving a certain market share.

2 Growth

In the growth phase there is a focus the 'early majority' or the 'followers'. This segment must be convinced of the qualities of the product by promotion and references from other customers. The enterprise will in this phase have to make a choice to go for high profits or a large market share. With similar promotion costs and prices, due to higher production and experience with production, the costs per product will become lower. This generates high profits. If the enterprise wishes to increase its market share, then the price will have to be adjusted (lower) to persuade the large group of price-conscious buyers to purchase the product or service. Promotion at the right time is then vitally important. When the initial buyers decide to make repeat purchases, the introduction phase ends and the growth phase begins. At around the same time, the investment in the product should also be paid back and thus, the break-even point should be reached. In this phase the teething troubles are gone and sales of the product will quickly increase.

A risk in the growth phase of new products is the appearance of competition. They have meanwhile discovered and investigated the new product and will also try to capture part of the market. An improved version of the product or service is an answer to the arrival of competition in this phase.

3 Maturity

In the maturity phase, the growth of the product or service will decline due to the competition, which brings comparable versions, cheaper versions or imitations onto the market. The market share is in this phase under strong pressure due to such competition. Improved versions, lowering the prices and more promotion of brand loyalty should retain market share. The degree of penetration is maximal in this phase because the product or service has been purchased by the vast majority of the customers. Here, the highest profits are attained in the PLC of the product or service. To retain market share and profits, the enterprise will have to pay attention to other segments, make adaptations for existing users or opt for different positioning of the product or service. Possible new customers can be attracted by adjusting the quality or style of the product or service.

4 Saturation

When the products of the competition are equal to those of the enterprise and there is only demand for replacement, the saturation phase commences. In order to not lose further market share with respect to the competition, promotional efforts must be increased. Due to the increasing costs (and possibly lower prices), profits will be lower. Because the demand for the product is slowly declining due to fewer replacements, the product can exclusively remain in production due to lower costs. The savings in costs are then usually in the area of the use of amortised machines.

5 Decline

Through over-capacity, price competition, new technologies, cheaper imported products or changes in needs, it will become increasingly difficult to keep the product or service on the market without loss. The enterprise should plan when the product or service will be taken off the market.

Result

The result of the use of the product life cycle model is that the enterprise receives insight into a possibly expected sales prognosis for the product or service and it becomes clear that the enterprise must start with the development of new products or services to replace the existing ones.

Focus areas

It is not always good to determine in which phase in the life cycle a product or service is placed. The usefulness of the model diminishes by this. Furthermore, it becomes proportionally more difficult to make prognoses as the cycle becomes longer and a product remains on the market for longer.

Literature

- Saaksvuori, A., Immonen, A. (2009). *Product Life Cycle management*. Springer-Verlag Berlin Heidelberg.
- Niemann, J., Tichkiewitch, S., Westkämper, E. (2009). *Design of Sustainable Product Life Cycles*. Springer-Verlag Berlin Heidelberg.
- Levitt, T. (1965). Exploit the product life cycle. *Harvard Business Review*, 43, 81-94.

75
Progress reporting

Author	M. Mulders
Year developed	1996
Also known as	–
Objective	Providing insight into the future status of a project on a financial basis, time basis and deliverables basis

Model

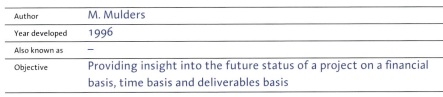

	Hours	Budget	Deliverables	Milestones
Additional		0%		
Internal	82%	79%		
External	106%	92%		
Total	89%	85%	97%	100%

	Relative index	12%	
Start	1-Apr-07		
End	31-Dec-08		
Day's	640		

Background

In the execution of projects, it is expected that insight is given into the state of affairs at different times. This is called progress reporting. In between times, developments in different subjects are explained to the clients. The clients will require insight into the budgetary status of the project in relation to the time and the realisation of the deliverables. If milestones and products or deliverables are included in the project, they are reported on.

What is also important to include in these reports are the bottlenecks that arise

273

during the execution of the project. Good progress reporting thus gives complete insight into the current status of the project.

The reporting comprises two components:

1 Substantive report

With the substantive report, on the basis of text it is indicated what the status of the project is at that time. In this report the following subjects are covered in the reporting period[12]:

- results of previous period
- conclusions to be drawn
- bottlenecks
- actions for the coming period

2 Report in figures

The report in figures gives insight into the progress of the project on the basis of concrete data. These data comprise the following components:

- budget
- hours
- mileposts
- deliverables

With this report it is also important to provide future insight into the status of the project on the mentioned data components. After all, merely looking back, establishing retroactively that things did not go well, makes little sense. Therefore, in the report there will also have to be a component that indicates the future situation. Due to this, before any actual problems occur, adjustments can be made in time.

Budget. Budget is always one of the most important components to which adjustments are made. Budgets are established in advance and are often difficult to adjust afterwards. If there are budget problems, this will also always be at the expense of the functionality produced.

			€			
	Budget	Project plan	Planned	Spent	Still to do	O/B
Additional costs	350 000	0	0	0	0	0
Internal	0	211 900	179 500	160 969	0	18 531
External	0	150 075	150 075	143 128	1 500	5 447
Total	*350 000*	*361 975*	*329 575*	*304 096*	*1 500*	*23 979*

Vertically are the cost types, in this situation additional, internal and external. These costs are reported on in various categories. Firstly, the initial budget is indicated. Secondly follows the overview from the project plan. Thirdly, the actual budget is shown for which the project is accountable. Subsequently, what has been spent on the project up to and including the reporting period is updated. Then follows an important item and this is the 'still to do' budget. For this, in every report the remaining part of the project is calculated and input anew. Subsequently, via the following calculation, it can be worked out whether the project comes out below or above the planned budget in the financial sense.

budget = (planned – spent) – still to do

Hours. Reporting in relation to the hours is in accordance with the lay-out of the budget.
Milestones. During the period the project is running, there are a number of important moments that are already known at the beginning. These are, for example, go/no-go moments, approval of partial deliverables or the completion of an analysis. These moments are called milestones and are achieved on time or not.
Deliverables. Ultimately, it is about the results that must be produced by the project. These are called deliverables. This can encompass anything, such as a software-system, a business plan, a building or a recommendation.
Total overview. There is now reporting on four subjects: hours, budget, deliverables and mileposts. Separately, they give a certain insight into each subject, as in the figure on the first page of this model. The following step is to put these four subjects together, so that a total picture is created with regard to the project. Graphically, the percentages can be put side by side. A relative index can also be calculated to give a total overview of the project. The relative index is a percentage that indicates what the general status of the project is. This is calculated based on the difference from averages of deliverables/milestones and hours/budget.
The calculation is:

$$\text{Relative index} = \frac{\text{deliverables} + \text{milestones}}{2} - \frac{\text{hours} + \text{budget}}{2}$$

Result

The most important result from this method is that the enterprise is able to establish in a timely manner whether the project will overrun in terms of time or budget and thus adjust it in time.

Focus areas

The reporting in question should be seen as a guideline in relation to the status of the project. There could be products, for example, that must be delivered and first require a great deal of effort before they are completed. This gives a somewhat distorted picture of the report.

Literature

- Grit, R. (2008). *Project Management, English edition*. Groningen: Noordhoff Uitgevers.

[12] In relation to the frequency of the report, it can be remarked that the period reported on is dependent on factors like throughput time, complexity, priority, importance in the organisation and size of budget. The reporting period often encompasses a period of a week to two months. A monthly report is common.

76
Purchasing Process

Author	R.M. Monczka (supplemented by M. Mulders)
Year developed	1998
Also known as	Procurement process
Objective	Assessing and organising the purchasing process

General management

Strategy

Marketing

Sales

Purchasing

Project & Planning

Production

Quality

Logistics & Distribution management

Information management

Financial

HRM & HTM

Internationalisation

Model

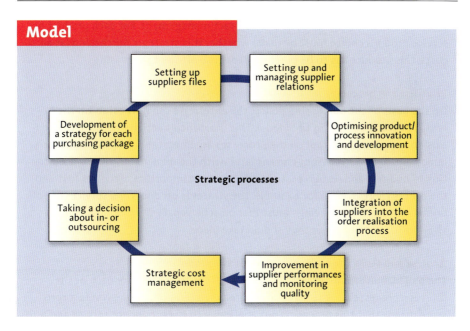

Setting up suppliers files

Setting up and managing supplier relations

Development of a strategy for each purchasing package

Optimising product/process innovation and development

Strategic processes

Taking a decision about in- or outsourcing

Integration of suppliers into the order realisation process

Strategic cost management

Improvement in supplier performances and monitoring quality

Background

The attention of enterprises is mainly focused on their customers because that is where turnover can be obtained. Enterprises sometimes do not realise sufficiently that on the purchasing side, there are also possibilities to save costs and achieve better backward integration. This is necessary because in the Supply Chain, companies are increasingly dependent on each other. A well-structured Purchasing Process is an important contribution towards this. The Michigan State University (MSU) purchasing model, with eight strategic processes and six supporting processes, produces a model with which the Purchasing Process can be assessed and structured.

The model is actually a benchmark of the Purchasing Processes and can thus be used in enterprises to compare the different purchasing departments or the different divisions with each other. Furthermore, the model can be used to compare the Purchasing Processes of the enterprise with those of others. For this, it is then necessary that a database exists in which the comparable data is stored and managed privacy-securely.

Application

The application of the model comprises the steps below:

1 Determine the purchasing policy
From the business strategy, there should be a policy present with regard to the total Purchasing Process. Subsequently, choices are made with regard to, among other things, the internal purchasing department(s), single sourcing or multi sourcing, supplier management and contract management. For each product or service group, a choice must be made whether it is strategic purchasing (at all costs, this product has to be purchased) or cost-efficient purchasing.

2 Prioritise the processes
On the basis of the purchasing policy, the enterprise can now establish the priorities of the processes in the model. This is a difficult activity because the conclusion is easy to draw that all the processes are important. Still, this activity is important to make the right choices later, with the implementation and allocation of budgets and resources, to tackle the most important activities first and the others thereafter. If, for example, the strategic products and services are of primary interest, cost savings must first be achieved. Even more important is the prioritisation of when they should take place.

3 Analyse and score the eight processes of the model
The model indicates assessment criteria and maturity levels for each of the fourteen processes. These levels are scored on a ten-point scale, where a zero score means that this process is not applicable to the product or service and a 10 is 'best in class'. The processes of the enterprise are analysed and scored on the basis of the assessment criteria.

4 Gap analysis
Via a Gap analysis the difference between what is desired and what is reality is is analysed. For each process it is indicated on which aspects the process does not comply with the desired situation. These differences form the basis for coming to a professional Purchasing Process. It is important to formulate clear objectives in this step by means of success factors and performance indicators, to steer the realisation in a planned manner.

5 Adaptation of Purchasing Processes
For each aspect in the Gap analysis, the activities that must take place to ensure that the Purchasing Processes are adapted are now drafted, a project plan is

drafted and resources and means are linked to the realisation of the project. A substantial component is monitoring the realisation to establish whether the adaptations to the purchasing process also lead to the desired results, which are established in the success factors and performance indicators.

Result

The result that use of the model produces is the structuring and professionalisation of the purchasing organisation. Many companies focus only on the cost aspect and consequently take incorrect decisions, which sometimes even leads to higher costs. With the professionalisation of the purchasing the relationship between supplier and customer becomes increasingly important due to the Supply Chain integration.

Focus areas

The MSU model was drafted by Prof. Monczka and was set up for internationally operating manufacturing companies. Due to this, it takes too little account of service-providing companies. In collaboration with the Dutch Association for Purchasing Management (NEVI) and Purchasing Excellence (PIA), an MSU Public model was developed in the Netherlands for service-providing companies and government institutions.
A second aspect is that the model focuses too much on the cost aspect of the purchasing function and less on the strategic objectives a purchasing organisation strives for.

Literature

- Monczka, R., Handfield, R., Giunipero, C., Patterson J. (2008). *Purchasing and Supply Chain Management*. Mason, OH: South-Western Publishers.
- www.kingston.gov.uk/1steps_prior_to_purchase_2006_.pdf

77
RASCI Matrix

Author	Ministry of Defense, USA
Year developed	1991
Also known as	Responsible, Accountable, Supportive, Consulted, Informed, RACI, ARCI, RACI-V
Objective	Mapping out responsibilities and authorities in teams

Model

	Mr. Swart (Client)	H. Maas (Sales support)	K. Grint (Sales support)	B. Bastiaan (Logistics)	A. Miller (Dispatch)	K. Borg (Supplier)	C. Bender (Shipper)
Order to be transported		A		I			
Selection of orders			A	R	S		
Journey planning				A	R		C
Acceptance of orders				A	I		
Delivery of pallets of end product					A	R	
Loading trailer				A	R		I
Reporting loading list				A	R		
Printing bill of loading				S	A		
Communication of planning to shipper			R	A			I
Driving truck			A				R
Delivery of end product to client	I		A				S
Reporting of delivery complete		I	I	A			S

R = Responsible
A = Accountable
S = Supportive
C = Consulted
I = Informed

Background

Everywhere where people collaborate, this can lead to great successes and excellent results. The opposite is unfortunately also true. Collaboration can also lead to fiascos and squabbling. Teams that cannot collaborate well usually achieve less good or disappointing results. There are of course countless events that stand in the way of collaboration. One of them is blaming the other when things do not go as envisaged. And then a confusing discussion arises, which never leads to a good result. A simple and effective aid is the RASCI Matrix, in which responsibilities are established so that everyone knows what he or she must do or what he or she is responsible for. In this way, the right people can be addressed about achieving the agreed results or not.

Application

Especially in risky, complex and time-consuming projects, but also in simple projects, it is sensible and advisable to consider the roles that the different employees have in the different activities. Without these clear agreements, overlap and gaps will arise, which in themselves lead to frustration, inefficiency and unsatisfactory results. The RASCI Matrix is a model that brings clarity and structure into the responsibilities and authorities of people with different roles in projects.
RASCI stands for:
R = Responsible. Person responsible for the result: this person ensures that the result is achieved.
A = Accountable. Finally responsible person: is held responsible if things go wrong, addresses the 'R' person.
S = Supportive. Provides support or performs the activities.
C = Consulted. Must be consulted.
I = Informed. Must be informed.

The overview of the RASCI Matrix comprises the activities and the responsibilities of the people involved in the activities. This always involves individuals because they can be addressed about the result. If, for example, departments were used, this produces problems because a department cannot be addressed about anything.

To compile the RASCI Matrix, the following steps must be carried out:
1 Determine the activities that must be performed in the project.
2 Determine the people who participate in the project.
3 Make the matrix: the activities vertically and the people horizontally.
4 For each activity fill in the roles of the people that have something to do with it. If a person has nothing to do with an activity, the matrix is left open on that point. The roles can best be filled in as follows:
   a For every activity first fill in the 'A'. For each activity only one person can be finally responsible. If nobody is finally responsible, nothing will happen and no-one can also be addressed about it. When several people are finally responsible, then the final responsibility is not borne by anyone and everyone will point to someone else if things go wrong. The person with the final responsibility must also have the knowledge, training and the authorities to perform this role.

b Thereafter, the 'R' is filled in. For every activity there must be at least one person responsible for its execution. It is also advisable to let only one person be responsible because otherwise, there could be 'finger-pointing' at each other if the activity is not carried out or not performed well.

c Thirdly, the other roles can be filled in.

5 After the matrix has been filled in, it must be checked that only one person has the final responsibility for each activity (A) and at least one person is responsible for the execution of the task (R).

6 Next to the check on the A's and the R's, the matrix must be further checked by answering the questions below. This can best be done by looking at the R's, the S's, the C's and the I's vertically for every person and seeing which of them are linked to them.

a Has one person too many responsibilities? If this is so, there is a risk that this person cannot perform the tasks satisfactorily.

b Has one person too many or all the A's? If this is the situation, then it is recommended to reconsider the function of this person and see if some tasks can be delegated.

c Is one person involved in all the activities? This is probably unnecessary and unwise. It must be investigated how the activities can be shared.

7 As the last step, the matrix is communicated so that everyone knows which roles and responsibilities are for whom.

Result

With the aid of the RASCI Matrix, the responsibilities and authorities of people can be mapped out with regard to the activities to be performed. Through this, an even balance is created between the activities to be performed and the people involved in them.

Due to this, the risk of gaps in responsibilities and haziness about who must be informed and consulted for the correct performance of the activities is reduced. In this way, a more effective and efficient team is created

Focus areas

With the application of the RASCI Matrix, special care must be taken with what the division of roles is between the 'A' for Accountable and the 'R' for Responsible. These two are sometimes confused.

If politics and personal matters play a role, this model has less added value.

Literature

None.

78
Ratio Delay Studies

Author	L. Tippet
Year developed	1938
Also known as	Work-Sampling and Random Sampling method
Objective	Determining inefficiency and bottlenecks in processes

General management
Strategy
Marketing
Sales
Purchasing
Project & Planning
Production
Quality
Logistics & Distribution
Information management
Financial
HRM & HTM
Internationalisation

Model

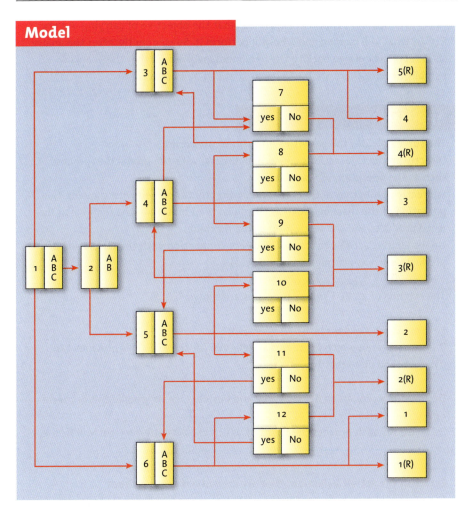

Background

The objective of the Ratio Delay Studies (RDS) is finding those activities or actions where time can be saved or unnecessary time is wasted. The three best known applications are:

- Obtaining insight into how people spend their time.
- Obtaining insight into the running, set-up and breakdown times of machines.
- Obtaining basic data for the remit (time standard) for activities.

Ratio Delay Studies (RDS) is a collection of snapshots of the activities of a group of people and/or machines over a certain period. These observations also have the objective of determining the percentage share of a certain activity. For the success of a RDS survey, it is essential that this is carefully prepared, analysed and reported.

Here it is important that it is explained what the objective of carrying out the RDS is, what will happen and who will perform it. Subsequently, after the analysis, a report should go back to the personnel involved, so that they can also establish where there are bottlenecks that can be improved.

Application

The survey divides the activities into three categories:

- Directly productive: actions concerned directly with the production process, such as the operation of machines.
- Indirectly productive: actions that are indirectly concerned with allowing the operation of the machine, such as the delivery of materials, the removal of finished products and the setting-up of the machine.
- Unproductive: actions that have no direct connection with the realisation of products, such as waiting times and breaks.

The method of an RDS survey proceeds as follows:

1 First establish a proper research question
It is investigated which processes are eligible for the RDS. This provides the overview and demarcation.

2 Define the processes to be measured and business items (people and/or machines)
Establish for each process the items of which the activities/actions will be measured.

3 Establish the activities/actions that are carried out for each item
For personnel, these are usually the activities related to the main task and some sidelines, also including waiting times and pauses (talking, telephoning and answering e-mails are also activities). For machines, this is often during

operational standstill. Standing time will have to be further elaborated into, for example, maintenance, cleaning, resetting and repairs. It is important not to define too many categories because further division is then no longer possible later. Activities that do not often occur can possibly be combined with other activities.

4 Establish the desired accuracy and reliability of the outcomes
The more observations that take place, the more accurate the survey. Because the RDS is a snapshot, accuracy is not 100%. Many RDS surveys are performed with the aid of software and formulas are included for accuracy.

5 Establish the number of observations for each situation
During a certain period, the activities of the people or machines are observed in a large number of rounds. For each person or machine, a tick is put beside the activity being carried out at the time of observation. After this period, the observations for each activity are accumulated. All the activities together total 100%. Each activity is now calculated as a percentage of the total time.

6 Do trial rounds and pay attention to measurement effects
Measurement effects occur when the personnel observed displays a deviational work pattern due to the presence of the observer. This measurement effect can be eliminated as much as possible by involving the personnel in the preparation for the survey.

7 Perform the survey
Draft an observation schedule. Determine the duration of the observation period by determining the average round interval, the number of rounds per day, the size of the group, the minimum number of observations and the times of the rounds. The cycle time for production is, for example, 20 minutes. For the round time, an average interval of 10 minutes is thus selected.
Per day, 45 rounds can be made with 7.5 hours of direct productive working. The size of the group is 40 personnel. Measuring the group takes 2.5 minutes. The minimum round interval is set at 3 minutes.

8 Analyse the data
To what extent the data from the survey are valid outside the observation period is dependent on the representativeness of the measurement period. Some performance indicators can help to find the answer, namely: productivity, effectiveness and efficiency. Items such as order intake and absence due to illness can provide an answer to the question of whether the data obtained are representative for the normal operational situation. It is advisable with the choice of the observation period to assess the representativeness of this period. At later stages, this saves a great deal of discussion about the correctness of the information obtained.

9 Report and present

A RDS produces a great many figures. These must be ordered and processed. On the one hand, to come to conclusions and recommendations and on the other, to present it in an orderly fashion.

Result

The result of the RDS is insight into those activities or actions in the business process where time can be saved or where too much time is wasted. Furthermore, the RDS lends itself well to tracing bottlenecks in the business process. By performing the RDS, insight is obtained into the activities the personnel perform, into the running, setting-up and breakdown times of machines and insight into the standard times for the activities that must be performed.

Focus areas

Personnel on the work floor should be involved in the RDS and receive an explanation of the objectives. If not, then the risk is run that people become uncertain and do not cooperate or influence the results, due to which the RDS will not produce a representative result.

Literature

None.

79
Research method

Author	M. Saunders
Year developed	2003
Also known as	'Onion research process'
Objective	Choosing the correct research method

Model

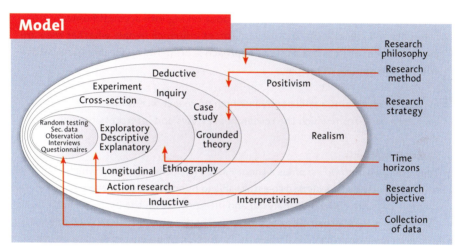

Background

Everywhere around us, research is being done. The term 'research shows' is very often used to express standpoints and convince others or prove a certain point. The importance of research is thus so great that it must be comprehensively examined. Asking a few questions or a survey filled in cannot provide the foundations on the basis of which important decisions have to be taken. Even more: the collection of data, next to analysis and interpretation, is exactly one of the most important aspects of the performance of research. Data are systematically collected to aspire towards a certain objective. Systematic means that there is a certain structure and logical sequence involved. Striving towards a certain objective means that it serves a specific objective. The onion research process provides the framework within which research can be carried out: systematic and leading to a certain objective.

Within the process of the onion research, a number of layers are distinguished.

Research philosophy

The research philosophy relates to the interpretation of data and the situations in which the research takes place. These influence the manner in which the researcher(s) perform the research over whole research programme. There are three angles of approach:

- *Positivism*. Assumes an observable reality and quantifiable observations that can be statistically analysed and is primarily applicable to the exact sciences.
- *Interpretivism*. Assumes changes and the fact that there can be no generalisations. The researcher searches for the underlying reality, also called social constructivism, and seeks the subjective meanings behind the actions of people. This angle of approach is primarily applicable to research within enterprises.
- *Realism*. Assumes an existing reality without taking into account human thoughts and ideas. Social and societal forces influence people whether they are aware of them or not. This angle of approach is primarily applicable to research within large groups of people.

In itself, this remains a philosophy in which no real choice is made. It can, however, be a basis from which the researcher reviews and interprets the data.

Research methods

The *deductive method* assumes a theory and a hypothesis, within which a research strategy is designed to establish the hypothesis. With the *inductive method*, data are collected, analysed and interpreted, on the basis of which the theory is established. The deductive method is primarily used with scientific principles, seeking causal links, the collection of quantitative data and the application of checks to ensure the validity of the data. The deductive method assumes a structured approach and ensures the independence of the researcher and the sufficient scope of random testing.

The inductive method emphasises understanding the meaning that people ascribe to events, to gain a proper understanding of the context of the research and the collection of high-quality data. This method has a flexible structure to put the emphasis on possible other aspects and assumes that the researcher is part of the research process. Furthermore, little importance is attached to possibilities for generalisation.

Research strategy

The research strategy goes into the manner in which the research will be tackled. The research questions and objectives and which people belong to the target group must be clear. The researcher can choose from the following strategies:

- *Experimental*. The actual performance of activities in practice on the basis of a hypothesis. This is a deductive method.

- *Investigation*. The collection of data via questionnaires. Used for the collection of large quantities of data from an extensive population. This is a deductive method.
- *Case study*. Makes use of empirical research (practical research) with the use of different types of evidence. Suitable for the why, what and how questions. Data are collected by means of interviews, observations, document analysis and questionnaires. This is a deductive method.
- *Grounded theory*. Research by means of the construction of a theory. This is a combination of deductive and inductive methods. The theory is generated based on the collected data, predictions from this are tested by further observations.
- *Ethnography*. Research into the descriptive study of the lifestyles of groups of people such as tribes, ethnic groups, professional groups, residents of a closed institution, adherents to a sect in which the studied people live in the reality they themselves experience. It is a time-consuming method that must be flexible and able to respond to changes. This is an inductive method.
- *Action research*. A research method that is focused on change and not only on describing, understanding and explaining. This is an inductive method.

Time horizons
Studies can be snapshots (cross-sectional study) or can run over longer periods, similar to a kind of diary (longitudinal research). Cross-sectional studies are used to explain a certain phenomenon at a certain time. Longitudinal studies, on the other hand, can investigate changes and developments.

Research objective
The research objective indicates to what type of questions answers must be given. Is it an exploratory, descriptive or explanatory study?
- Exploratory research provides answers to questions like: what is happening? What new insights are there? What questions are there for assessing phenomena in a new light? This research can be performed via literature study, talking with experts and focused interviews.
- A descriptive study gives an accurate picture of the reality and is more a means than a study.
- Explanatory research establishes connections between variables.

For research, several methods can be used together. Quantitative research often follows qualitative research. This has two advantages: there is a focus on the most important matters and the use of triangulation is possible. This is the collection of data via several methods to establish whether the data tell you what you think they do.

Result

The onion model gives a greater guarantee of the fact that the results of the research can only be interpreted in one way. The research should be representative, reliable and valid.

Focus areas

The model does indicate that several methods can be used together, but goes no further into it.

Literature

*   http://managementhelp.org

80

Resource Based View

Author	B. Wernerfelt
Year developed	1984
Also known as	RBV
Objective	Adequate deployment of available resources

Model

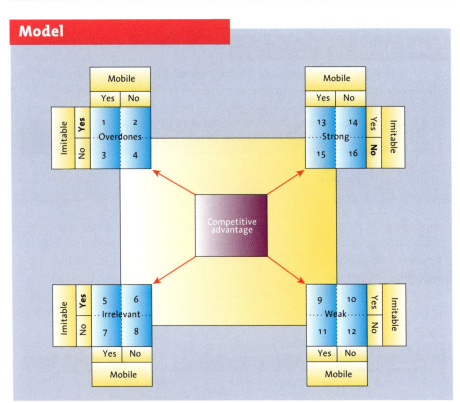

Background

Enterprises that devise a strategy to service a market always have the same external analysis, in principle. This market is the same for everyone. It is thus important in which way the enterprise can best capitalise on the market to be successful. To this end, we review the possibilities the enterprise has, on the basis of resources (means) and capabilities (skills), to service this market. The

General management

Strategy

Marketing

Sales

Purchasing

Project & Planning

Production

Quality

Logistics & Distribution management

Information management

Financial

HRM & HTM

Internationalisation

resources and capabilities should fulfil the following characteristics to obtain a permanent competitive advantage:

- They must be valuable.
- They must be impossible or difficult to duplicate.
- There may be no equivalent substitutes with the competition.

This creates strategic resources. They must fulfil two criteria:

- degree of imitability
- degree of mobility

If a resource cannot be imitated by the competition or is not mobile (for example, a machine cannot be purchased on the market), this produces a long-term advantage. In the further discussion of this model, resources and capabilities are seen as resources.

Application

In the analysis of the resources, we first look at the degree of importance and the degree of strength. Four categories of resources are thus created.

Importance / Strength	Not important	Important
Stronger than the competition	overdones	strong resources
Weaker than the competition	irrelevants	weak resources

Overdones

These resources are not important with regard to the environment. They are, however, stronger than the those of the competition. This means that the enterprise has put too much money and energy into this resource. In almost all situations, the enterprise will have to put less effort into this resource, except in the situation where it is non-imitable and non-mobile.

Overdone resource	Mobile	Non-mobile
Imitable	sell outside the market _disinvest_	do not sell _do not invest_
Non-imitable	sell outside the market _disinvest_	look for new applications _look for other markets_

The mobile resources can be sold. The non-mobile but imitable resources cannot be sold. They have no added value however, so no more investment. The non-imitable and non-mobile resources could possibly become a strategic resource in a different market or application.

Irrelevants

These resources are worse than those of the competition. Enterprises are thus quickly inclined to invest in these resources to make them better. This makes little sense however, because these resources are unimportant for the market. It also makes no sense to pay any attention to these resources. The enterprise must look whether other enterprises in the market view this resource as strategic in order to subsequently outsource it.

Irrelevant resource	Mobile	Non-mobile
Imitable	remains with core competences *outsource or ignore*	remains with core competences *outsource or ignore*
Non-imitable	remains with core competences *outsource or ignore*	remains with core competences *outsource or ignore*

In all situations the enterprise will have to make a choice to either outsource the resource or ignore it, depending on the effects of its performance on the market.

Weak resources

Weak resources are important in the environment in which the enterprise operates but they are less good than those of the competition. Here too the enterprise must pay attention to the choices that are made and not try headlong to strengthen all the resources. Depending on imitability and mobility, the enterprise has the following choices:

Weak Resource	Mobile	Non-mobile
Imitable	buy or imitate at least at level of competition *buy or imitate*	at least at level of competition *imitate*
Non-imitable	buy on the market buy from the competition *buy*	ignore compete on other resources *ignore*

Weak resources will have to be purchased or imitated. The non-mobile and nonimitable resources must be ignored. It requires too much effort and cost to strengthen them.

Strong resources

Strong resources are those resources that are important in the market and are better than those of the competition. These resources must be cherished, but not always. The imitable and non-mobile resources can be turned into strategic resources by making them non-imitable. The non-mobile and non-imitable resources are the strategic resources of the enterprise; they can be invested in.

The enterprise can achieve a long-term competitive advantage with them.

Strong resource	Mobile	Non-mobile
Imitable	use of temporary advantage *attack*	make resource non-imitable *invest*
Non-imitable	use now to harvest the fruits later *harvest*	use strategic advantage cherish and build up the enterprise on it *harvest and invest*

Mobile resources can leave the company and are thus less suitable for the long term. The knowledge and training for these resources must be transferred to the enterprise before the resource disappears.

Result

The Resource Based View offers an alternative to the SWOT analysis. Proceeding from the resources an enterprise has available, it is investigated in which way the market can best be approached. The enterprise can in this way select from sixteen different strategies.

Focus areas

In the model, the mutual relationships between the resources are not included. The management must also consider the consequences for other resources when making choices.

Literature

- Wernerfelt, B. (1984). A resource based view of the firm. *Strategic Management Journal*, 5 (2), 171-180.
- Barney, J. (1991). Firm Resources and Sustained Competitive Advantage. *Journal of Management*, 17 (1), 99-120.
- Barney, J., Clark, D. (2007). *Resource Based Theory*. Oxford University Press.

81
Sales Funnel

Author	Cap Gemini
Year developed	1989
Also known as	Buying Funnel, The Sales Pipeline
Objective	Turnover forecast

Model

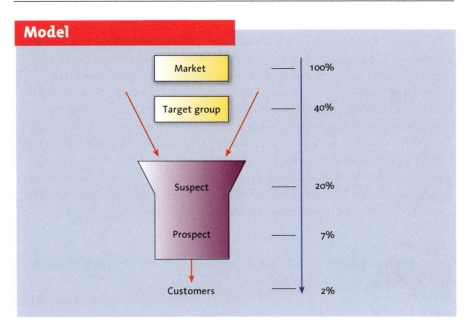

Background

Enterprises spend a lot of time and energy on achieving turnover via marketing and sales instruments. The efforts that account managers and sales people make to bring in orders are in keeping with this. When it concerns products that are simple and sell like hot cakes, it is a question of adding up the turnover and extrapolating a prediction or *forecast*. With larger and more expensive products and especially with services, it is much more difficult to establish what the possible forecast is and what priorities must be set, in order to approach the right customers and achieve turnover. To guide these efforts by the account managers and sales people and achieve a possible forecast, use can be made of the *Sales Funnel*.

The Sales Funnel is filled in for each account manager or sales person, thus for each person. Depending on the strategy of the enterprise, the market in which it operates is divided into segments, which together form the target group. Within the segments, one or more account managers may be actively approaching the market. This is depends on a number of factors like geography, number of customers, size of customers and the structure of one's own enterprise. Next to dividing the market into segments, the groups of accounts to be cultivated are established and divided among the account managers. They can subsequently make a forecast. Totalised, this produces a total forecast for the enterprise. This total forecast can moreover contain a number of subtotals, such as a one for each account manager, segment or sector.

Suspects, prospects and customers

The account manager will now make an analysis of the present situation for each account in the portfolio. Here it is important to distinguish between suspects, prospects and customers. A *suspect* is an account of which it has been established that there is a need for a product or service that is marketed by the enterprise, but there has still been no actual contact between the account and the account manager. A *prospect* is an account of which it has been established that a need for a product or service exists, where there has been contact between the account and the account manager and it has been established that the account will in time purchase an equivalent product or service from the enterprise or one of its competitors. A *customer* is defined as an account if between now and a year ago, it has purchased a product or service from the enterprise.

Forecast

In order to produce a good forecast, for each account the following criteria are established:
- budget
- need
- will
- Decision Making Unit (DMU)
- time

The forecast for each account manager is drafted on the basis of empirical figures that apply to this sector and the enterprise. The market of the enterprise is set at 100%. Of this, 40% is determined by the target group. After the inventory, within the target group 20% are selected as suspects. From the suspects, 7% are selected as prospects. Of these, 2% will ultimately become customers who will actually switch to the product or the service. The account manager or sales person can thereafter draft a sequence in which to approach the accounts, on the basis of the prioritisation of the criteria of the forecast. Here it applies that in the sequence, the customers are first, then the prospects and only then the suspects. Within these groups there can then be further sorting, on criteria determined by the account managers themselves.

Result

An overview is achieved for every account manager or sales person, where it can be seen what turnover can be expected for each account and which accounts should be approached first.

Focus areas

The model is rigid but has proven useful in practice. The account manager or sales person cannot follow this overview blindly. There are sometimes companies that suddenly turn up and can produce a high turnover. This phenomenon is called 'Blue bird'. A Blue bird is an order from a company from an unexpected direction or at an unexpected time.

Literature

- Feigon, J. (2010). *Smart Selling on the Phone and Online*. Amacom.
- Lambert, B. (2010). *10 Steps to Successful Sales*. American Society for Training & Development.
- http://alumni.actonmba.org/PDFs/Fall_Semester/Customers/The%20Sales%20Funnel%202007.pdf

82
Segmentation

Author	E. McCarthy
Year developed	1978
Also known as	Cluster Analysis, Decline Analysis, Market Segmentation
Objective	Division of the market into homogeneous customer groups to achieve a specific market approach for each segment

Model

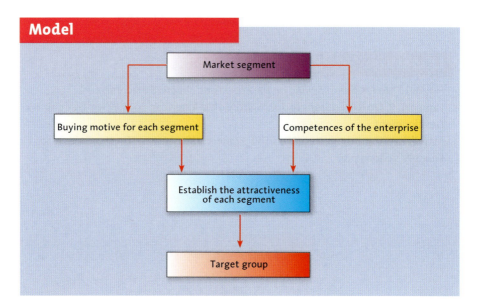

Background

The approach to customers cannot take place in the same way for all of them. Every person or company buys products and services on the basis of how they match this person or company. Moreover, the purchase depends on the need at the time. Enterprises can capitalise on this by seeing if groups of people or companies on which the marketing and sales efforts can be focused can be formed, so that a successful sales can be achieved. The process of division into groups is called segmentation. After the segmentation has been accomplished, the enterprise will have to choose one or more segments on which the marketing and sales efforts will be focused. This group of segments is called the target group of the enterprise. Good segmentation can only take place if there are sufficient customers with the same needs. If this is not the case, the enterprise will have to switch to personal sales and approach each customer separately in the right manner.

Application

To arrive at proper segmentation, the following steps are followed:

1 Demarcation of the market

Theoretically, the whole world is a market in which products and services can be sold. Dependent on the products or services the enterprise brings onto the market, there will exclusively be looked at the proportion of customers in the world that could possibly actually use the products or services. The demarcation of the market is an arbitrary process because not all the customers in the world can be investigated on their needs. There must, however, be a clear connection with the vision and mission of the enterprise. This connection must be such that the demarcated market falls within the objectives of the enterprise.

2 Collection of needs

For the selected customers, a survey will have to take place into their needs (see Research method). This is an important component of segmentation because the enterprise wishes to capitalise precisely on the needs of the customers with its products and services and is not approaching the market from the functions of its products or services.

3 Provisional segments

On the basis of the survey into their needs, the customers are classified in accordance with the different needs, from which groups of customers are created. These groups are then the provisional segments.

4 Elimination of similar characteristics

If all customers have given the same characteristic, for example price, this is then an overall need and not one that can be used for segmentation. Therefore, all the same characteristics are eliminated for segmentation. In this way, segmentation is created exclusively on the basis of the unique characteristics of each segment.

5 Definitive segments

Because all the same characteristics have now been filtered out, the definitive segments remain. If one or more segments are near enough the same in terms of characteristics, it will have to be seen if these segments can be combined into one segment. This is an arbitrary process.

6 Additional data

Any data lacking in the segments can be supplemented in this step to describe the segments fully. To this end, the following segmentation criteria can be used:

- Consumer market and B-2-B market
- Geographic criteria
- Demographic criteria
- Psychographic criteria
- Behavioural criteria

Next to the criteria for segmentation, each segment that is established will also have to comply with the following conditions:

- *Size*: the segment should be big enough to achieve turnover and profits.
- *Measurability*: the segment must be measurable, both in size and purchasing power.
- *Distinguishability*: the segments must be distinguishable from each other, otherwise mass marketing arises and there is thus only one segment.
- *Accessibility*: every segment must be accessible via the communications and distribution resources available to the enterprise.
- *Cultivability*: the enterprise will have to have the right methods and resources available to be able to cultivate the segment.

7 Quantification of segments

In order to be able to choose the target group, the segments are now supplemented with quantifiable data. A number of criteria for this are:

- size and growth
- degree of homogeneity
- competition intensity
- competition strategies
- product differentiation
- phase in product life cycle

Together with the purchasing motives and the competences of the enterprise, the most attractive segments can subsequently be selected as target groups. Furthermore, the enterprise can establish which segments are the most attractive to approach.

Result

The result of the segmentation is a demarcated market with customers that the enterprise can prioritise per segment on the basis of attractiveness. Moreover, the enterprise can approach each segment in a different way via the marketing mix, to achieve as much as possible turnover.

Focus areas

With segmentation of the market, it is easy to create over-segmentation, that is to say, segmentation carried through too much, due to which too many segments are created. Because of this, the positioning of the enterprise becomes more difficult, the products and/or services will in many cases have to be adapted for each segment and a separate marketing mix will have to be set up for each segment. The costs of over-segmentation often cannot compare to somewhat less segmentation.

Literature

- Weinstein, A. (2004). *Handbook of Market Segmentation*. The Haworth Press Inc.
- Cahill, D. (2006). *Lifestyle Market Segmentation*. The Hayworth Press Inc.

83
SERVQUAL

Authors	Parasuraman, Zeithaml and Berry
Year developed	1985
Also known as	Service Quality Model, GAP Model, RATER, P&B Model, American Model
Objective	Measuring the quality of the service of an enterprise

Model

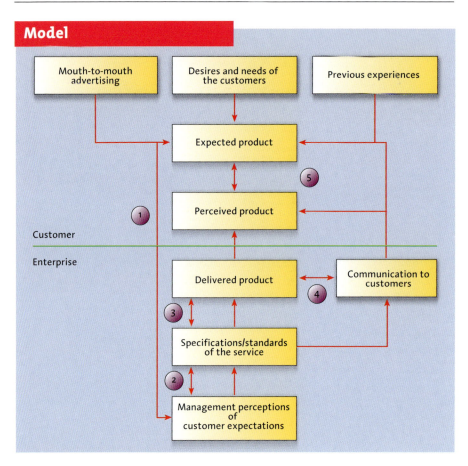

Background

To an increasing extent, enterprises are shifting their attention to the customers. Due to various developments, where information technology developments have played an important role, customers are much more knowledgeable about what can and cannot be done. Moreover, customers are much more mature, due to the information available and increased competition. Due to this, companies are compelled to focus more strongly on the satisfaction of their customers. With the SERVQUAL model, it is possible to gain insight into this satisfaction.

Application

An important starting point of the model is the definition of satisfaction. With the SERVQUAL model, satisfaction is understood to be: the difference between what the customer expects and what the customer experiences. It is therefore not about what the enterprise itself thinks but what the customers think, on the basis of their experience with the product or service of the enterprise. To measure this satisfaction, the model assumes nine variables to map out the quality of the service:

- reliability: keeping to promises
- responsiveness/response speed: immediate answers to questions
- competence/professional knowledge: rapid and effective response or referral
- accessibility/respect: and politeness towards customers
- communication: explaining to and informing the customer
- credibility: reputation of the organisation
- safety/security: the feeling of being at the right address
- understanding the customer: customised service/empathy
- tangible matters: facilities

The above variables are obtained through a market survey or a customer-satis-faction survey. To establish whether there is a difference in what the customer is promised and what the customer experiences, the same survey should take place among the personnel involved. In these questionnaires, at least the following questions should be included:

- What is for you the minimum service level for this variable?
- What is for you the desired service level for this variable?
- What is your perception of the service level for this variable?

These questions are necessary to establish what tolerances there are in the service levels (minimum and desired) and whether the score of the customers experience lies between these tolerances.

The model provides four causes (gaps) that enterprises must take into account with regard to the customer satisfaction of the service. The fifth gap is ultimately the result of the model: the difference between the expected service and the experienced service, expressed as the satisfaction of the customer. The size of these gaps depends on the following factors, which can be influenced by the enterprise:

- The management has a good picture of the expectations of the customer.
  - Carry out further surveys into the needs of the customer.
  - Improve vertical communication within the enterprise.
  - Reduce the number of hierarchical layers in the enterprise.
- The expectations of the customers are not correctly interpreted by the enterprise.
  - Increase the commitment of the management.
  - Establish objectives in a SMART way
  - Standardise tasks.
  - Develop a perception of the feasibility of customer wishes.
- The product or service is not delivered according to the specifications.
  - Increase the teamwork.
  - Put the right employees in the right positions.
  - Deploy the right machines and equipment.
  - Increase the responsibility of employees.
  - Measure both quantity and quality.
  - Ensure a good process flow (transfer) between the processes (employees) from one process (department) to the other.
- The marketing communication arouses false expectations.
  - Promise less to the customers, especially not what cannot be lived up to.

The total of these four gaps indicates the degree of customer satisfaction.

Result

On the basis of the questionnaires among the customers and the personnel, the satisfaction of the customers can be established compared to what the enterprise itself thinks. On the basis of this comparison, the enterprise can steer towards the aspects mentioned in the four gaps, to increase satisfaction.

Focus areas

For every enterprise and in every situation it should be established whether the five gaps are indeed all gaps. This also applies to the nine variables for measuring satisfaction.

Literature

- Zeithaml, V. & Bitner, M. (2002). *Services Marketing*. Irwin/McGraw-Hill.
- Carr, D. (2002). A Psychometric Evaluation of the Expectations, Perceptions and Difference Scores Generated by the IS-Adapted SERVQUAL Instrument. *Decision Sciences* 33 (2), 281–296.
- http://www.businessadvantageuk.biz/SERVQUAL.htm

84
Seven-S Model

Authors	R. Pascale, T. Peters, R. Waterman
Year developed	1980
Also known as	7-s Framework, McKinsey 7-S model
Objective	Analysis of internal organisation

Model

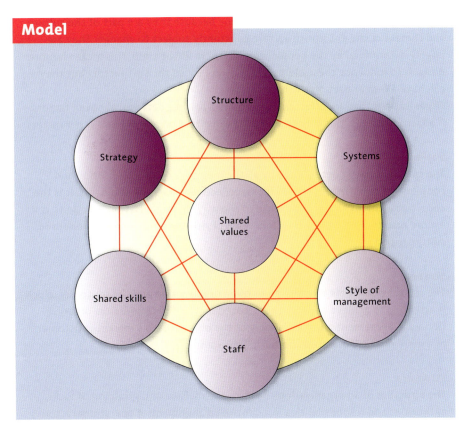

Background

The 7-S model describes the seven important aspects of an organisation and functions as a diagnostic checklist for these most important organisational aspects. The system is intended to assess the quality of organisations. Thereby attention is paid not only to the hard side of the enterprise, such as strategy and organisational structure, but also to the soft elements, such as management style and personnel. The 7-S model indicates what an organisation must pay attention to. The model also indicates that there are relationships between the factors; for example, management style and the versatility of the personnel are related.

The model is called the 7-S model because all the factors with which an organisation is concerned begin with the letter S.

Application

The seven factors in the model are divided into 'hard S's and 'soft S's. The hard factors can easily be established and identified. They are established in the strategy of the enterprise, the structure of the organisation and in documents. These are the Strategy, Structure and Systems.

The soft factors are more difficult to define because they are part of the culture and climate of the enterprise and are constantly subject to change. They are largely determined by the people working there at the time. This makes it more difficult to influence these elements. They are called the soft factors but they can have a firm impact on the hard factors.

Organisations that are effective have found a balance between all seven factors. If a factor changes, this almost always has an effect on one or more other factors.

Shared values

The culture is partly determined by all the members of an organisation and contains the sum total of shared ideas, collective values and standards. It is the collective element that makes sense of the way the organisation functions. Is it a more results-oriented culture (takes lots of risks) or a more process-oriented culture (risk-avoiding)?

Strategy

The strategy concerns the objectives of an organisation and the routes by which it attempts to achieve them. Is there, based on the defined mission, organisation-wide agreement and consistency of the objectives in a market-, customer- or a more product-oriented approach, for example?

Structure

The structure of an organisation concerns the division and grouping of tasks, authorities and responsibilities in a controlled alignment of operational activities and functions. If the organisation is more centralised, with few authorities for individuals or does the organisation comprise several autonomous units, each with its own authorities?

Systems

The systems encompass all formal and informal methods, procedures, regulations and agreements, according to which the processes should proceed. It is essential to compare their performance with the established standards, identify the differences and in case of a significant difference, take measures to ensure that all the resources are used in an effective and efficient manner to achieve the objectives of the organisation.

Style of management

Style refers to management style. This does not mean the personalities of the people in (top) management, but the way in which the actions and behaviour of the managers are perceived by the personnel in the organisation. Are the managers directive or more coaching towards the personnel? It is not what the management says but what it does that is determinative.

Shared skills

Shared skills focus on what makes ones own organisation stand out. What is the organisation good at? One could think of organisations that are well-known for their service, innovative strength or production capacity. Are there many experienced personnel in the organisation that need freedom to act or more inexperienced personnel for whom a certain amount of guidance from above is desirable?

Staff

Staff refers to a number of matters. On the one hand it concern things like non-appearance, absenteeism and training levels. On the other, it concerns more abstract matters, like the motivation and flexibility.

Result

The result indicates whether the factors of the enterprise are in balance. The effectiveness of the enterprise is thereby determined. The model provides the possibility with a strategic plan to compare the seven factors of the current situation with the seven factors of the new situation and so establish whether the new strategy is not only supported in the hard factors, but also in the soft ones.

Focus areas

Many enterprises steer exclusively on the hard factors and are consequently hardly effective.
Researchers often follow the model as a checklist and describe the seven factors separately. Connecting them mutually and bringing them into balance is often not done.
The model aims to be a diagnostic tool. This can exclusively be used correctly if the diagnosis is compared with the results of many other companies that have undergone the same diagnosis. This data base is only available via McKinsey.

Literature

- Peters, T.J. & Waterman, R.H. (2004). *In search of excellence: lessons from America's best run companies*. Harper Business Essentials.
- Pascale, R. & Athos, A. (1982). *The Art of Japanese Management*. Penguin Books Ltd.

85
SIT Method

Author	Roni Horowitz
Year developed	2001
Also known as	Systematic Inventive Thinking
Objective	Thinking up successful new ideas

Model

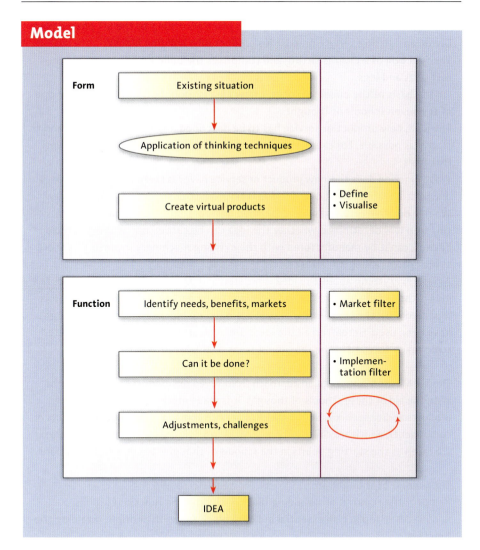

General management

Strategy

Marketing

Sales

Purchasing

Project & Planning

Production

Quality

Logistics & Distribution management

Information

Financial

HRM & HTM

Internationalisation

Background

Thinking up new inventions is reserved for very few people. Thinking up new ideas from nowhere on the basis of brainstorming sessions and 'out of the box' thinking can lead to non-feasible ideas, because they do not take into account the existing situation of the enterprise with regard to finances and machinery inventory. There are more possibilities if you start from the existing product range and go to work on innovations 'closer to home'. The SIT Method offers enterprises the possibility to think up new ideas on the basis of existing products or services, with the aid of seven different schools of thought. These seven schools of thought have proven themselves in the past and are now combined in the SIT Method.

Application

The actual thinking up of new ideas takes place according to the SIT phased plan:

1 Divide an existing service or existing product into building blocks.
   The function of a chair is sitting and comprises the building blocks back, armrest, seat and legs.
2 On the basis of the building blocks, a new idea is thought up with the aid of one of the seven schools of thought.
3 The idea, new product or service has to be described and visualised as well and as clearly as possible. For example: what does a washing machine with two drums look like?
4 What function does this new product or service have? Is there demand for it or can one be stimulated? What benefits does this product or service have for the user?
5 When a positive result has been obtained in step 4, step 5 can commence. In this step it is determined whether the idea can be carried out. Is there sufficient budget, can it be manufactured with the existing machinery inventory, is there sufficient knowledge in-house?
6 As last, everything about the idea is ordered and parts are possibly adjusted. The idea is then ready and the SIT phased plan can be performed again. This cycle is repeated until the time is over and all the building blocks or schools of thought have been used. Hereafter, all the ideas are evaluated and the best are selected to be taken forward in the remaining steps of the SIT project.

The SIT Method comprises an approach from seven different schools of thought. With the aid of these schools of thought, it is made much easier to devise new products and/or services. Each product or service comprises a number of aspects or components, which are called building blocks in SIT. Precisely these building blocks are taken as the starting points in the schools of thought, to come to innovations.

The schools of thought are:
- *Removal*: the removal of a building block, including the function it fulfils.
- *Replacement*: replace an essential building block and with another, retaining the function.

- *Connection*: make a connection between the product and the environment, through which the product takes over an extra task from the environment.
- *Copy*: copy a building block of the product, change something in the copy and put it back in the original product.
- *Divide*: divide the product into building blocks.
- *Rearrange*: rearrange the building blocks in time and/or space.
- *Disruption of symmetry*: a variable has different values in different places and/or times.

These seven different schools of thought do not *per se* need to be carried out in this order. Regardless of which method is used first, it turns out that the school of thought used often produces fifty per cent of the ideas.

Result

The result of the SIT Method consists in a number of ideas for new products or services that can be brought onto the market. These products or services usually require no heavy or high investments because this method starts from existing products or services.

Focus areas

Innovations usually lie in simplicity and creativity. The method supports simplicity but the creativity is in the freedom of thinking through which new concepts are devised. Due to the systematic model, the creativity can be destroyed. Because the method is still very young, these suppositions have not yet been substantiated, however.

Literature

- www.start2think.com/new.html
- www.sitsite.com

86

Situational Leadership Theory

Authors	**Hersey & Blanchard**
Year developed	**1969**
Also known as	**SLM, Situational Leadership Model (SLM), the parcipative leadership style, Contingency Models**
Objective	**Providing effective leadership**

Model

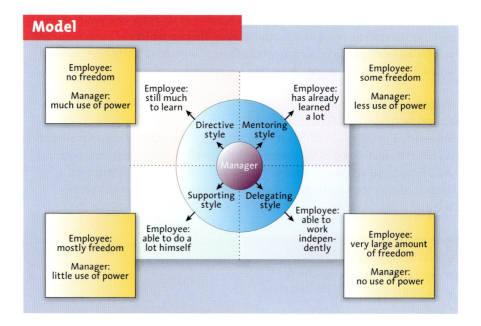

Background

The model of Hersey & Blanchard falls under the heading of situational leadership. Situational leadership means that the leader adapts his leadership style to the necessary style in every situation. To this end, it is necessary that the leader, if he wishes to be successful, is able to understand his or her own behaviour and that of the personnel and properly assess the current situation.

Application

The starting point with the application of this model is the task maturity of the personnel. For this, the leader must first of all establish: which style of leadership suits

Sidebar navigation labels:
General management | Strategy | Marketing | Sales | Purchasing | Project & Planning | Production | Quality | Logistics & Distribution | Information management | Financial | HRM & HTM | Internationalisation

him or her best, how many styles of leadership suit him or her and to what extent it is possible for him or her to adapt to the situation and the personnel under their leadership. The model of Hersey & Blanchard identifies four leadership styles:

- directive style
- mentoring or coaching style
- supporting style
- delegating style

Two of these leadership styles are task-oriented, the directive and mentoring style, and two are relationship-oriented, the supporting and delegating style. The task-oriented styles are on the basis that the manager explains concretely to the personnel how and what to do and monitors this closely. The relationship-oriented styles assume a great degree of independence for the personnel. The leader will steer in a results-oriented fashion and he facilitates the personnel. Furthermore, the model assumes a certain task maturity of the personnel. This task maturity is indicated in two components: the competence to carry out a task and preparedness to accept the corresponding responsibility. Due to this, the following levels of task maturity arise:

- Disillusioned trainee: not competent, not prepared
- Enthusiastic beginner: not competent, but prepared
- Reluctant employee: competent, not prepared
- Top performer: competent and prepared

On the basis of the above starting points, four styles of leadership arise: delegation, consultation, persuasion and instruction.

Delegation
The manager gives little direction and steers towards results. The personnel are assigned the responsibilities and authorities needed to carry out their tasks. The personnel report on results and bottlenecks.

Consultation
The manager supports the employees in the performance of their activities. The personnel receive little direction and decisions are taken jointly by employees and managers.

Persuasion
Both relationship- and task-oriented behaviour is maintained by the manager. Next to actual direction the personnel receive, a great deal of attention is paid to support in their performance.

Instruction
The manager indicates what and how activities must be carried out. They are also checked in detail by the manager. Further support is lacking.

The model provides the personnel with the possibility to grow in the development of task maturity. This consists in the development of:

- D1, the leader tells the personnel what they must do.
- D2, the leader shows the personnel what to do.
- D3, the leader allows the personnel to try it themselves, where some risk is entailed.
- D4, the leader observes the results and focuses on the positive.

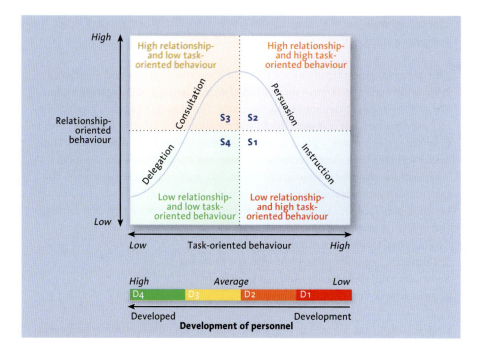

Result

The result that can be achieved is broad and supports the realisation of self-governing teams that work in a results-oriented fashion on the objectives of the enterprise. The leader needs less time for these teams and still gets the right results. This makes it possible to situate the tasks, responsibilities and authorities lower in the organisation: *empowerment*.

Focus areas

The qualities of the leader are often underestimated and adaptation to situations and personnel on the basis of a leadership style that is not one's own can lead to a breach between manager and personnel.

Literature

- Hersey, P., Blanchard, K. & Kenneth, H. (2008). *Management of Organizational Behaviour: Leading Human Resources.* Upper Saddle River, NY: Pearson Prentice Hall.
- Dubrin A. (2010). Leadership: research Findings. Practice, and Skills, Cengage Learning.
- www.leadership-expert.co.uk/

87
SIVA

Authors	Chekitan, S. Dev and Don E. Schultz
Year developed	2005
Also known as	Solution-Information-Value-Access
Objective	Development of a more customer-oriented marketing mix

Model

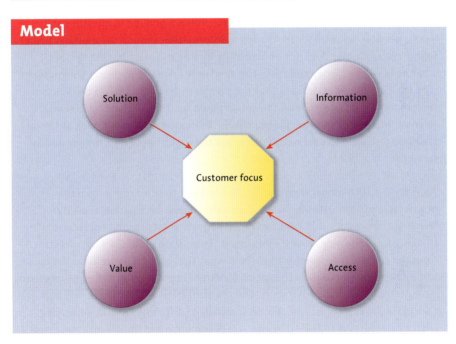

Background

The '4 Ps' in the marketing mix have a strong focus on thinking from the product towards the customer. The enterprise produces new products and tries to bring them to the customers via promotion, with an attractive price and via the distribution channels. Due to the developments the Internet has introduced, there is more and more information available. Information should be seen from a broader perspective in this context. Via the Internet, there are already possibilities to experience the 'look and feel' of the products. Due to the possibilities of the Internet, the requirements of the customers are becoming increasingly individualised. Enterprises should capitalise on this. The framework in which enterprises communicate with customers has consequently changed radically. Product has been replaced by *Solution*; Promotion by *Information*, Price by *Value* and Place for *Access*, or SIVA. The enterprise will hence think in a more customer-oriented manner.

Application

To apply the SIVA model in practice, employees will have to assume a different pattern of thought, namely from the viewpoint of customers with a need. Naturally, one must also know if this need also requires a solution. Customers search for a solution to satisfy their needs or resolve a problem. From this train of thought, the customer searches for information to establish whether the solution satisfies the wishes and requirements he has set. This search proceeds via various channels and the different media to friends, colleagues and acquaintances, who also know something about the problem or need in question and have a possible solution for it. As soon as information about a solution has been found, the customer does not immediately look at the price but establishes what he is willing to pay to satisfy the need or resolve the problem. The moment that the customer has decided that the price is in accordance with the value of the product or service, follows the actual purchase. The customer also wants to know where this solution is obtainable. The customer does not look at the standard distribution channels for this, but the easiest access to the product or service for him or her.

To apply the SIVA model, employees will also have to think more from the perspective of the customer: what does he/she want to do or achieve? SIVA thinking can produce different and much larger markets for the enterprise than thinking from the older four P's viewpoint. There is no more thinking directly from the customer's viewpoint but from what the solution delivers for the customer. Here, the focus is on the social, functional and emotional dimensions that a solution fulfils for the customers. The segmentation of the market will also take place differently, in any case on the basis of different criteria. Observing what customers do and why they do it is becoming more important than dividing communities or companies on the basis of sex or sector.

Solution

When devising the solution, it is no longer all about the product that is available, but more about what solution can be found for the problem or need. A solution is nowadays often a combination of a physical product and an information component. Look at the mobile telephone, with which the physical phone calls can be made and where, with all kinds of software ring tones, the solution can be personalised.

Information

The promotion is attuned to the size of the group of customers. The greater the market scope, the lower the quality and detail in the content of the message can be. Thus the more people approached, the simpler the message. This has disadvantages because many customers then receive too vague a message and do not know whether their needs will be covered. Due to the technology that is available, modern promotions can be rich in information and still appeal to a very broad target group. Here, the customers search for information on the solution to their problem or fulfilling their needs. Both when searching for the solution and the development of it, the Internet provides the possibility to make this wealth of information available

Value

Value is what the customer bases the acquisition on, usually benefits and price. But this concerns the benefits of the functions of the item. Nowadays, customers see value in a much broader spectrum. Sources of value are:

- confidence
- image
- returned products
- customisation
- relationship with the brand
- service
- user groups
- access to information
- correct information
- speed and ease
- being taken seriously
- accessibility 7 days a week 24 hours a day

This is not an exhaustive list but it indicates that the value of the solution no longer lies solely in the benefits or functionality of the product. The digitised aspects of the solution have the advantage that they can be attuned to the specific wishes of customers and that customers can simply download new solutions via the Internet, separately from the physical distribution channels.

Access

When doing business via a 'wire' (the Internet) it does not matter how long that wire is. This provides customers all over the world with the possibility to look up the information required at the time. This wire also makes it possible to order from and have delivery to anywhere in the world. If the information the customer requests is not available, one can simply switch to suppliers or partners who perhaps do have this information. Formerly, vertical and horizontal integration, Mergers and Takeovers were *the* means to keep on servicing customers. With the current possibilities of information technology, enterprises collaborate by linking their information systems. Due to this, customers also have direct access to the data of the suppliers. Enterprises should however realise that a Multi-channel approach is still desired. People want to see and feel some solutions before the purchase actually takes place.

Result

The result is a different perspective on the market, due to which the market can be serviced in a different way. It concerns a market that is much more diverse and bigger. This approach also fits in with the manner in which increasingly more customers are searching for their solutions in the market. If an enterprise wishes to remain in existence in the longer term, then it currently seems to be necessary to step away from the 4 P's and make use of the SIVA model.

Focus areas

SIVA is an ongoing development in the market. There is still little theoretically substantiating literature. The application of SIVA thus requires a change in the thinking of the employees of the enterprise and the involved partners.

Literature

- Dev, S. & Schultz, Don E. (2005). A Customer-focused Approach Can Bring the Current Marketing Mix into the 2lst Century. *Marketing Management*. 1 January/February 2005.
- Christensen, C., Cook, S. & Hall, T. (2005). Marketing Malpractice: The Cause and the Cure. *Harvard Business Review*, 83 (12).

88
Six Sigma

Author	Motorola, Mikel Harry
Year developed	Initially, in 1979
Also known as	$6\sum$
Objective	Quality and process improvement

General management

Strategy

Marketing

Sales

Purchasing

Project & Planning

Production

Quality

Logistics & Distribution

Information management

Financial

HRM & HTM

Internationalisation

Model

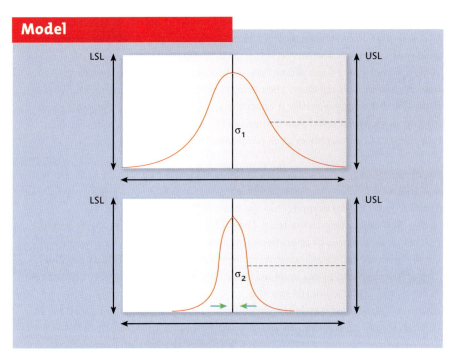

Background

Six Sigma ($6\sum$) is a method for improving the quality of the processes in an enterprise. Each time that process is executed, variation can occur with respect to the results of the previous time.

Sigma	% good	% bad	DPMO
1	30.9%	69.1%	691.462
2	69.1%	30.9%	308.538
3	93.3%	6.7%	66.807
4	99.38%	0.62%	6.210
5	99.977%	0.023%	233,0
6	99.9997%	0.00034%	3.4

These deviations are called 'defects' and expressed in the number of deviations per million possibilities or 'Defects Per Million Opportunities'(DPMO). The deviation expressed in sigma comes from statistics, where the value of sigma goes from 0 to 6 inclusive. The aspiration here is to have as few as possible defects. With six sigma there are maximally 3.4 defects per million opportunities, where 99.9997% good products are produced. An important aspect of this method is that it departs from the wishes of the customer and the defects are based on solid measurements and not on intuition or average values.

With this method, a fixed phased plan is followed to achieve the process improvements. This concerns the business processes of the enterprise, where it makes no difference whether it concerns a manufacturing or a service-providing company. The phased plan comprises the steps *Define, Measure, Analysis, Improve* and *Control*, abbreviated to DMAIC.

Application

The Six Sigma model is applied on the basis of five steps:
1 *Define*. Before starting to measure, the problem must first be properly defined. Furthermore, the area of operations should be demarcated to narrow the survey area so that measurable objectives are attained as quickly as possible. Thereafter, the employees involved must be selected to investigate the process in detail and propose improvements.
2 *Measure*. The second step is the collection of data and making preparations for its analysis and interpretation.
3 *Analysis*. After documentation and verification of the data, the analysis can begin. Activities where the employees are insufficiently able to act effectively or do not succeed in applying efficient supervision, are selected and identified.
4 *Improve*. For each activity, it is established from the analysis step in what way it can be improved.
5 *Control*. The last step is the development and maintenance of the improvement objectives and implementing them on the work floor. Moreover, a system is set up to ensure maintenance of the improvements.

To carry out these steps properly, employees (internal and external) are needed with knowledge of the method. The project should be supported by the (top) management. Within Six Sigma, four roles are distinguished:

- *Master Black Belts*: trainers, usually from an external bureau.
- *Black Belts*: project leaders, with specialist training (1% of personnel).
- *Green Belts*: project employees with basic training (10% of personnel).
- *Project employees*: employees with only internal training.

Result

The results that the application of this method can deliver are immense. Every process of the enterprise can be improved with this model. Deployment of this model on the critical processes helps an enterprise to better achieve its objectives. Examples of improvements are:
- extremely low defect levels
- at least 99% customer satisfaction
- higher productivity
- drastic reductions in throughput time
- spectacular cost reductions
- total approach with regard to quality

Focus areas

Although Six Sigma almost always leads to good results, a consideration should be made with regard to the investment in time and money. The method requires time and energy from the employees of the enterprise at both high and low levels.

Literature

- Snee, R., Hoerl, R. (2009). *Leading Six Sigma*. Financial Times Management.
- Pries, K. (2007). *Six Sigma for the next Millennium*. Quality Press.
- http://www.leaninstituut.nl/publications/ASQ%20story%20quality,sigma%20and%20olean.pdf
- www.sixsigma.eu

89
Stakeholder Management

Authors	D. Wheeler and M. Sillanpää, Gilmore and Beilin
Year developed	1997
Also known as	Stakeholder mapping, Socially responsible capitalism, Expectations Management
Objective	Stakeholder analysis

Model

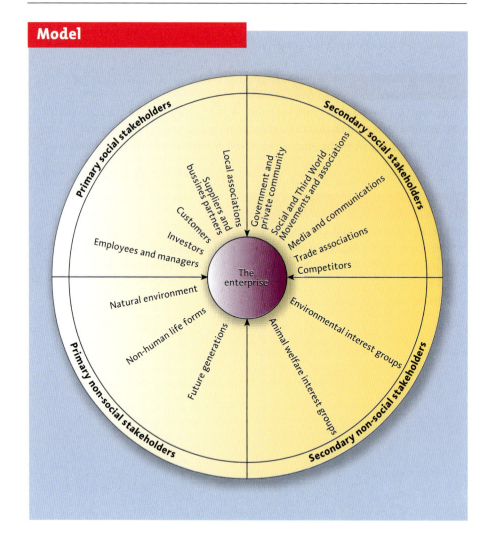

Background

According to Freeman, a *stakeholder* is:

> 'any individual or group of individuals that can influence the enterprise or be influenced by the enterprise's activities.'

It immediately becomes clear that mapping out the stakeholders is important to the enterprise. Stakeholders must not be confused with *shareholders*, who have purchased a share in the enterprise. Where the management of an enterprise was until recently focused on these shareholders and the value of the shares, directed by socially responsible capitalism, the management now, focuses more on all the stakeholders in the enterprise. Wheeler and Sillanpää have applied the classification shown in the diagram (page 322). Further mapping out via this classification is assisted by determining how great the involvement of the stakeholders is and whether they are for or against the policy of the enterprise.

Application

To map out the stakeholders, according to Gilmour and Beilin (2006), the following steps must be undertaken:
1 identification of the stakeholders
2 analysis of the stakeholders
3 visualisation of the stakeholders
4 deployment of the stakeholders

Mapping out the stakeholders takes place in order to achieve the objectives established by the organisation. This can be done more successfully if the enterprise knows which interests the stakeholders have. The enterprise should take into account not only those stakeholders who support these objectives, but also those who are against it.

1 Identification of stakeholders
To identify all the stakeholders, the environmental factors must first be established. This occurs based on the following questions:
- Are we looking for the local, national or international stakeholders?
- What type of stakeholders must be mapped out?
- What data are of interest?

Hereafter follows a brainstorming session with internal employees to inventory all the relevant stakeholders. Here, the questions 'Who can influence the enterprise?' and 'Who is influenced by the enterprise?' are foremost. Subsequently, every stakeholder is contacted to establish whether via these stakeholders more stakeholders of interest can be approached.

2 Analysis of the stakeholders

The following step is the collection and analysis of the stakeholders by means of the following questions:

- How great is their involvement (expressed in involvement and interest)?
- How much power has the stakeholder?
- What is their attitude? (Is the stakeholder for or against?)
- What relationships are there with other stakeholders?

This overview can best be put in a matrix.

Stakeholder	Involvement	Power	Attitude	Relationships

3 Visualisation of stakeholders

To obtain a picture as quickly as possible, a graphic overview of the stakeholders can be made.

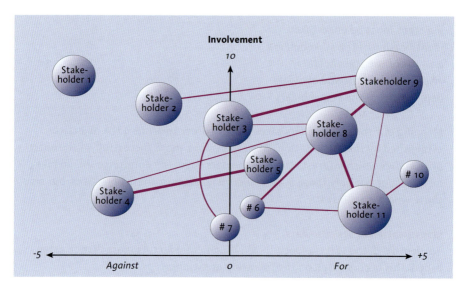

In the above diagram, the various stakeholders are represented as circles. The size of the circle indicates the power of the stakeholder. Vertically, the involvement of the stakeholder is represented, comprising the involvement of the stakeholder in the subject or the enterprise and interest that the stakeholder has in the subject or the enterprise. On the horizontal axis are proponents and opponents. It is also important to look at stakeholders that are neither for nor against. These stakeholders still have to make a choice and can thus be directly influenced. Finally, the lines indicate the relationships between the stakeholders. The thickness of the line indicates the strength of the relationship.

With the aid of this overview, the following role models can be defined:

- Change champion: this person helps personally, is for and is highly involved.
- Friendly helper: this person likes to help.
- Doubter: waits to see what happens before making a decision.
- Cynic: is negative about everything and tries to tempt everyone 'to spill the beans'.
- Enemy: is by definition against and does everything to oppose.

Important about the doubters is that they have not yet made a choice and thus can be persuaded into the position of friendly helper.

4 Deployment of stakeholders
Now it is clear which stakeholders play what roles, activities can be organised directed towards involving these stakeholders in the achievement of the established objectives. The table from step 2 'analysis of stakeholders' can now be extended by two columns.
- What expertise of the stakeholder can be used?
- How can the stakeholder become involved in the project?

Result

Because it is clear who has what interests in achieving the established objectives, each stakeholder can also better be steered towards actually achieving them. Stakeholder mapping also provides a picture of governmental and non-governmental organisations that play a role in, usually large, companies. By paying better attention to the stakeholders, they become more loyal to the enterprise. Long-term results can be achieved with this.

Focus areas

Filling in the model completely and the activities to be performed takes time and energy. The results are certainly worth it. It is important that the model is filled in objectively and not by one person. The latter is too arbitrary.

Literature

- Wheeler, D. & Sillanpää, M. (1997). *The stakeholder corporation: A blueprint for maximizing stakeholder value.* London: Pitman publishing.
- Bourne L. (2010). *Stakeholder Relationship Management.* Ashgate Publishing Company.
- Gilmour, J. & Beilin, R. (2006). *Stakeholder mapping for effective risk assessment and communication.* University of Melbourne.

90
Strategic Alignment Model

Authors	J. Henderson and N. Venkatraman
Year developed	1993
Also known as	SAM, SAME, The Alignment Paradox, Business and IT alignment
Objective	Alignment of organisation and information technology

Model

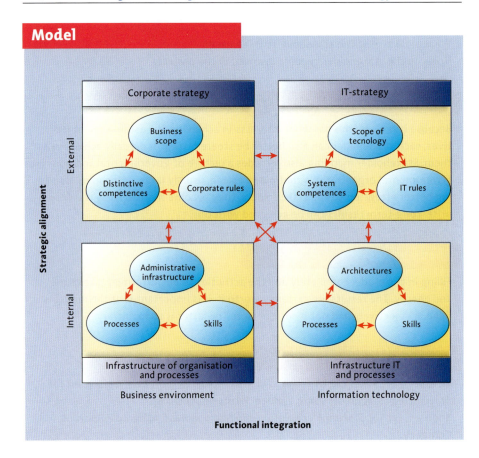

Background

Changes in the processes of organisations have a direct influence on the support provided by its IT systems. Due to new technological developments, it is increasingly easy for enterprises to adapt their IT systems to new situations. This does not mean that an analysis positively has to be made to establish which IT systems must be adapted in what way to be able to support the new or changed processes in the enterprise. This is usually called Business and IT alignment.

Application

The SAM model departs from two viewpoints: functional integration and strategic alignment. Moreover, the model is based on four fundamental domains, namely:
- corporate strategy
- IT strategy
- infrastructure of the organisation and processes
- infrastructure of the IT and processes

Each domain has its own dimensions: for each domain there are three dimensions. A model is thus created with twelve components on the basis of which the corporate strategy and the IT strategy can be attuned to each other.

Corporate strategy
- Business scope: all aspects concerned with an enterprise, such as markets, products, service, segments, locations, competition.
- Distinctive competences: critical success factors and core competences with which the enterprise distinguishes itself from the competition, such as brand name, innovation, cost and price structure, sales and distribution channels.
- Corporate rules: how alignment is arranged between management, shareholders, stakeholders and the board of management. Furthermore, the mutual relationships and alignments with the partners of the enterprise fall under this.

Infrastructure of the organisation and processes
- Administrative structure: how is the enterprise organised?
- Processes: what processes are there in the enterprise and how do they add value?
- Skills: personnel policy with regard to hiring/firing, motivation and training, as well as the culture within the enterprise.

IT strategy
- Technology scope: the computerised information systems (applications and technology).
- System competences: the distinctive capacity of the IT services (making the necessary information available to support the strategy).
- IT rules: how is the alignment on the deployment, acquisition and use of IT systems between management, users, IT personnel and service providers?

IT infrastructure and processes
- Architecture: the design of the IT systems with regard to technology, applications and infrastructure.
- Processes: the activities that must be performed for the development and maintenance of the IT systems.

- Skills: personnel policy with regard to hiring/firing, motivation and training, as well as the culture within the enterprise.

Strategic alignment and Functional integration

Because the four domains must collaborate as a whole, there are mutual relationsips. The first is strategic alignment. This alignment determines the processes and activities the enterprise must undertake to implement the strategy. The second alignment concerns functional integration. Functional integration is the most direct alignment between company and IT. When the business processes change, their IT support must also be adapted. A lead is gained over the competition if the IT systems can quickly be adapted to changes in the organisation.

The alignment between the company and its IT can subsequently take place in eight different ways. This is schematically represented in the following figure. For each block with an arrow, the following principles apply:

- Starting point: what is the starting point? The domain that is strongest. The starting point is the place where the arrow begins. This is the fundamental domain and changes first.
- Adaptation: what must be adapted? The arrow runs from one domain via a second domain to a third, where the arrow ends. The second domain must be adapted due to the change in the domain at the starting point.
- Effect: what does the adaptation affect? This is the domain where the arrow ends. As a consequence of the changes in the preceding domains, these changes will have an effect on the domain where the arrow ends.

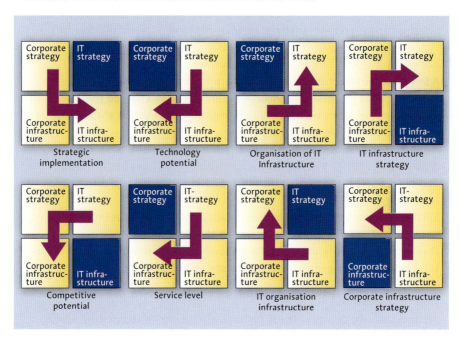

In these eight different ways, the IT can be attuned to developments within the company. Each of these eight ways has its own name on the basis of the angle of approach taken.

Result

From different approach angles, the corporate strategy and the corporate infrastructure with respect to the IT strategy and infrastructure can be mutually aligned. Due to this mutual alignment, the enterprise can quickly satisfy the wishes and requirements of the market with the aid of the IT systems and so achieve competitive advantage.

Focus areas

The model includes no approach for the ultimate change process itself.

Literature

- Henderson, J.C. & Venkatraman, N. (1993). Strategy alignment: Leveraging information technology for transforming organizations, *IBM Systems Journal,* 32 (1), 1993.
- Chew, E., Gottschalk, P. (2009). *Information Technology Strategy and Management*. IGI Global.
- Cater-Steel, A. (2009). *Information technology Governance and Service Management* (Chapter XII). IGI Global.

91
Strategy Clock

Authors	C. Bowman and D. Faulkner
Year developed	1995
Also known as	Strategic clock, Customer Matrix
Objective	Establishing competitive position

Model

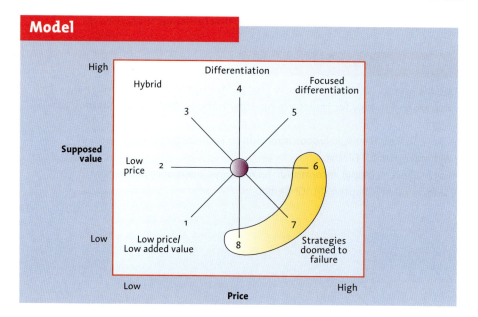

Background

Customers usually select a product/service on the basis of price and added value. The higher the added value and the lower the price, the more interesting the customers regards it. With the model of Bowman and Faulkner, the enterprise can choose from eight strategies with regard to price and added value.

Application

The application of this model is not so much in the steps to be carried out as in the choices an enterprise can make on the basis of the matrix. These choices are based on the price a customer has to pay for a product or service and the added value the customer experiences.

1 Low price and low added value

This strategy comprises a low price and low added value. There is focus on those market segments that exclusively buy on price and expect no further added value. Furthermore, there is no regard for what the competition is bringing onto the market. For example, Lada and Aldi.

2 Low price

This strategy comprises retaining a low price but in combination with at least the same added value as the competition offers.

Strategies 1 and 2 are low-price-strategies and can only be successful if the enterprise:
- Is cost-leader: this is a very ambitious strategy and only a few enterprises can achieve this. Exclusively those enterprises that routinely manufacture products are able to achieve this position. In all aspects of the enterprise, all costs must be kept as low as possible. For example, no more face-to-face selling but only a web-shop where the customers can order themselves. Due to this, no showrooms or shops are necessary either.
- Can outsource activities that do not produce customer value.
- Operates in a segment that considers low prices important and where the enterprise can achieve cost benefits with respect to the competition.

3 Hybrid strategy

The hybrid strategy starts from a low price but with higher added value than the competition. The challenge in this strategy is the insight that the enterprise must obtain to achieve greater added value, by both understanding the customers' needs and also actually fulfilling them. This will have to be achieved simultaneously at a low price. For example, Ikea.
This strategy is one where, with the aid of information technology, among other things, customer benefits can be achieved, for example, in consumer electronics. With the aid of information technology, everyone can organise their mobile telephones as they wish. However, these devices are still mass produced. This is called *mass customisation*.

4 Differentiation strategy

This strategy comprises a distinctive capacity with respect to the competition with regard to added value for customers. Better products and services are produced at the same price as the competition with this strategy.

5 Focused differentiation

This strategy is similar to the differentiation strategy, the difference being that the enterprise now focuses on one segment.

Strategies 4 and 5 are successful if the enterprise:
- continues to produce distinctive products/services
- knows better than the competition what the customer wants; branding and image are important here
- remains close to its core competences

Strategies 4 and 5 lend themselves excellently for production to customer specifications. Information can first be made available via web sites, after which the details are elaborated in face-to-face discussions.

Wrong strategies
Strategies 6, 7 and 8 are the undesired strategies. These strategies do not lead to a successful enterprise. Strategy 6 produces a higher price for the customer but the added value remains the same. Strategy 7 increases the price for the customer while the added value is reduced. Strategy 8 finally, reduces the added value for the customer at the same price.

Result

The two aspects price and added value are by definition at odds with each other. More added value often means a higher price. Depending on the product or service provided, a structured choice can be made for the basic strategy of the enterprise. Depending on the strategy selected, operational implementation will be different. Price-associated strategies focus more on scale. Differentiation strategies focus on the distinctive capacity of the enterprise with respect to the competition.

Focus areas

When following the different strategies, the enterprise must pay attention to the fact that from strategy 2, it is easy to fall back on strategy 1. Furthermore, there is a clear difference between strategies 4 and 5. With strategy 5, the focus is on only one segment. Here it is necessary that the enterprise knows exactly what needs of the customers in this segment are and how to capitalise on them.

Literature

- Bowman, C. & Faulkner. D. (1995). *The Essence of Competitive Strategy*. Harlow: Prentice Hall.
- Johnson G., Scholes K. & Whittington R. (2006). *Exploring Corporate Strategy*. Harlow: Prentice Hall.

92
Strategy Map

Authors	R. Kaplan and P. Norton
Year developed	2004
Also known as	Strategic Linhage Model
Objective	Transition from strategy to measurable indicators

Model

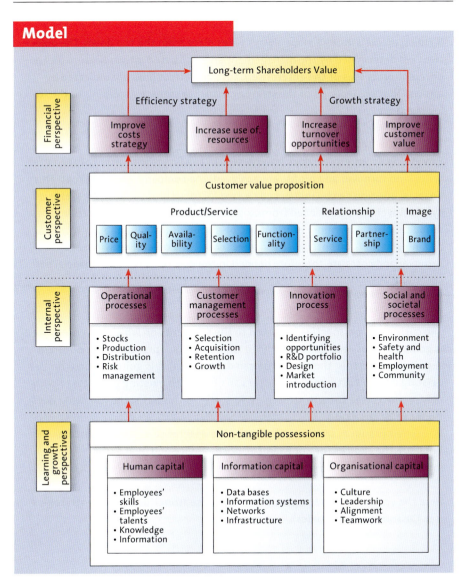

General management
Strategy
Marketing
Sales
Purchasing
Project & Planning
Production
Quality
Logistics & Distribution
Information management
Financial
HRM & HTM
Internationalisation

Background

For enterprises, the question is how they must translate the policy of the management correctly into concrete guiding variables for the employees. The policy is still too vague for the employees. Employees are more and more involved in the policy but have difficulty translating abstract policy into their own activities. Due to this, an instrument like the Balanced Scorecard (BSC), also by the authors Kaplan and Norton, will not lead to insight for the management to steer the enterprise effectively. To make the transition and the link with the BSC and the indicators, Kaplan and Norton have developed the strategy map or strategy maps. These link the actions that the employees must perform to the four perspectives of the BSC and thereby directly to the policy.

Application

Building up the strategy maps always takes place from the top down. The objectives are determined by the management and translated into indicators for the different processes of the enterprise. Cause and effect links are indicated by arrows. The construction of the strategy maps takes place according to the following steps:

1 Describe the financial perspective

Everything an enterprise does is expressed in the financial position of the enterprise. If no turnover and profits are achieved, the company goes bankrupt. This financial position can be influenced by two factors: turnover and costs (efficiency). Turnover can be achieved from existing customers, new customers and new products. By making more efficient use of resources (machines, people, capital and information), an enterprise can lower costs. The objectives with regard to turnover and costs are therefore defined in the description of the financial perspective.

2 Describe the customer's perspective and define the strategy

The customer's perspective is related to the segments on which the enterprise is going to focus. It is also determined what needs are present in the different segments. From this, the enterprise can determine if it is going to focus on existing or new customers. The latter can occur with existing products or with new products (see Growth strategies, Ansoff). On this basis, the following questions can be answered:

- With what products and/or services does the enterprise supply its customers?
- What are the choices for, for example, price, service and quality?
- In what ways does the enterprise distinguish itself from the competition (USPs)?

Here the enterprise has the possibility to choose from the following strategies (see Customer Value Profiles):

- *Cost leadership*: the enterprise strives for the best price-performance ratio.
- *Product leadership*: the enterprise starts from high quality products and/or services. Higher prices and margins can be achieved.
- *Customer partnership*: the enterprise constantly ensures an appropriate solution for the customer.
- *Distinctive capacity*: the enterprise will have to maintain its strategy over the long term and constantly pick one of the other three and maintain the remaining two.

3 Translate the customer's perspective into internal processes

Once an enterprise has determined in which way the customers can best be serviced, it must then determine which internal processes best satisfy the strategy established in the customer's perspective. When this is successfully achieved, the strategy in the financial perspective will also automatically be achieved. The enterprise has the following possibilities for this:
- Differentiation: new products and/or services with new markets and new segments.
- Increase the added value to the customers by further expanding existing relations.
- Increase product leadership by improvements in costs, supply chain management and quality, reducing the throughput time and optimal use of resources.
- Improve relations with the stakeholders (see Stakeholder Management).

It is important for enterprises that next to the costs and quality of the production processes, the innovation processes and customer processes are included, otherwise it will be difficult for the management to implement the strategy.

4 Bring the learning and growth perspectives into line with the strategy

In the learning and growth perspectives, the skills and knowledge of the employees are determined, the necessary information systems are set up and the qualities of the organisation are established with regard to change management.
- The skills and knowledge of the employees must be in line with those required for the internal processes. Employees should from their competence profiles (experience, knowledge, behaviour and attitude) be able to carry out the activities necessary for the internal processes.
- The information systems will have to make the desired data available to enable the employees to make the decisions necessary for the execution of the internal processes.
- The organisation will have to be able to implement the changes imposed by the strategy.

The last step, bringing in line the learning and growth perspectives, is often only partly implemented because the management too quickly assumes that the employees know what they must do and can also do it. This is unfortunately not true. Establishing the competences of the employees necessary to carry out the processes is often missed out, due to which employees are responsible for processes for which they do not have the competences.

Result

In the model, the emphasis is put on the *learning and growth perspectives*. Due to this, enterprises are able to translate the strategy from general objectives into concrete measures. The resources deployed are developed such that they support the *internal processes*. The internal processes are attuned to the customer processes that have added value for the *customers*. The effect of this is visible in the *financial perspective*: more turnover and profits.

Focus areas

The model focuses on shareholders and not on stakeholders. This is also logical because the three underlying perspectives (the four approach angles from the Balanced Scorecard) are focused on the financial perspective.

Literature

- Kaplan, R.S. & Norton, D. P. (2004). *Strategy Mops. Converting Intangible Assets into Tangible Outcomes.* Boston: Harvard Business School Publishing Corporation.
- Kaplan, R.S. & Norton, D.P. (2000). Having Trouble with Your Strategy? Then Map It. *Harvard Business Review, 78 (5),* 167-176.
- www.sas.com/offices/asiapacific/taiwan/document/sm.pdf (or click on the 'search' button and thereafter on the 'advanced search' button and enter the following text 'strategy maps' in the advanced search field and subsequently, 'Converting Intangible Assets into Tangible Outcomes').

93
Supplier Selection

Author	M. Mulders
Year developed	2006
Also known as	–
Objective	Selecting the most suitable supplier(s)

General management

Strategy

Marketing

Sales

Purchasing

Project & Planning

Production

Quality

Logistics & Distribution management

Information management

Financial

HRM & HTM

Internationalisation

Model

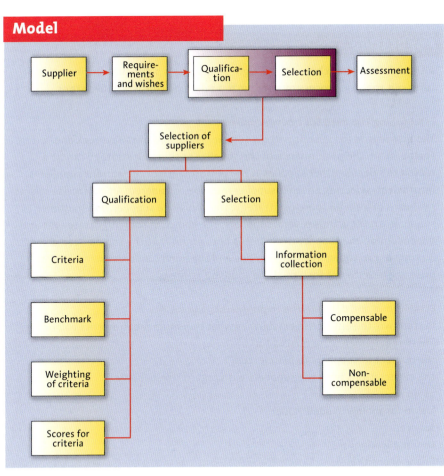

Background

With the increasing (chain) integration between companies, the selection of suppliers has become more important. Companies are forced to lower costs and avoid the slingshot effect between the companies. Customers depend for their production on timely delivery of the raw materials and other materials necessary for production. Suppliers therefore must be able to guarantee a certain reliability of delivery. Due to the greater provision of information via the internet, more information is available and buyers are able to look at suppliers more critically. Conversely, the suppliers have also developed further and there are more suppliers in the market. Every supplier indicates that it can fulfil the requirements of the customers and can often show this via references. Due to this, the selection process has become a complex consideration. Furthermore, the personal preference of an employee for a certain supplier can play a role.

Application

Although the actual choice of the right supplier(s) is a difficult consideration, it turns out that the process of arriving at a selection consists in five steps.

1 Establishing the need for a new supplier

The first reason for selecting a new supplier is the loss of the current one. Furthermore, the performance of the supplier or sourcing strategy can be a reason to select another supplier. If the performance of the current supplier is insufficient, selecting another supplier must be considered. An enterprise selects by means of a single sourcing strategy, thus only one supplier, or a multiple sourcing strategy, thus several suppliers. The choice of sourcing strategy is also dependent on the supplier itself. If it is not certain that the supplier can deliver on time or can supply the right service and the minimum order size, the enterprise will have to opt for a multiple sourcing strategy.

2 Establishing and defining the requirements and wishes

In step two, the enterprise establishes what minimum requirements will be set. These requirements are related to:
- the number of suppliers to be selected
- the expectations from the suppliers with regard to reliability
- quality
- 'value-for-money' (added value)
- service
- communication
- financial position
- 'fit-for-purpose' (useable as intended)
- innovation
- error and complaints handling
- packaging of the product and transportation packaging

- payment terms
- contractual requirements
- knowledge of the sector
- pricing
- price increases

An important component is the functional requirements to which the product or service must comply. These need to be clearly defined because otherwise, a discussion could arise about their use.

Furthermore, the enterprise must make a clear distinction between requirements, wishes and 'nice-to-have'. If the *requirements* ('knock-out criteria') cannot be complied with, the supplier is immediately rejected. If they cannot comply with the wishes, a clear weighing must be made against other suppliers and, when it concerns 'nice-to-have' components, the supplier gets a plus with regard to the other suppliers.

3 Qualification of suppliers

With the qualification of the suppliers, a long list of suppliers is narrowed down to a short list of suppliers from which the final choice is made. For qualification, the criteria, benchmarks, weighting and score play the most important roles. They are, however, influenced by the following factors:

- Product type
  - standard product with no problems
  - procedural problem product: functionality is sufficient but learning to use the product is causing problems in practice
  - functional problem product: the product does not (entirely) do what it was acquired for
  - political problem product: a product that requires large investments, due to which many departments are involved in the choice
- Production strategy
  - MTO (make-to-order): production to customer order
  - MFS (make-from-stock): semi-manufactures are produced, end products are assembled to customer order
  - MTS (make-to-stock): end product is produced to stock
- Geographic location
  - local supplier(s)
  - international supplier(s)
- Decision-making process
  - one person
  - DMU: decision-making unit
- Decision-making criteria with which the supplier must comply as a company
  - single sourcing
  - multiple sourcing

4 Selection of supplier(s)

The ultimate selection of supplier(s) depends on the criteria and their scores.

For this, the criteria, benchmarks, weighting and score are entered in a decision table and thereafter totalised. An important question is if there can be compensation in the consideration. If compensation is possible, a weak point of the supplier will be weighed against a strong point. If no compensation is allowed, this has consequences for the scores.

With the final selection, the supplier will in practice have to prove that it fulfils the functional requirements before contract negotiations can start. In these negotiations, the legal aspects are covered as well as the extra agreements made between supplier and customer. Here, one could think of payment and delivery terms, warranties and guarantees, responsibility and liability.

5 Assessment

After the supplier(s) has (have) been finally selected, it has to be checked that the agreements made are indeed being lived up to. This is not a snapshot but will take place periodically. A score table with weightings is also set up for this.

Result

The result of this model is a considered choice on the basis of actual criteria, for the supplier who can best fulfil the needs of the enterprise at the time. This is thus not always the supplier with the lowest price. By using this model, the selection of suppliers on the basis of personal interest is prevented.

Focus areas

Although a thorough consideration can be made, it cannot be established in advance that a supplier will fully comply with the set requirements. This will have to become apparent in practice. To this end, monitoring the performances of the supplier is necessary.

Literature

- Mahmut Sonmez (2006). *A Review and Critique of Supplier Selection Process and Practices*. UK: Business School Occasional Papers Series.
- Garfamy, R. (2009). *Supplier Selection and Business Process Improvement*. Lap Lambert Academic Publishing.
- www.projectsmart.co.uk/docs/supplier-selection-checklist.pdf

94
SWOT

Author	Standford University
Year developed	1960-1970
Also known as	TOWS Matrix, TOWS Analysis, Internal and External Assessment
Objective	Determining strategy for an enterprise

Model

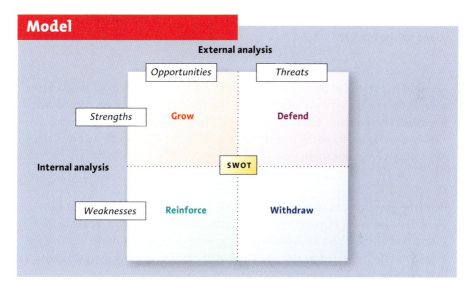

Background

Enterprises regularly evaluate whether their strategy is still in line with developments in the market. To this end, the strong and weak sides of the enterprise are often inventoried. Moreover, enterprises consider developments on the market in terms of possible opportunities and potential threats. The strong and weak sides of an enterprise concern the internal survey of the enterprise, while the opportunities and threats concern the external survey. Subsequently, the enterprise can analyse its strategy on the basis of the combination of the internal and external surveys. This combination is called the SWOT analysis (*Strengths, Weaknesses, Opportunities, Threats*).

General management

Strategy

Marketing

Sales

Purchasing

Project & Planning

Production

Quality

Logistics & Distribution management

Information management

Financial

HRM & HTM

Internationalisation

Application

With the SWOT analysis, the external analysis is first applied to establish if the market offers possibilities for the enterprise to do business. If, for example, in a certain segment there is no need for the product or service marketed by the enterprise, it is pointless to further analyse the strong and weak sides of the enterprise in context of this market segment. If the market offers possibilities, then the enterprise can proceed with the internal survey to inventory the strong and weak sides of the enterprise.

Strengths

Here, the question can be asked: what is the enterprise really good at? Strengths always concern the internal affairs of the enterprise. Everything concerned with the market falls outside the internal survey. Does the enterprise have good sales staff, for example? Are the products of good quality. Has the enterprise a good image on the market?

Weaknesses

Here, the question can be asked: what is the enterprise not good at? Weaknesses always concern the internal affairs of the enterprise. Everything concerned with the market falls outside the internal survey. Does the enterprise have a poor view of developments in the market, for example? Are delivery times unreliable? Are mutual communications poor?

Opportunities

Here, the question can be asked: from which developments in the market can the enterprise profit? Opportunities are related to matters that take place in the market or the direct environment of the enterprise. For example, if there are extra subsidies provided by the government, if extra needs for customers arise or if a competitor goes bankrupt.

Threats

Here, the question can be asked: which developments in the market can hinder the enterprise? Threats are related to matters that take place in the market or the direct environment of the enterprise. For example, if more competition appears in the market, if the product can no longer be sold due to government regulations or if customers become more critical.

To establish the strong and weak sides of the enterprise and the opportunities and threats in the market, the following surveys are important (see table).

Internal research	External research
Value chain	Macro
Marketing	Sector
Clients	Customers
Financial	Competitors
Organisation	Suppliers
	Distribution

The results of these surveys produce a great many strengths, weaknesses, opportunities and threats. Because large numbers are difficult to organise, the SWOT analysis will have to be concentrated. For each component of the SWOT analysis, four or five items are the maximum to take along for further analysis with the confrontation matrix (see Confrontation Matrix). With the concentration of the analysis, no items may be left out. However, items that are related can be combined. If, for example, a competitor implements a new advertising campaign and hires new, very experienced account managers, these threats can be combined into one threat called intensive competition. After concentration of the strengths, weaknesses, opportunities and threats has taken place, the ultimate SWOT analysis can be compiled.

On the basis of expanding the items in the SWOT analysis, the enterprise can define its strategy. The following strategies are possible:

Grow

The combination of the strong sides of the enterprise and the opportunities in the market offers the enterprise the possibility to further expand its activities. To this end, the enterprise uses its core competences to take advantage of the opportunities.

Withdraw

If the enterprise is not good in a number of areas and there are also a number of threats in the market, then it will be very difficult for the enterprise to remain operating at a profit. It is then a question of setting up the right strategy to slowly, with as little as possible loss, think for example about investments in machinery, withdraw from the market in question and invest time and money in markets that do offer opportunities on the basis of the strong sides of the enterprise.

Defend

In any market, at a given moment developments can occur that constitute a threat to the enterprise. The enterprise will have to defend against this by, depending on the threat, undertaking actions to avert it. If, for example, a competitor lowers its prices, the enterprise can do the same or devise a different counter campaign, but doing nothing leads in most situations to loss of turnover and profits.

Reinforce

It is good to know what weak points are present in an enterprise. Above all because the weak sides can be the cause of not being able to use an opportunity in the market. It is thus important that the enterprise, if it wishes to seize these opportunities, reinforces this weak side.

Result

On the basis of the SWOT analysis, the enterprise is able to determine its long- and medium-term strategy in terms of grow, defend, reinforce or withdraw.

Focus areas

Next to the mentioned strategic options, the SWOT analysis provides no transition to the actual strategy and its impact on the enterprise. It is too complex for this. A choice from a number of strategic alternatives cannot be made on the basis of the SWOT analysis.

Literature

- Ferrel, O., Hartline, M. (2009). *Marketing Strategy*. Thomson South-Western.
- Fine, L. (2009) *The SWOT Analysis*. Booksurge Lic.

95
Talent Branding

Author	H. van Zwieten
Year developed	2005
Also known as	Employee Branding, Personal Branding
Objective	Distinguishing yourself as a professional

Model

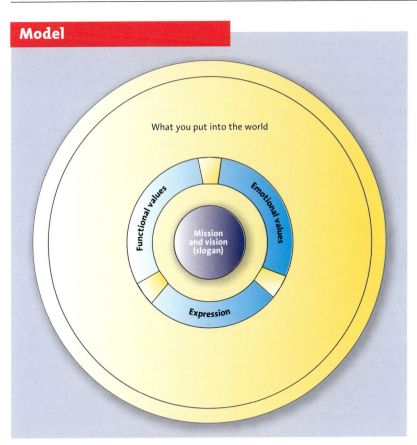

Background

Enterprises select their employees increasingly less on training and more and more on the skills they bring with them. Cognitive skills can always be learned later. It is also quite a bit easier than learning personal skills. This means that

General management

Strategy

Marketing

Sales

Purchasing

Project & Planning

Production

Quality

Logistics & Distribution

Information management

Financial

HRM & HTM

Internationalisation

training and experience is regarded as a minimum requirement. Due to this, it is increasingly difficult for young professionals to distinguish themselves in the labour market. With Talent Branding, young talent can look at themselves in a different way and also communicate about themselves to others in a different way. In this way, someone can distinguish himself from others and communicate this in the correct way.

Application

Talent Branding comprises an action plan in ten steps. The person takes themself as the starting point, listens to where he or she thinks his or her passion lies and what they want themselves. The ten steps are:

1 Inventory your functional skills

Your knowledge and experience are inventoried with the functional skills. This concerns your basic education and your further studies. You can also include any additional courses, knowledge of languages and other knowledge. Think here primarily of everything for which you have received a certificate, diploma, medal, and so forth. Make this list as long as possible; everything goes in. Selection of the relevant items is done later. Look also at your professional experience as a person. What have you done? Your career, side jobs, associations, voluntary aid work, volunteer work and any hobbies. After you have done this, select your most important functional skills. These choices may be based on your own preferences, it is about you after all. Then describe your functional skills in a few brief sentences.

2 Survey what else you have to offer

The functional skills can also be learned by others. Enterprises select on more than just these skills. Above all, personal skills are important. They are divided into in emotional traits and expressive attributes. Emotional traits are those characteristics of which you can say that they are your unique talents, mainsprings, qualities, passions and peculiarities. Expressive properties are those characteristics of which you can say you present yourself to the outside world with them, such as clothing, manner of walking and talking, patterns of thought, colours and the things you surround yourself with. This is your style and your image to others.

3 Retain only those emotional traits that you assess as genuinely authentic

These are the characteristics that genuinely belong to you. What is necessary for a job you are applying for or is socially desirable cannot be considered authentic. To select these characteristics, you give all the characteristics a score on a scale of one to ten. A ten for the characteristics that suit you best, a nine for the characteristics that suit you a little less and a one for the characteristics that do not suit you. Score all the characteristics in this way and then select the fifteen highest scoring ones.

4 Select the three most important traits

From the list of fifteen highest scoring traits, three are now chosen with the aid of the PAD method (passion and fun, aptitude and development potential, objective and ambition). To this end, assess all fifteen traits on:

- Passion and fun: from which traits do you have the most fun and about which you are really enthusiastic?
- Aptitude and development potential: which traits are the most natural and can develop further?
- Objective and ambition, which traits will help you most to achieve your objectives and ambitions?

Select five traits per point and prioritise them on a scale of one to five, where five is the most important and one the least important. Now select the three traits that have received the most points.

5 Translate the traits into specific terms

Check that there are no container concepts among the three traits. These are concepts that can be interpreted in many ways. One person sees it one way and another can understand it completely differently. Accurately describe what is intended with the trait thereafter.

6 Determine your expressive characteristics

Proceed with these characteristics in the same way as for the traits and come down to maximally three. Describe these characteristics.

7 Make your brand template

Fill in the functional skills, emotional traits and the expressive characteristics discovered in the template. Think up a slogan for the centre of the template on the basis of the skills, traits and characteristics.

8 Describe your positioning

Describe now your positioning on the basis of the template, in a few sentences. You must learn this positioning by heart. When you encounter someone and you wish to introduce yourself quickly, it can be done in this manner. This is called an elevator-pitch after an American example, where an employee is standing next to his most senior boss in the lift and has to bring himself to his attention within one minute.

9 Make a communication plan

A communication plan for your brand template comprises one of the following components:

- *Selectivity*: select a small number of subjects in your message.
- *Consistency*: ensure a consistent message and do not blow with the wind.

- *Repetition*: a message is powerfully communicated and lingers through many repetitions.
- *Creativity*: with high creativity, the message will linger better.

Within the communication plan, a number of communication resources can be used, for example:
- behaviour
- CV or profile sketch
- CV via e-mail
- letter
- visiting card
- e-mail signature
- personal brochure
- web site
- advertisement
- elevator pitch
- bumper sticker
- voice mail, answering machine
- work environment
- clothing
- network discussion
- job interview
- logo and mood board
- publishing articles
- telling stories
- your communication idea

10 Implement your communication plan
Carry out the steps that you have included in your communication plan and check the results with what you have in your ten objectives. If necessary, adjust your plan.

Result

With the aid of the brand template inventory, any person can map out his or her skills, traits and characteristics and profile themselves such that he or she makes use of their own strengths and training. The chance that the right person will end up in the right place on this basis is then strongly increased. People explore everything from their own strengths and the enterprise can see whether the person fits in with the enterprise as regards their traits and characteristics. Due to this, the success of a career is increased.

Focus areas

It is very important to perform the self-analysis properly. Compiling a profile too quickly decreases the chances of success enormously.

Literature

- Schuman, M., Sartain, L. (2009). Brand for talent. John Wiley & Sons Ltd.
- Mobray, K. (2009). The 10Ks of Personal Branding. iUniverse.
- http://www.masternewmedia.org/news/2008/07/22/selfmarketing_online_the_personal_branding.htm

96
Target marketing

Author	P. Kotler
Year developed	1996
Also know as	Market operation strategy
Objective	Classification of the market to define marketing approaches for each segment

Model

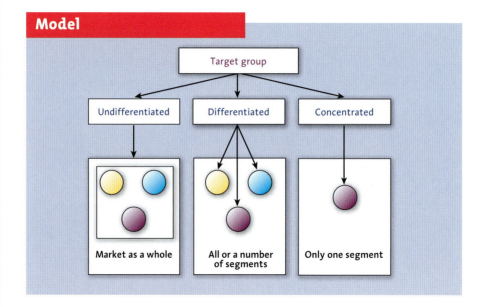

Background

The target group on which an enterprise focuses comprises one or more segments (see Segmentation). It is important for an enterprise to approach each segment such that the service or product has the greatest chance of success, leading to more sales. To do this properly, far-reaching knowledge of the segments is necessary. When this is present, the enterprise can determine in what way the segments will be approached. The most successful is the individual approach: each customer is approached separately. The cheapest method is the mass approach, where all customers are viewed as one segment. Furthermore, there is an intermediate form where several segments are approached in different ways. These three forms of marketing strategy are:

- undifferentiated approach
- differentiated approach
- concentrated approach

Application

The marketing strategies assume the approach to the market via the marketing mix, where the aspects of the marketing mix for each segment can differ from the other segments.

Undifferentiated approach

With the undifferentiated market approach, the enterprise approaches the segments in the target group with the same marketing mix. This is a form of mass approach, where the marketing mix is attuned to the average wishes of the target group. Advertising is directed at the target group in the same manner, the pricing is the same, the product is the same and the distribution points are the same. This method of market approach has above all advantages of cost.
A risk with this form of segmentation is that the competition focuses on those segments that fall short of the average wishes of the target group. In this way, the enterprise can quickly lose a number of segments to the competition.

Differentiated approach

The differentiated approach assumes that for each segment or for several groups of segments, a specifically adapted marketing mix is compiled. The customers' desires have now been specifically addressed and they will be more inclined to take the services or products in question away from the enterprise. Due to this, there is greater market penetration, the revenues for the enterprise are relatively higher. The enterprise should however, take account of rising costs due to the different marketing mix for several segments or groups of segments. If a separate advertising campaign is designed for each segment, for example, costs rise dramatically.
If this is too expensive for the enterprise, a solution can be found by applying exclusively product differentiation. Here, there is exclusively differentiation in the product and the other aspects of the marketing mix remain unchanged.

Concentrated approach

The concentrated market approach means that the enterprise attunes its marketing mix to only one or a limited number of segments of the target group. The enterprise specialises on this segment. This will be approached in an extremely effective manner. In this way, the enterprise can get a foot in the door and possibly gain a sustainable position in the market. This form of market approach is primarily of interest to companies with a limited budget, such as starters and small businesses. After a solid position has been obtained in the segment in question, the enterprise can focus on another segment and so expand further. In this way, a differentiated market approach is ultimately created.
A risk connected with this approach is that during the build-up of the first

segment, the wishes of this segment change and the enterprise is unable to respond. Another risk is that the competition will make a better offer for exactly the same segment. The enterprise has little chance of survival in these cases because its turnover is obtained from only one segment.

Result

A proper analysis of the segments leads to choosing the correct approach. This means that the effort invested in the market approach will turn out to be effective and will provide more turnover.

Focus areas

With the differentiated market approach, the enterprise can break through the segmentation of the target group and consequently push the segmentation too far. This is called hyper-segmentation. The most significant risk with hyper-segmentation are the high costs involved and the huge efforts the enterprise must produce.

Literature

- Kotler, P., Armstrong, G. (2009). *The Principles of Marketing*. Prentice Hall.
- Friedmann, S. (2009). *The Compete Idiot's Guide to Target Marketing*. Alpha Books.
- www.theamericancollege.edu/docs/129.pdf

97
Team Buying Team Selling (TBTS)

Author	**Cap Gemini**
Year developed	**1995**
Also known as	–
Objective	**Organisation of the sales process**

Model

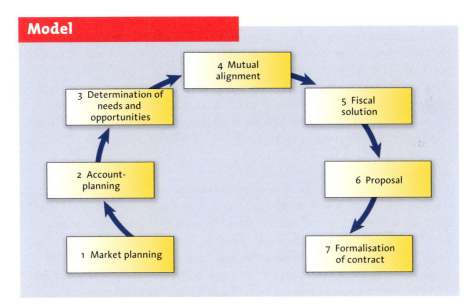

Background

In proportion as more information becomes available and the requirements of customers increase, the sales process has also become more complex. Due to this continuing excess of information, it is becoming increasingly difficult for consumers and sales people to align the right aspects with each other and come to an agreement. In view of the increasing importance of buying in exclusively products and services that produce an added value for the enterprise in a business environment, companies are becoming increasingly critical of their suppliers. The suppliers in turn have also become more critical and will involve several people in the sales programme, to provide clearer and substantively more specialist explanations. In this way, it is accomplished that several people are involved in the sale on both sides.

To plan the sales process properly, it is necessary to make a number of agreements. These agreements can be found in Team Buying Team Selling (TBTS).

Application

From the start up to and including a signed contract, seven steps are taken. These steps are:

1 Market planning
In the first step, the market is inventoried in detail and attractive segments are established and on that basis, the target group is determined. On the basis of the needs of the market and the possibilities the enterprise can offer, a marketing strategy is set up.

2 Account planning
Within the selected segments, all the accounts are identified and allocated to the account managers. The account managers fully inventory the accounts. This concerns all the relevant aspects related to bringing in an order. Subsequently, the account manager determines what position the enterprise will assume with the account in question, to establish whether it makes sense to compete with the other suppliers. If this turns out positively, the account manager determines how this account can best be serviced.

3 Determining the needs and opportunities
As soon as the account has been selected and an account plan has been drafted, it will have to be filled in, in detail. To this end, the account manager inventories all the possibilities to obtain an order from this account. The most important possibility for an order is subsequently taken up. The account manager inventories all those involved with the customer and maintains contact with them. In this way, it is possible for the account manager to inventory all the needs of the different buyers and capitalise on them. These needs can be both business needs and personal needs.
In a TBTS, the following roles are recognised:
- *User*: this is the person who will use product or service.
- *Technical buyer*: this person is responsible for all the technical ins and outs of the product or service.
- *Financial buyer*: this person disposes of the budget.
- *Decision maker*: this is the person who ultimately has the last word and makes a decision based on the other buyers.
- *Coach*: this is the person who can answer any questions the account manager has.

For each of these roles it has to be established who has them and on the basis of what arguments the decision to say yes or no to the proposal will be taken.

4 Mutual alignment

In the phase of mutual alignment, the relationships with the buyers are further expanded, to build up mutual confidence. This can take place during the further alignment between the parties, to come to possible solutions to the problem. The subjects are reviewed in detail and described. Finally, the content of the contract is defined in outline.

5 Final solution

The organisation of the contract is now further developed into a definitive solution, which is carefully discussed with the buyers so that no more discussions arise in this context.

6 Proposal

After all the ingredients of the proposal are known, the final proposal can be written. One's own enterprise must be fully behind the proposal however, and the presentation of the proposal to the buyers is then prepared. The objective of this presentation is removing the last doubts of the buyers and obtaining their consent.

7 Formalisation of the contract

The last step is ultimately drafting and signing the contract. Here, the legal experts of the enterprises often play a role and negotiations will take place on the conditions under which the solution will be accepted. This is still an important event because it is still possible that the buyer will not sign and there will be no contract.

Result

The structure of TBTS brings the enterprise into a positive position with buyers and provides a well-considered structure along which the sales cycle can proceed for both parties. If it does not ultimately lead to a contract, both parties have done everything to reach a consensus but there remains an element that cannot be covered by the proposal.

Focus areas

The seven steps are gone through in every sales cycle, whether it involves a small or a large enterprise. With small enterprises, the different roles can be fulfilled by one person and some of the steps in the process can be combined. If one step is missed out, then the contract somehow always leads to problems.

Literature

None.

General management
Strategy
Marketing
Sales
Purchasing
Project & Planning
Production
Quality
Logistics & Distribution
Information management
Financial
HRM & HTM
Internationalisation

98
The Ten Steps Plan

Authors	P.M. Kempen and J.A. Keizer
Year developed	1995
Also known as	TSP, Programme for organisational advice
Objective	Phased plan for a successful advice project

Model

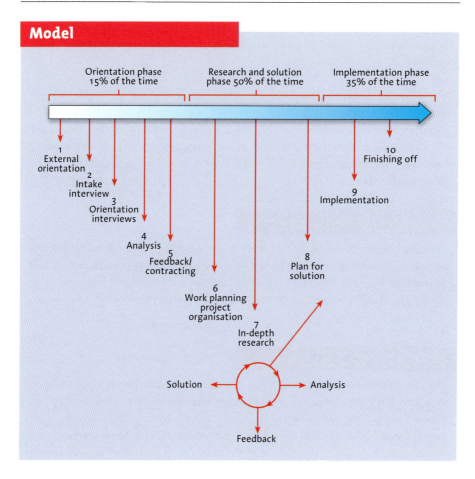

Background

Almost every change in an enterprise is carried out in a project. This change can be inspired by the wishes and strategy of the management, but can also originate from a changed market situation to which the enterprise must react. An advice programme is the foundation for this. From the moment an assignment is formulated to the moment that the solution is actually implemented, it is important to review what steps must be undertaken to come to a successful advice programme. Exactly here, the Ten Steps Plan can play a large role.

Application

A successful advice programme is systematically carried out. In this case, the following ten steps have been established, on the basis of which an advice programme can be designed:

1 External orientation

Before an agreement is made with the company, the advisor collects information on the company and the sector to which it belongs. This occurs in preparation for the first discussion with the employees of the enterprise and ensures that the advisor is well prepared and shows the participants in the discussion that he is familiar with the context.

2 Intake interview

The intake interview is the first introduction to the client of the enterprise. In this interview, the expectations and possibilities envisaged by the client are discussed. Furthermore, it is established whether the advisor is able to carry out the assignment, given the wishes and requirements of the client.

3 Orienting interviews

On the basis of the assignment definition, interviews are held with the personnel involved in the enterprise. Based on these interviews, the advisor can establish how urgent the problem is, whether there is support within the enterprise for tackling the problem and whether the previously formulated assignment is the right one to carry out. On the basis of these data, the advisor can determine if the assignment is feasible and form an opinion in relation to it.

4 Analysis

During the analysis step, information obtained during the previous steps is reviewed and the feedback interview with the client is prepared. This means the formulation of a draft definition of the problem and a draft assignment. An overall plan of approach is also drafted for the remaining time to be worked on the project.

5 Feedback/contracting

In this step, the advisor gives his view of the problems occurring in the enterprise and in what way the solution will be found. Here, there is a clear search for support within the enterprise. This support is necessary for a successful project. The proposals for the follow-up programme (definition of the problem and definition of the assignment) are discussed and established in formal agreements. These agreements are put on paper (contract).

6 Work planning and project organisation

After the client and advisor have reached agreement on the execution of the project, a detailed plan is drafted. Furthermore, a project organisation is set up to perform the activities within the project.

7 In-depth research

This step in the advice programme costs the most time and effort. The objective of this step is the collection of the necessary information to be able to give solid and well-founded advice.

8 Solution plan

The collected information should lead to a solution for the previously established problem. In this phase, all the collected data are analysed and translated into possible solutions for the enterprise. From the different alternatives, one solution that best fits with the assignment is ultimately selected.

9 Implementation

The implementation of the proposed solution is connected to the budget, the activities, the resources and the time (BART). In this step it is established what budget is necessary. With budget is intended a cost-benefits analysis; what will it produce for the enterprise? Furthermore, it is established which activities must be carried out to come to the implementation of the proposed solution. And it must be established what is necessary to implement the solution: the resources in means and manpower. Lastly, the total throughput time and the net hours spent by employees on the project are reviewed.

10 Conclusion

The conclusion concerns the transfer of the project to the enterprise. This must occur such that the enterprise is subsequently able to actually implement the proposed solution.

Result

With the aid of the Ten Steps Plan, the advisor can lay down a solid and well-founded plan with which the enterprise can actually achieve the project in question and the objectives defined therein.
The Ten Steps Plan is used a great deal in higher education to ensure the quality of graduation programmes.

Focus areas

The Ten Steps Plan is quite detailed and exactly following these ten steps will have to take place with the necessary attention. Every advisor must determine how much attention which step in the process receives. In many situations steps 1 to 6 are carried out in the first three to four weeks of a project that takes around twenty weeks. Step 7 will take the longest because a lot of information must be collected and it takes about ten weeks. The last six weeks are for the solution, implementation and delivery of the project to the enterprise. The advisor must take care that in week fourteen, the end of in-depth research, he stops with the collection of information to have enough time for the implementation phase. Information that is collected hereafter may no longer have any great influence on the advice. If the latter is the case, then something has gone wrong during the in-depth research and a new plan must be drafted.

Literature

- Kempen. P.M. & Keizer, J.A. (2006). *Business Research projects*. Oxford: Butterworth-Heinemann.

General management
Strategy
Marketing
Sales
Purchasing
Project & Planning
Production
Quality
Logistics & Distribution
Information management
Financial
HRM & HTM
Internationalisation

99
Two Factory Theory

Author	F. Herzberg
Year developed	1959
Also known as	Motivator-Hygiene Theory
Objective	Motivation of personnel

Model

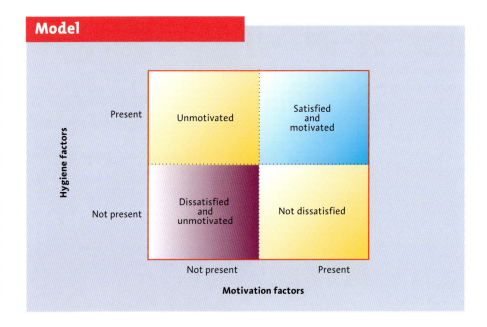

Background

Although this theory of Herzberg is already fairly old, it can be very handy in the current development of companies. The old adage 'a kick-in-the-ass' (KITA) to motivate personnel no longer fits in with current styles of leadership. Managers are currently more coaches, creating the conditions under which the personnel perform best. Due to the flatter organisation (empowerment) the personnel receive more responsibilities and authorities. The work has also become more complex and requires better trained personnel. These personnel are not primarily motivated by KITA but more by two factors described by Herzberg: motivating factors and hygiene factors.

Application

Personnel are influenced in two ways at work:

- *Motivation factors*: these are factors that influence their work satisfaction and mental growth. Due to the motivation factors, the personnel are satisfied. These factors influence motivation in the longer term.
- *Hygiene factors*: these are factors which, when there is a lack of them, lead to dissatisfaction in the personnel. This concerns short-term factors that have hardly or no influence on motivation in the longer term. If these factors are present, this does not necessarily mean that this leads to satisfaction. These factors only mean that the personnel can become dissatisfied.

Hygiene factors that lead to dissatisfaction are, in order of importance:

- corporate policy
- supervision
- relationship with direct superior
- working conditions
- salary
- relationship with colleagues

Motivation factors that lead to satisfaction are, in order of importance:

- performances
- recognition
- the work itself
- responsibility
- development
- growth

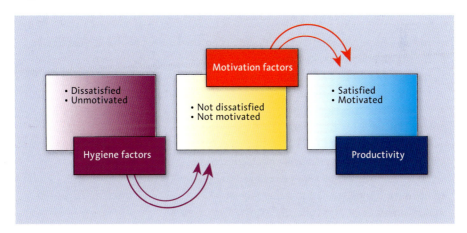

To motivate personnel, they will first have to become less dissatisfied on the basis of the hygiene factors. To achieve this, rewards and punishments can be initiated. These all fall under KITA and are external stimulators. This creates personnel who are not dissatisfied but not yet motivated. Motivation does not come from an external stimulator but from inside (intrinsic motivation). To achieve this, the management can enrich the roles of the personnel. Enrichment can only take place via vertical enrichment (more or new tasks) and not horizontal enrichment (making existing tasks heavier). Horizontal enrichment is, for example, that personnel who at first have to pack 100 boxes a day, have to pack 200 boxes a day after an increase in productivity. Vertical enrichment comprises the number of resources the enterprise can deploy. Vertical enrichment influences intrinsic motivation positively (see table).

Measure	Motivation
remove a number of checks	responsibility and performance
increase the responsibility and authorities of personnel	responsibility and recognition
give a worker full responsibility over a part (for example, division, department, results)	responsibility, performance and recognition
more authorities	responsibility, performance and recognition
make the periodic reports accessible to everyone and not just the management	internal recognition
introduce new and difficult tasks that have not been introduced before	growth and training
offer personnel the opportunity to become a specialist in a specific task	responsibility, growth and development

To implement these measures, the enterprise can use the following steps:
1 Select those functions in which:
   a the investment in industrial design does not make the change too expensive
   b the attitude is slack
   c the hygiene factors are too expensive
   d the motivation factors tend to increase productivity
2 Approach these functions with the conviction that they can be changed. Years of tradition have led to the conviction that functions cannot change and personnel can only be stimulated.
3 Make a list of changes that will enrich these functions.
4 Remove from the list all changes related to hygiene factors.
5 Remove from the list the too general changes, such as 'give them more responsibility'. In practice, this is hardly followed.
6 Remove the horizontal expansions.
7 Avoid the direct involvement of the personnel in whose functions are involved. Experience shows that they only add hygiene factors.
8 Start with a controlled pilot project.
9 Take into account a reduction in production in the beginning.

Result

Modern personnel are much more independent than a few decades ago. It is therefore important to make sure that these personnel are genuinely motivated. Motivated employees produce better performances. Not only in the area of productivity, but also in acquiring, possessing and sharing the knowledge and experience. Managers can in this way also better achieve the objectives of the enterprise or their own department.

Focus areas

There has been a great deal of criticism of Herzberg in connection with the small population on which the theory is based. Other studies have been performed in which different results have been presented. In studies with larger samples, it turns out that Herzberg's theory is supported.

Enrichment of tasks is an important pillar in the motivation of personnel. The enterprise will have to thoroughly investigate to what extent this is possible. The costs tend to be very high and not everyone can handle a more responsible job. Moreover, it is important that the objective (vision and mission) of the enterprise is ultimately aspired to and not the personal objectives of the personnel.

Literature

- Herzberg, F., Mausner, B., & Snyderman, B. (1959). *The Motivation to Work*, (second edition). New York: John Wiley & Sons.
- Herzberg, F. (2008) One more time: How do you motivate employees? *Harvard Business Review*, Sept–Oct 1987, pp 1–16, Reprint 87507.

100
Value Chain, Porter

Author	M. Porter
Year developed	1985
Also known as	Value Chain Analysis
Objective	Mapping out the activities of the enterprise to create value and competitive advantage

Model

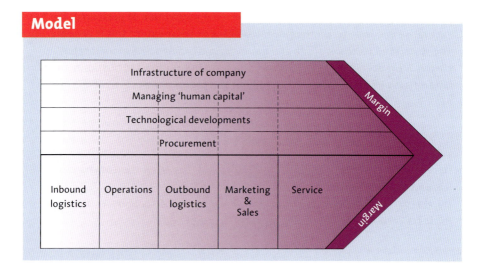

Background

When an enterprise puts services or products onto the market, this is achieved by one or more activities performed by the enterprise. The performance of these activities costs money. If the enterprise can perform these activities cheaper that another enterprise, a competitive advantage is created.

Porter has divided these activities into two categories: primary and secondary activities. The primary activities are exclusively related to the realisation of the service or product, while the secondary activities are indirectly related to them. By primary activities is understood:

- ingoing logistics (receipt of goods)
- operations (the actual production)
- outgoing logistics (distribution)
- marketing and sales
- service

General management
Strategy
Marketing
Sales
Purchasing
Project & Planning
Production
Quality
Logistics & Distribution
Information management
Financial
HRM & HTM
Internationalisation

By secondary activities is understood:
- infrastructure of the enterprise (planning, finances, general management, legal affairs)
- human capital and management (personnel management)
- technological development (R&D)
- acquisition (purchasing)

Application

To map out the Value Chain for the enterprise, the following steps are important:

1 Establish what primary and secondary activities take place
To be able to recognise the primary activities it is important to map out the primary process. This can be done via the logistics model in which the stock points and the processes of the enterprise are shown. Depending on the type of logistics model, push or pull, a start is made with mapping out the processes for ingoing and outgoing logistics. Subsequently, it is investigated which processes ensure that the activities of the logistics model can be adjusted, for example the order process and the planning process. All the other activities performed by the enterprise belong to the secondary activities and have an indirect influence on the primary process.

2 Establish which activities are strategic
By strategic activities is understood activities that can achieve success for the enterprise. For some, this is the quality of the product from the production process, for example, and for others it can be advertising that creates success. All the other activities are necessary to realise the end product but are not strategic in nature.

3 Establish what costs belong to which activities
With the execution of activities, the enterprise will deploy resources to produce the end product. Resources are machines, buildings, people, capital, raw materials and auxiliary materials, for example. Costs are involved with the use and consumption of these resources. For each activity, the use and consumption of resources is established. This can be with the aid of Activity Based Costing, in short ABC (See Activity Based Costing).

4 Establish how these activities are managed
Insight into the costs of the primary, secondary, strategic and non-strategic activities provides the management of the enterprise with the possibility to optimise the total Value Chain, to obtain a better competitive position.
Porter gives the following ten motives for this:
- benefits of scale
- learning capacity
- degree of utility
- connections between activities

- relationships between business units
- degree of vertical integration
- timing of market entry
- corporate policy with regard to the costs of differentiation
- geographical location
- institutional factors

If the enterprise is able to better control these motives than the competition, a competitive advantage is created. With regard to the costs of the activities, the enterprise can choose from:
- Reducing the costs of the activity and leaving the added value of the activity intact
- Increasing the added value of the activity at similar cost
- Reducing the capital of the activity at similar cost and added value

On the basis of the analysis of the Value Chain, various activities can be adjusted to obtain a better competitive position. These adjustments can be simple and not imply a great many changes, but they can also be structural changes, due to which the chain as a whole has to be adapted.

Result

The result is optimisation with regard to the costs of the enterprise, through which a better competitive position is obtained. Furthermore, the model gives insight into the strategic activities of the enterprise that have a direct effect on the realisation of customer value.

Focus areas

Enterprises must be aware that they are dealing with suppliers and customers. The optimisation of one's own Value Chain can then lead to sub-optimisation because, with an eye to fewer intermediate stocks, the whole chain must be reviewed. The enterprise then becomes involved in supply-chain management. The analysis of the Value Chain is relatively clear for manufacturing companies because they work with physical goods. For companies that provide services it is more complex, because it is not always easy to define the added value of services.

Literature

- Porter, M. (1998). *Competitive advantage: creating and sustaining superior performance*. Free Press.
- www.value-chain.org
- www.de.capgemini.com/m/de/tl/2016_The_Future_value_chain.pdf

101

Value Stream Mapping

Author	Toyota
Year developed	1990
Also known as	VSM, Manufacturing process evaluation technique
Objective	Streamlining the primary process so that customers get what they want

Model

Step 4: mapping out the existing processes

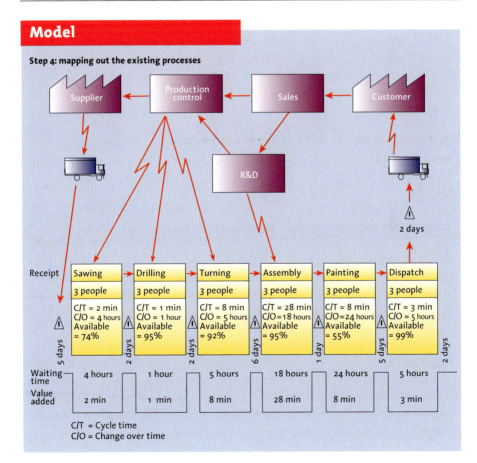

C/T = Cycle time
C/O = Change over time

Background

Value stream mapping is a method of mapping out the whole value stream of an enterprise, starting with the order from the customer up to and including the order from the supplier. Initially, with value-stream mapping it was only looked at where value was added and where waste occurred in the production process. Nowadays, it is used to discover the possibilities that can:

- save costs
- improve production processes
- save time
- lower stocks
- improve environmental conditions

Value stream mapping is part of the larger lean manufacturing concept (optimisation of production processes).

Application

Value stream mapping maps out the processes of an enterprise to ensure that the customers' wishes can be realised. In the mapping out, important indicators are shown that affect the performance of the processes. Examples of indicators are:

- waiting times
- throughput times
- processing times
- transfer times
- forms used
- documents

Value stream mapping is performed according to the following steps:

1 Establishing the scope

The first step is to establish the product or service groups to be analysed. Every enterprise subdivides the products or services it supplies to its customers into groups. Because these groups often make use of the same resources, value stream mapping is applied at group level.

2 Determining the team

The personnel who will participate in the project are selected. These are process owners and personnel that have good insight into the process. The process owners must have the decision-making ability to adjust the processes. The team comprises optimally six to eight people but certainly no more than ten.

3 Collection of data

All the indicators of importance are determined and the data from the processes are recorded. Furthermore, it must be known in which IT systems data will be

input and which IT systems will make the data available. For each activity it is investigated who performs it. The ongoing work is also established. Also the reasons why something does not proceed as desired are established, such as:
- queuing
- postponed processing
- machine standstill
- personnel not available due to too many tasks at once
- shared resources
- too much travelling or vacancies
- interruptions and setting times of the machines

Some very important indicators are:
- Process Time (PT)): the actual time that an activity takes to finish, if it can be worked on without interruptions.
- Lead Time (LT): the time elapsed from the start of the activity until the moment the activity is finished and is passed on to the following person or the following process in the value stream. The lead time is the process time + waiting and delays.
- Activity ratio (AR): the percentage of the total time that is worked on the product throughout the whole process.

$$AR = \frac{\text{Total PT}}{\text{Total LT}} \times 100\%$$

4 Mapping out existing processes
The following step is mapping out the existing processes and the indicators of interest. This is done as shown in the figure.
- Customers and their requirements and wishes.
- Supplier.
- How is the order placed and planned.
- Main process steps (five to maximally fifteen).
- Add details, such as process indicators, why something does not work, ongoing work at that moment, personnel complement, arrows that link the processes.
- Information flows and physical flows.
- Calculate the indicators for each process step.
- Nominate the process steps that add value and those that do not.
  Process steps that add value are the steps for which the customer is prepared to pay. Process steps that do not add value are steps that require time or resources but add no value to the product or service that is sold to the customer.

5 Setting up new processes
The new processes are leaner and no longer contain waste, such as over-production, stocks, queues, errors and defects, understaffing and transport. To set up these processes properly, use is made of the following questions:
- What are the requirements and wishes of the user?
- Is there production to stock or to customer specifications? (With services, it is almost always production to customer specifications).

- Where can a continuous production flow be set up? (Processes that follow each other without intermediate stops or intermediate stocking.)
- Where must pull systems be implemented to manage earlier production processes?
- At which step in the process (pacemaker process) is there planning according to task time? Task time is the frequency at which production occurs according to the number of orders from customers.

$$\text{Task time} = \frac{\text{Production time per shift}}{\text{Number of products per shift ordered by customers}}$$

- How much work is supplied and taken away with the process that runs on task time (pacemaker process)?
- What improvements are necessary to define the value stream on the basis of the future design specifications?

6 Establishing an action plan

The action plan that can subsequently be set up from the previous step is carried out via a normal project.

Result

Waste such as over-production, waiting times, resetting times and undermanning of personnel are mapped out with the aid of value stream mapping. By organising processes afresh, costs can be saved and the wishes and requirements of the customers, such as delivery time, functionality and pricing, can better be satisfied.

Focus areas

Analysis of the value stream can only be accomplished if there is sufficient data present. If these data are never established, the project can take a lot longer. Moreover, it is important that everyone also actually keeps to the new process steps and does not fall back into the old methods. The personnel have had a great deal of freedom from way back and this can lead to falling back on old principles.

Literature

- Ono, T. (1988). *Toyota Production Systems, Beyond Large-Scale Production.* Productivity Press.
- Rother, M. & Shook, J. (1999). *Learning to see.* Lean Enterprise Institute. www.leaninstituut.nl
- www.lean.org

Index by Discipline

#		General management	Strategy	Marketing	Sales	Purchasing	Project & Planning	Production	Quality	Logistics & Distribution	Information management	Financial	HRM & HTM	Internationalisation
1	360° feedback												●	
2	AAA Triangle													●
3	Activities schedule						●							
4	Activity Based Costing											●		
5	Balanced Scorecard		●											
6	BART						●							
7	BCG Matrix		●											
8	Belbin Team Roles												●	
9	Benchmarking		●											
10	Blue Ocean Strategy		●											
11	Brainstorm	●												
12	Brand Asset Valuator			●										
13	Business Intelligence		●											
14	CAGE Distance Framework													●
15	Colour Print Thinking												●	
16	Competence management												●	
17	Competing Values Framework, Quinn												●	
18	Competitive Forces, Porter			●										
19	Competitive Positions, Kotler		●											
20	Competitive Strategies, Kotler		●											
21	Competitive Strategies, Porter		●											
22	Complaints Management								●					
23	Conflict handling												●	
24	Confrontation Matrix		●											
25	Core Competence		●											
26	Core Marketing System			●										
27	Core Qualities												●	
28	Costs-Benefits analysis											●		
29	Cultural dimensions, Hofstede													●
30	Customer Order Decoupling Point							●						
31	Customer Pyramid, Curry				●									

		General management	Strategy	Marketing	Sales	Purchasing	Project & Planning	Production	Quality	Logistics & Distribution	Information management	Financial	HRM & HTM	Internationalisation
32	Customer Relationship Management		●											
33	Customer Satisfaction				●									
34	Customer-Value Profiles				●									
35	Decision Table	●												
36	Deming Circle								●					
37	DESTEP			●										
38	Diamond, Porter		●											
39	Employability Scan												●	
40	Entry Mode Decision													●
41	F-PEC scale		●											
42	Functional and process management	●												
43	Gantt Chart						●							
44	Global Sourcing													●
45	GPS for Enterprises	●												
46	Growth Strategies, Ansoff		●											
47	Image and Identity			●										
48	Industrial column									●				
49	INK / EFQM								●					
50	Intelligence Pyramid		●											
51	International Market Research													●
52	International Pricing Strategy													●
53	ITIL V3										●			
54	Karasek's Job Strain Model												●	
55	Knowledge management										●			
56	Kraljic Matrix					●								
57	Lead time/net time						●							
58	Levers of Control								●					
59	MaBa Analysis		●											
60	Managerial Grid												●	
61	Mergers and Takeovers		●											
62	Multichannel Marketing			●										
63	Organisation Chart	●												
64	Organisational Climate Index		●											
65	Organisational growth, Greiner		●											
66	Organisational Management		●											

	General management	Strategy	Marketing	Sales	Purchasing	Project & Planning	Production	Quality	Logistics & Distribution	Information management	Financial	HRM & HTM	Internationalisation
67 OSO model		●											
68 Pareto Analysis					●								
69 Performance matrix for family businesses		●											
70 Physical Distribution									●				
71 PMT, Abell & Hammond		●											
72 Positioning		●											
73 PRINCE2						●							
74 Product Life Cycle			●										
75 Progress reporting						●							
76 Purchasing Process					●								
77 RASCI Matrix												●	
78 Ratio Delay Studies							●						
79 Research method	●												
80 Resource Based View		●											
81 Sales Funnel				●									
82 Segmentation			●										
83 SERVQUAL								●					
84 Seven-S Model		●											
85 SIT Method	●												
86 Situational Leadership Theory												●	
87 SIVA			●										
88 Six Sigma								●					
89 Stakeholder Management		●											
90 Strategic Alignment Model										●			
91 Strategy Clock		●											
92 Strategy Map		●											
93 Supplier Selection					●								
94 SWOT		●											
95 Talent Branding												●	
96 Target marketing			●										
97 Team Buying Team Selling (TBTS)				●									
98 The Ten Steps Plan	●												
99 Two Factory Theory												●	
100 Value Chain, Porter		●											
101 Value Stream Mapping							●						

Index by Objective

Objective category	No	Model	Description
Analyis of the environment	18	Competitive Forces, Porter	Sectoral analysis
	26	Core Marketing System	Establishing players with a direct influence on the enterprise
	37	DESTEP	Sectoral analysis at macro level
	38	Diamond, Porter	Determining the international competitive capacity of a nation or enterprise
	51	International Market Research	Considering the potential of countries
Determining distribution	48	Industrial column	Selection of distribution channels
	70	Physical Distribution	Establishing transport movements
Determining strategy	11	Brainstorm	Generation and development of ideas
	24	Confrontation Matrix	Determining strategic options based on a SWOT analysis
	40	Entry Mode Decision	Determining in which way the enterprise can best start abroad
	49	INK / EFQM	Formulation of organisational objectives and policy
	50	Intelligence Pyramid	Translation of raw data into action-focused strategic decision making
	67	OSO model	Strategy formation
	94	SWOT	Establishing strengths and weaknesses of the enterprise and the opportunities and threats from the market
Management/ responsibility	5	Balanced Scorecard	Development of organisational strategy and focusing activities on it
	13	Business Intelligence	The collection, interpretation and translation of data into goal-oriented decision making by the enterprise
	15	Colour Print Thinking	Streamlining changes in enterprises
	28	Costs-Benefits Analysis	Financial justification of projects/investments
	41	F-PEC scale	Shows the degree and quality of the influence of the family
	42	Functional and process management	Reducing logistics throughput time and improving communication between processes
	63	Organisation Chart	Formal management and responsibilities of the enterprise
	69	Performance matrix for family businesses	Determining the relationship between business and family dimensions in relation to the performance of family businesses
	77	RASCI matrix	Mapping out responsibilities and authorities in teams
	81	Sales Funnel	Turnover forecasting
	89	Stakeholder management	Managing the enterprise, taking the influence of stakeholders into account
	92	Strategy Map	The translation from strategy to measurable indicators

Objective category	Nr.	Model	Description
Management/ leadership	12	Brand Asset Valuator	An aid to understanding and managing brands
	17	Competing Values Framework, Quinn	Effective management
	60	Managerial Grid	Determining personally-oriented or business-oriented leadership to provide more effective management in proportion to what is needed
	65	Organisational growth, Greiner	Overcoming internal crisis situations with the growth of the enterprise
	86	Situational Leadership Theory	Providing effective management
Development/ innovation	45	GPS for Enterprises	Innovation
	85	SIT Method	Thinking up successful new ideas
Development of staff	1	360° feedback	Awareness process to achieve self-development
	8	Belbin Team Roles	Working in teams successfully
	16	Competence manage-ment	Deploying staff optimally based on knowledge, training and skills
	27	Core Qualities	Increasing personal effectiveness
	23	Conflict Handling	Preventing conflict situations from escalating
	39	Employability Scan	Correct deployment of personnel
	55	Knowledge management	Managing the production factor knowledge
	95	Talent Branding	Distinguishing oneself as a professional
	99	Two factor Theory	Motivating staff
Optimisation of external factors	2	AAA Triangle	Profiling on the international market
	31	Customer pyramid, Curry	Mapping out the customer base
	33	Customer Satisfaction	Establishing customer satisfaction
	44	Global Sourcing	Purchasing and outsourcing on a global scale
	46	Growth Strategies, Ansoff	Determining growth strategy based on market and product
	62	Multichannel Marketing	Balanced use of Marketing Channels
	71	PMT Abell & Hammond	Determining the growth markets of the enterprise
	82	Segmentation	Dividing the market into homogeneous customer groups to achieve a specific market approach for each segment
	87	SIVA	Developing a more customer-oriented marketing mix
	96	Target marketing	Division of the market to establish a market approach for each segment

Objective category	Nr.	Model	Description
Optimisation of internal factors	3	Activities schedule	Establishing the sequence of activities and their responsibilities in processes
	4	Activity Based Costing	Assigning costs to the activities that incur them
	22	Complaints Management	Turning complaints into an improved relationship with the customer
	25	Core Competence	Determining the most important competences that contribute towards the result of the enterprise
	29	Cultural Dimensions, Hofstede	Providing insight into cultural differences in order to try to bridge them
	30	Customer Order Decoupling Point	Optimising the physical flow of goods by the enterprise
	32	Customer Relationship Management	Determining business strategy for customers
	34	Customer-Value Profiles	Establishing core values at which the enterprise excels
	35	Decision Table	Making considered choices from different options
	47	Image and Identity	Determining the personality of the enterprise
	52	International Pricing Strategy	Determining correct pricing on the international market
	54	Karasek's Job Strain Model	Prevention of work-related stress
	57	Lead time/Net time	A planned approach to working
	58	Levers of Control	Finding a balance between empowerment of the personnel and steering towards the objectives of the enterprise
	61	Mergers and Takeovers	Determining forms of collaboration
	64	Organisational Climate Index	Mapping out the culture of the enterprise
	66	Organisational Management	Managing an enterprise in the short, medium and long term
	76	Purchasing Process	Assessing and organising the purchasing process
	78	Ratio Delay Studies	Determining inefficiency and bottlenecks in processes
	79	Research method	Selecting the right research methods
	80	Resource Based View	Adequate deployment of available resources
	83	SERVQUAL	Measuring the quality of the services provided by an enterprise
	88	Six Sigma	Quality and process improvement
	90	Strategic Alignment Model	Aligning organisation and information supply
	93	Supplier Selection	Selecting the most suitable supplier(s)
	97	Team Buying Team Selling (TBTS)	Organisation of the sales process
	98	The Ten Steps Plan	Phased plan for a successful advice project

Objective category	Nr.	Model	Description
Optimisation of internal factors	84	Seven-S model	Analysis of internal organisation
	100	Value Chain, Porter	Mapping out the activities of the enterprise to create value and competitive advantage
	101	Value Stream Mapping	Streamlining primary processes so that customers receive what they want
Planned working	6	BART	Setting up the planning for an implementation plan
	36	Deming Circle	Circle of rules for monitoring achieved results
	43	Gantt Chart	Giving an overview of activities to be performed
	53	ITIL V3	Management of information systems
	73	PRINCE2	Managing complex projects
	74	Product Life Cycle	Insight into the sales prognoses of a product or service
	75	Progress reporting	Providing insight into the future status of a project on the basis of financials, time and deliverables
Portfolio analysis	7	BCG Matrix	Portfolio analysis
	56	Kraljic Matrix	Portfolio analysis for purchasing
	59	MaBa Analysis	Establishing in which PMCs to invest
	68	Pareto Analysis	Examination of range of articles
Improving competitive position	9	Benchmarking	Creation of a better performance for customers than the competition
	14	CAGE Distance Framework	Establishing and identifying the impact of differences on a cultural, administrative and economic level
	19	Competitive Positions, Kotler	Establishing distinctive competitive strategy
	20	Competitive Strategies, Kotler	Determing competitive strategies
	21	Competitive Strategies, Porter	Establishing distinctive competitive strategy
	72	Positioning	Obtaining a place in the view of customers with regard to the competition
	91	Strategy Clock	Establishing competitive position

Index by Research or Advice Project

	General	Prilliminary Study	Internal research						External research						Analysis		Implementation	
			Organisatiion	Leadership	Management	Marketing	Financial	Primary process	Macro analysis	Sector analysis	Customer analysis	Competition analysis	Distribution analysis	Supplier analysis	Analysis	Interpretation	Solution	Implementation
1 360° feedback			●	●														
2 AAA Triangle																	●	
3 Activities schedule								●										
4 Activity Based Costing							●											
5 Balanced Scorecard																	●	
6 BART																		●
7 BCG Matrix						●												
8 Belbin Team Roles			●	●														
9 Benchmarking												●						
10 Blue Ocean Strategy	●																	
11 Brainstorm	●																	
12 Brand Asset Valuator						●												
13 Business Intelligence	●																	
14 CAGE Distance Framework																	●	
15 Colour Print Thinking			●															
16 Competence management			●															
17 Competing Values Framework, Quinn				●														
18 Competitive Forces, Porter										●								
19 Competitive Positions, Kotler																	●	
20 Competitive Strategies, Kotler						●												
21 Competitive Strategies, Porter						●												
22 Complaints Management											●							
23 Conflict handling			●															
24 Confrontation Matrix																●		
25 Core Competence	●																	
26 Core Marketing System										●								
27 Core Qualities				●														
28 Costs-Benefits Analysis																	●	
29 Cultural Dimensions, Hofstede			●															
30 Customer Order Decoupling Point								●										
31 Customer Pyramid, Curry						●					●							

#		General	Preliminary Study	Internal research						External research						Analysis		Implementation	
				Organisation	Leadership	Management	Marketing	Financial	Primary process	Macro analysis	Sector analysis	Customer analysis	Competition analysis	Distribution analysis	Supplier analysis	Analysis	Interpretation	Solution	Implementation
32	Customer Relationship Management	●																	
33	Customer Satisfaction						●												
34	Customer-Value Profiles																	●	
35	Decision Table																●		
36	Deming Circle	●																	
37	DESTEP									●									
38	Diamond, Porter									●									
39	Employability Scan				●														
40	Entry Mode Decision																	●	
41	F-PEC scale	●																	
42	Functional and process-management			●															
43	Gantt Chart																		●
44	Global Sourcing														●				
45	GPS for Enterprises	●																	
46	Growth Strategies, Ansoff																	●	
47	Image and Identity						●												
48	Industrial column										●	●							
49	INK / EFQM	●																	
50	Intelligence Pyramid	●																	
51	International Market Research															●	●		
52	International Pricing Strategy																	●	
53	ITIL V3	●																	
54	Karasek's Job Strain Model																	●	
55	Knowledge management	●		●															
56	Kraljic Matrix															●			
57	Lead time/net time																		●
58	Levers of Control			●	●														
59	MaBa Analysis						●												
60	Managerial Grid				●														
61	Mergers and Takeovers	●																	
62	Multichannel Marketing																	●	
63	Organisation Chart			●															
64	Organisational Climate Index			●														●	
65	Organisational growth, Greiner			●															
66	Organisational Management			●															

#	Method	General	Priliminary Study	Organisation	Leadership	Management	Marketing	Financial	Primary process	Macro analysis	Sector analysis	Customer analysis	Competition analysis	Distribution analysis	Supplier analysis	Analysis	Interpretation	Solution	Implementation
				Internal research						External research						Analysis		Imple-men-tation	
67	OSO model	●																	
68	Pareto Analysis														●				
69	Performance matrix for family businesses	●																	
70	Physical Distribution													●					
71	PMT, Abell & Hammond						●											●	
72	Positioning																	●	
73	PRINCE2	●																	
74	Product Life Cycle						●												
75	Progress reporting	●																	●
76	Purchasing Process														●				
77	RASCI Matrix																		●
78	Ratio Delay Studies								●										
79	Research method		●									●							
80	Resource Based View																	●	
81	Sales Funnel											●							
82	Segmentation																	●	
83	SERVQUAL															●			
84	Seven-S Model			●															
85	SIT Method	●																	
86	Situational Leadership Theory				●														
87	SIVA						●											●	
88	Six Sigma	●																	
89	Stakeholder Management	●																	
90	Strategic Alignment Model	●																	
91	Strategy Clock																	●	
92	Strategy Map	●																	
93	Supplier Selection														●				
94	SWOT															●			
95	Talent Branding	●		●															
96	Target marketing																	●	
97	Team Buying Team Selling (TBTS)											●							
98	The Ten Steps Plan	●																	
99	Two Factory Theory			●															
100	Value Chain, Porter								●										
101	Value Stream Mapping								●									●	

Index by Author

Abell 260
Ansoff 55, 168
Astrachan 153

Beilin 322
Belbin 36
Berry 302
Birkigt 171
Bitner 126
Blakee 218
Blanchard 312
Boston Consulting Group 32
Bowman 330
Bunt 246

Caluwé, de 63
Cap Gemini 295, 353
CCTA 266
Chan Kim 42
Chekitan 315
Cock, de 234
Cooper 23
Curry 118

Deming 136
Dev 315

European Foundation of Quality
    Management 178

Faulkner 330
Flanders District of Creativity
    165

Gantt 159
Gartner Group 122
General Electric 215
Ghemawat 16, 58
Gilmore 322
Greiner 237

Hamel 97
Hammond 260

Harry 319
Haspeslagh 222
Henderson 326
Hersey 312
Herzberg 360
Hoekstra 114
Hofstede 111
Hollensen 39, 149, 184, 187
Horowitz 309

Jemison 222
Juran 250

Kaplan 23, 26, 241, 333
Karasek 195
Keizer 356
Kempen 356
Kersten 162
Kilmann 91
Kotler 78, 82, 350
Kraljic 203

Leeflang 101
Levitt 269

Mauborgne 42
McCarthy 298
Ministry of Defense, USA 280
Monczka 277
Motorola 319
Mouton 218
Mulders 29, 94, 97, 207, 273,
    277, 337

Nieuwenhuis 67
Norton 26, 241, 333

Ofman 104
Osborn 47

Parasuraman 302
Pascale 305
Peters 305

Porter 74, 85, 143, 364
Prahalad 97

Quinn 70

Ries 263
Rodenberg 181
Romme 114
Roos 133
Rubicam 51

Saunders 287
Schultz 315
Sharma 253
Sillanpää 322
Simons 211
Stadler 171
Standford University 341

Theorell 195
The Stationary Office 191
Tippet 283
Toyota 367
Treacy 129
Trout 263

Van Goor 175
Venkatraman 326

Ward 13
Waterman 305
Weggeman 199
Wernerfelt 291
Wheeler 322
Wiersema 129

Young 51

Zeithaml 126, 302
Zwieten 345

Index by keyword

5 forces Porter 74
6 ∑ 319
7-s Framework 305
7-S model 305
80-20 rule 250
360° feedback 13

AAA Triangle 16
A-, B- and C-countries 185
ABC 23
ABC analysis 250
Absorption 223
Access 316
Accountability 231
Account managers 295
Account planning 354
Action research 289
Activities 30
Activities Schedule 21
Activity Based Costing 23
Activity Based Management 23
Activity ratio (AR) 369
Actual costs 25
Adaptation 17
Added value 330
Administrative distance 58, 60
Administrative processing 259
Affective components 173
Aggregation 17
American Model 302
Ansoff Matrix 168
Arbitration 17
ARCI 280
Attack Strategies 78
Autonomy 223
Avoidance 92
Avoidance of uncertainty 111

Background information 48
Balanced Scorecard (BSC) 26,
   57, 334
BAV 51
BBSC 26
BCG Analysis 32
BCG Matrix 32
Belbin Self-Perception Inventory
   36
Belbin Team Roles 36

Belbin types 36
Belief and Boundary Systems
   211
Belief systems 212
Benchmarking 39
BERI index 185
BI 55
Bilateral positioning 172, 265
Black Belts 321
Blue bird 297
Blue ocean 42
Blue Ocean Strategy 42
Bottleneck products 203, 205
Bottlenecks 273
Boundary systems 212
Brainstorm 47, 48
Brand 51
Brand Asset Valuator 51
Brand image 172
Branding 172
Brand levels 172
Brand stature 53
Brand strength 53
Brand valuation method 51
Break-even Analysis 108
Broker 71
BSC 26, 334
Budget 30
Budget Activities Resources &
   Time 29
Business and IT alignment 326
Business and Organization
   Climate Index (BOCI) 234
Business Attractiveness 215
Business Balanced Scorecard 26
Business chain 175
Business column 176
Business Definition Model 260
Business Intelligence 55
Business processes 22
Buying channels 227
Buying Funnel 295
Buy-out 222

CAGE Distance Framework 58
Calendar time 208
Cannibalisation 229
Capabilities 291

Case study 289
Cash cow 33
CBA 108
Chain 259
Chain-Guard Model 171
Challenger 82
Change process 63, 65
Change programme 64, 65
Channels 226
Cluster Analysis 298
Coach 354
CODP 115
Cognitive components 173
Cognitive skills 345
Collaboration 92
Colour of the enterprise 64
Colour Print Thinking 63
Communication-Identity Mix
   171
Competence management 67
Competence profile 68, 147
Competences 68
Competing Values Framework,
   Quinn 70
Competing Values Model 70
Competition 78, 82, 185
Competition analysis 79
Competitive advantage 83, 97
Competitive behaviour 84
Competitive Benchmarking 39
Competitive Forces, Porter 74
Competitive intelligence 181
Competitive position 25, 79,
   143, 215
Competitive Positions, Kotler 78
Competitive Strategies, Kotler
   82
Competitive Strategies, Porter
   85
Competitive strategy 78, 79
Competitive strength 215
Competitor prognosis 79
Competitors 86
Complaint 88
Complaints Management 88
Conative components 173
Concentrated approach 351
Concession 92

Conflict Handling 91
Conflicts 91
Conflict situation 91
Conflict Styles 91
Confrontation matrix 94, 95
Conservation 223
Contingency Models 312
Contract management 278
Control 231
Convergent flow 258, 259
Coordinator 71
Core business 97
Core Competence 97
Core Competitive Ability 97
Core Expertise 97
Core Marketing System 101
Core Quadrant 104
Core Qualities 104
Core Quality Quadrant 104
Corporate identity 171
Corporate image 171, 172
Cost causers 24
Cost drivers 24
Cost leadership 129, 335
Cost objects 24
Cost price 23
Costs-Benefits Analysis 108
Countries portfolio 58
Critical concerns 49
Critical path 21, 209
Critical success factor 27
CRM 122
Cultural Dimensions, Hofstede 111
Cultural distance 58, 60
Culture 63, 111
Culture of the enterprise 63
Currency differences 188
Customer intimacy 129
Customer Marketing Method 118
Customer Matrix 330
Customer Order Decoupling Point 114
Customer partnership 129, 335
Customer Profitability Analysis 118
Customer Pyramid, Curry 118
Customer relations 122
Customer Relationship Management 122
Customers 118, 296
Customer satisfaction 122, 126
Customer-Value Profiles 129

Data 56
DC 256
Decision latitude 196
Decision maker 354
Decision Table 133
Decline Analysis 298
Deductive method 288
Defects 320
Defects Per Million Opportunities (DPMO) 320
Defend 96, 343
Defend position 83
Deliverables 273
Delivery 258
Delivery times 259
Demand 143
Deming circle 136
Deming Wheel 136
Demographic 139
Descriptive study 289
DESTEP 139
Determining the needs and opportunities 354
Diagnostic control systems 213
Diamond model 143
Differentiated approach 351
Differentiation strategy 331
Dimensions in cultures 111
Direct distribution 257
Director 71
Distance from power 111, 112
Distinctive capacity 335
Distribution centres (DC) 256
Distribution channels 257
Distribution network 256
Distribution Requirements Planning 258
Distribution structures 257
Distribution via consolidation 257
Divergent flow 258
Divergent goods flows 259
Diversification 168
DMAIC 320
Dog 33
DRP 258

Early-adopters 270
Early majority 270
Ecological 139
Economic 139
Economic distance 58, 60
Economic order 143

EFQM Excellence Model 178
EFQM model 178
Employability 146
Employability Scan 146
Employee 68
Employee Branding 345
Empowerment 211, 314, 360
Enterprise Relationship Management 122
Entry Mode Decision 149
Entry Modes 149
Ethnography 289
Expand market share 83
Expectations Management 322
Experimental 288
Explanatory research 289
Exploratory research 289
Export 150
Export mode 150
External costs 24
Externalisation 150

Facilitator 48, 71
Factors affecting the foreign market entry mode decision 149
Family business 153, 253
Family Power Experience Culture 153
Final solution 355
Financial buyer 354
Flanking attack 80
Focused differentiation 331
Focus strategy 86
Follower 82, 270
Forcing through 92
Forecast 295
Formalisation of the contract 355
F-PEC 153
F-PEC scale 153
F-PEC scale of Family Influence 153
Frontal attack 79
Functional and process management 156
Functional integration 327
Functional management 157

Gantt Chart 159
Gap analysis 278
Gap Model 302
Gaps 303
GE Business screen 215

GE-Matrix 215
Generic strategies Porter 85
Geographical distance 58, 60
Globalisation 184
Global sourcing 162
Goals and objectives 243
GPS for enterprises 165
Green Belts 321
Grounded theory 289
Grow 343
Growth 96
Growth Matrix 168
Growth model Greiner 237
Growth Share Matrix 32
Growth Strategies 169
Growth Strategies, Ansoff 168
Guerrilla attack 80

Handling 258, 259
Handling costs 258
Hidden costs 25
Hierarchical levels 211
Hierarchical management 157
Hierarchical mode 150
Holding company 223
Horizontal Bar Charts 159
Horizontal enrichment 362
Horizontal integration 176
Human relations model 70
Hybrid strategy 331
Hygiene factors 360, 361

Idea generation 48
Idea selection 48
Identity of the enterprise 171
Image and Identity 171
Image of an enterprise 171
Implementation positioning 265
Improve productivity 83
Independence 223
Individualism 112
Individual versus collective 111
Inductive method 288
Industrial column 175
Inflation 188
Information 55, 316
Informational positioning 172,
   265
INK/EFQM model 178
Innovator 71
Institute for Dutch Quality
   Assurance (INK) 178
Integrated goods flow 259

Intelligence circle 182
Intelligence Pyramid 181, 182
Interactive control systems 213
Interest 259
Interest groups 103
Intermediate mode 150
Internal and External Assessment
   341
Internal costs 24
Internalisation 150
Internal process model 70
Internationalisation 143, 184
International Market Research
   184, 185
International Pricing Strategy
   187, 188
Interpretivism 288
Intervention techniques 65
Investigation 289
Irrelevants 293
ITIL 191
ITIL V3 191
IT Infrastructure Library 191

JDC Model 195
Job-demand job-control model
   195

Karasek's Job Strain Model 195
KITA 360
Knowledge acquisition 232
Knowledge management 199,
   200
Knowledge sharing 232
Knowledge value chain 199
Knowledge workers 232
Kraljic Matrix 203

Leadership 218
Leadership Grid 218
Lead time 21, 22, 31
Lead Time (LT) 369
Lead time/net time 207
Lean manufacturing 368
Learning roles 36
Letter-of-Credit 190
Leverage products 203, 205
Levers of Control 211, 213
Line organisation 230
Line-staff organisation 230
Logistics 256
Logistics costs 259
Logistics ground form 115

Long-term thinking 112
Low-price-strategies 331

MaBa Analysis 215
Macro-analysis 142
Macro factors 139
Making compromises 92
Managerial Grid 218
Manufacturing process evalua-
   tion technique 367
Market Attractiveness 215
Market development 168
Market growth 33
Marketing intelligence 181
Marketing mix 300, 301, 315
Market leader 82
Market operation strategy 350
Market-oriented 169
Market penetration 168
Market planning 354
Market Segmentation 298
Market share 83
Masculine versus feminine 111
Masculinity 112
Mass customisation 331
Master Black Belts 321
Matrix organisation 230
McKinsey 7-S model 305
Mentor 71
Merger 222
Mergers and Acquisitions 222
Mergers and Takeovers 222
MFS (make-from-stock) 339
Milestones 273
Mission statements 242
Model of Competing Values,
   Quinn Model 70
Monitor 71
Motivating factors 360, 361
Motivator-Hygiene Theory 360
MTO (make-to-order) 339
MTS (make-to-stock) 339
Multichannel E-commerce 226
Multichannel marketing 226
Multichannel network 227
Multichannel strategy 227
Multiple channel 227
Multi Rater Feedback 13
Multi-rating 14
Multi sourcing 278
Mutual alignment 355

National Competitive Advantage 143
Need for autonomy 223
Net time 31, 208
Network 143
Network organisation 230
New demand 83
New inventions 310
Niche 82

Offshore Development 162
Off-shoring 162
Onion research process 287
Open system model 70
Operational 241
Operational excellence 129
Operational positioning 172
Opportunities 95, 341
Opportunity 88
Opposing interests 91
Options 95
Order entry 258
Order-picking 258
Organisational climate 234
Organisational Climate Index 234
Organisational growth, Greiner 237
Organisational intelligence 182
Organisational Management 241
Organisation Chart 230
Organisation structure 230
Organogram(me) 230
OSO model 246
Out of the box 310
Outsourced activities 21
Outsourcing 18, 162
Overdones 292
Overhead costs 23, 25
Over-production 370
Over-segmentation 300

Pacemaker process 370
Packaging module 258
Packing 258
Packing density 259
Parallel activities 21
Pareto Analysis 250
Pareto's principle 250
Passing attack 80
Payback Period 108, 110
P&B Model 302
PDCA cycle (Plan-Do-Check-Act) 136

Penetration 83
Performance indicators 27, 57, 257
Performance matrix for family businesses 253
Performance of family firms 253
Personal Branding 345
Personal skills 345
Pest 139
Pestel 139
Pestle 139
Physical Distribution 256
Place of business 257
Plan-Do-Check-Act (PDCA) 136
Planning 208
PLC 269
PMT, Abell & Hammond 260
Politico-legal 139
Portals 57
Porters Diamond of Competitive Advantage 143
Portfolio diagram 32
Positioning 188, 263, 300
Positioning characteristics 264
Positivism 288
Price 188, 330
Pricing policy 188
Pricing strategy 188
Primary activities 364
PRINCE2 266
Problem definition 48
Process management 157
Process-oriented management 157
Process Time (PT) 369
Procurement process 277
Producer 71
Product development 168
Product image 172
Production factors 143, 199
Product leadership 129, 335
Product Life Cycle 269, 270
Product-market combination (PMC) 215, 216
Product Market Grid 168
Product-Market technology 260
Product-oriented 169
Products 273
Programme for organisational advice 356
Progress reporting 273
Project employees 321
Projects In Controlled Environments 266

Proposal 355
Prospects 119, 296
Purchasing 162, 203
Purchasing portfolio 203
Purchasing Process 277

Quanxi 113
Question mark 33

RACI 280
RACI-V 280
RASCI Matrix 280, 281
RATER 302
Ratio Delay Studies 283
Rational objective model 70
RBV 291
Realism 288
Reception 258
Reconstructionist view 42
Red ocean 42
Reinforce 96, 344
Relative market share 33
Reliability of delivery 259
Reliable 289
Repackaging 258
Representative 289
Research method 287, 288
Research objective 289
Research philosophy 288
Research strategy 288
Resetting times 370
Resource Based View 291
Resources 30, 291
Responsible, Accountable, Supportive, Consulted, Informed 280
Revised pricing policy 25
ROI (Return On Investment) 108, 110
Routine products 203, 205

Sales Force Automation 122
Sales Funnel 295
Sales people 295
Sales process 353
SAM 326
SAME 326
Secondary activities 364
Segmentation 298
Segmentation criteria 299
Segments 350
Self-assessment 15
Self-image 15

Service Level Agreement 193
Service Quality Model 302
SERVQUAL 302, 303
Seven-S Model 305
Shared skills 307
Shared values 306
Shareholders 323
Short-term thinking 112
Single sourcing 278
SIT Method 309, 310
Situational leadership 312
Situational Leadership Model (SLM) 312
Situational Leadership Theory 312
SIVA 315, 316
Six Sigma 319
Six Sigma (6 Σ) 319
SLA 193
Slingshot effect 257
SLM 312
Socially responsible capitalism 322
Social support 196
Socio-cultural 139
Solution 316
Solution-Information-Value-Access 315
Specialisation 18
Staff 307
Staff body 231
Staff employees 231
Stakeholder 323
Stakeholder Management 322
Stakeholder mapping 322
Standardisation 18
Star 33
Steep 139
Steeple 139
Steepled 139
Steer 139
Step-by-step plan 47
Stock 256, 257
Stock management 257
Storage 259
Storage of goods 258
Strategic 241
Strategic alignment 327

Strategic Alignment Model 326
Strategic Business Intelligence 55
Strategic clock 330
Strategic independence 223
Strategic Linhage Model 333
Strategic products 203, 205
Strategy 95, 244, 306
Strategy Clock 330
Strategy focus 241
Strategy Map 333
Strengths 95, 341
Structure 306
Style of management 307
Success factors 57
Supplier management 278
Suppliers 203
Supplier Selection 337
Suspects 119, 296
Sustainable relationship 124
SWOT 341
SWOT analysis 341
Symbiosis 223
Systematic Inventive Thinking 309
Systems 306

Tactical 241
Takeover 222
Talent Branding 345, 346
Target group 83, 298, 350
Target marketing 350
Task requirements 196
Task time 370
Team Buying Team Selling (TBTS) 353, 354
Team members 36
Team roles 36
Technical buyer 354
Technological 139
Ten Steps Plan 357
The Alignement Paradox 326
The Blue Ocean 42
The European Model for Quality Management 178
The parcipative leadership style 312
The Sales Pipeline 295
The Ten Steps Plan 356

Thinking in colours 63
Threats 95, 341
Throughput time 208
Time 30
Time Flow Charts 159
Time horizon 112, 289
TOWS Analysis 341
TOWS Matrix 341
Transformational positioning 172, 265
Transport 257, 259
Tri-component model 173
TSP 356
T systems 326
Turnover 118, 119
Two Factory Theory 360

Uncertainty avoidance 112
Undermanning 370
Undifferentiated approach 351
User 354

Valid 289
Value 316
Value Chain Analysis 364
Value Chain, Porter 364
Value density 259
Value disciplines 129
Value Stream Mapping 367, 368
Vertical enrichment 362
Vertical integration 176
Vision 242
VOKIPO 234
VSM, Manufacturing process evaluation technique 367

Waiting times 370
Warehouse 57, 256
Warehouse management 257
Weaknesses 95, 341
What-if analyses 161
Withdraw 96, 343
Work Breakdown Structure (WBS) 159
Work-Sampling and Random Sampling method 283
Work stress 195

Glossary Dutch-English

Dutch	English	Number of model
360°-Feedback	360° feedback	1
AAA Triangle	AAA Triangle	2
Activiteitenschema	Activities schedule	3
Activity Based Costing	Activity Based Costing	4
Balanced Scorecard	Balanced Scorecard	5
BART	BART	6
BCG-matrix	BCG Matrix	7
Bedrijfskolom	Industrial column	48
Belbin teamrollen	Belbin Team Roles	8
Benchmarking	Benchmarking	9
Beslissingstabel	Decision Table	35
Blue Ocean Strategy	Blue Ocean Strategy	10
Brainstorm	Brainstorm	11
Brand Asset Valuator	Brand Asset Valuator	12
Business Intelligence	Business Intelligence	13
CAGE Distance Framework	CAGE Distance Framework	14
Competentiemanagement	Competence management	16
Concurrentiebenadering Kotler	Competitive Positions, Kotler	19
Concurrentiegedrag Kotler	Competitive Strategies, Kotler	20
Concurrentiestrategieën Porter	Competitive Strategies, Porter	21
Conflicthantering	Conflict Handling	23
Confrontatiematrix	Confrontation Matrix	24
Core Competence	Core Competence	25
Core marketing systeem	Core Marketing System	26
Cultuurdimensies Hofstede	Cultural Dimensions, Hofstede	29
Customer Relationship Management	Customer Relationship Management	32
Demingcirkel	Deming Circle	36
DESTEP	DESTEP	37
Diamond Porter	Diamond, Porter	38
Doelgroepbenadering Kotler	Target Marketing	96
Doorlooptijd/nettotijd	Lead time/net time	57
Employability Scan	Employability Scan	39
Entry Mode Decision	Entry Mode Decision	40
F-PEC schaal	F-PEC scale	41
Functioneel en procesmanagement	Functional and process management	42
Fusie en overname	Mergers and Takeovers	61
Fysieke distributie	Physical Distribution	70
Gantt Chart	Gantt Chart	43
Global Sourcing	Global Sourcing	44
GPS voor ondernemingen	GPS for Enterprises	45
Groeimodel Ansoff	Growth Strategies, Ansoff	46
Groeimodel Greiner	Organisational growth, Greiner	65
Hefbomen van controle (beheersing)	Levers of Control	58
Het Tien Stappenplan	The Ten Steps Plan	98
Imago en identiteit	Image and Identity	47
INK/EFQM	INK/EFQM	49
Inkoopmodel Kraljic	Kraljic Matrix	56
Inkoopproces	Purchasing Process	76

Dutch	English	Page
International Market Research	International Market Research	51
Internationale prijsstrategie	International Pricing Strategy	52
ITIL V3	ITIL V3	53
Karasek Job Strain Model	Karasek's Job Strain Model	54
Kennismanagement	Knowledge management	55
Kernkwadranten	Core Qualities	27
Klachtenmanagement	Complaints Management	22
Klantenpiramide Curry	Customer Pyramid, Curry	31
Klantorderontkoppelpunt	Customer Order Decoupling Point	30
Klanttevredenheid	Customer Satisfaction	33
Klantwaardeprofielen	Customer-Value Profiles	34
Kleurentheorie	Colour Print Thinking	15
Kosten-batenanalyse	Costs-Benefits Analysis	28
Leiderschapsrollen Quinn	Competing Values Framework, Quinn	17
Leiderschapsstijl Hersey & Blanchard	Situational Leadership Theory	86
Leveranciersselectie	Supplier Selection	93
MaBa-analyse	MaBa Analysis	59
Managerial Grid	Managerial Grid	60
Multichannel marketing	Multichannel marketing	62
Multimomentopname	Ratio Delay Studies	78
Onderzoeksmethoden	Research method	79
Organisatiebesturing	Organisational Management	66
Organisatieklimaatindex	Organisational Climate Index	64
Organogram	Organisation Chart	63
OSO-model	OSO model	67
Pareto-analyse	Pareto Analysis	68
PMT Abell & Hammond	PMT, Abell & Hammond	71
Positionering	Positioning	72
Prestatiematrix van familiebedrijven	Performance matrix for family businesses	69
PRINCE2	PRINCE2	73
Productlevenscyclus	Product Life Cycle	74
RASCI-matrix	RASCI Matrix	77
Resource Based View	Resource Based View	80
Sales Funnel	Sales Funnel	81
Segmentering	Segmentation	82
SERVQUAL- of Gapmodel	SERVQUAL	83
SIT-methode	SIT Method	86
SIVA-model	SIVA	87
Six Sigma	Six Sigma	88
Stakeholder Management	Stakeholder Management	89
Strategic Clock	Strategy Clock	91
Strategisch Afstemmings Model (SAM)	Strategic Alignment Model	90
Strategy Map	Strategy Map	92
SWOT-analyse	SWOT	94
Talent Branding	Talent Branding	95
Team Buying Team Selling (TBTS)	Team Buying Team Selling (TBTS)	97
The intelligence pyramid	Intelligence pyramid	50
Two Factory Theory	Two Factory Theory	99
Value Stream Mapping	Value Stream Mapping	101
Vijfkrachtenmodel Porter	Competitive Forces, Porter	18
Voortgangsrapportage	Progress reporting	76
Waardeketen Porter	Value Chain, Porter	100
Zeven-S model	Seven-S model	85

Glossary English-Dutch

English	Dutch
360° feedback	360°-Feedback
AAA Triangle	AAA Triangle
Activities schedule	Activiteitenschema
Activity Based Costing	Activity Based Costing
Balanced Scorecard	Balanced Scorecard
BART	BART
BCG Matrix	BCG-matrix
Belbin Team Roles	Belbin teamrollen
Benchmarking	Benchmarking
Blue Ocean Strategy	Blue Ocean Strategy
Brainstorm	Brainstorm
Brand Asset Valuator	Brand Asset Valuator
Business Intelligence	Business Intelligence
CAGE Distance Framework	CAGE Distance Framework
Colour Print Thinking	Kleurentheorie
Competence management	Competentiemanagement
Competing Values Framework, Quinn	Leiderschapsrollen Quinn
Competitive Forces, Porter	Vijfkrachtenmodel Porter
Competitive Positions, Kotler	Concurrentiebenadering Kotler
Competitive Strategies, Kotler	Concurrentiegedrag Kotler
Competitive Strategies, Porter	Concurrentiestrategieën Porter
Complaints Management	Klachtenmanagement
Conflict Handling	Conflicthantering
Confrontation Matrix	Confrontatiematrix
Core Competence	Core Competence
Core Marketing System	Core marketing systeem
Core Qualities	Kernkwadranten
Costs-Benefits Analysis	Kosten-batenanalyse
Cultural Dimensions, Hofstede	Cultuurdimensies Hofstede
Customer Order Decoupling Point	Klantorderontkoppelpunt
Customer Pyramid, Curry	Klantenpiramide Curry
Customer Relationship Management	Customer Relationship Management
Customer Satisfaction	Klanttevredenheid
Customer-Value Profiles	Klantwaardeprofielen
Decision Table	Beslissingstabel
Deming Circle	Demingcirkel
DESTEP	DESTEP
Diamond, Porter	Diamond Porter
Employability Scan	Employability Scan
Entry Mode Decision	Entry Mode Decision
F-PEC scale	F-PEC schaal
Functional and process management	Functioneel en procesmanagement
Gantt Chart	Gantt Chart
Global Sourcing	Global Sourcing
GPS for Enterprises	GPS voor ondernemingen
Growth Strategies, Ansoff	Groeimodel Ansoff
Image and Identity	Imago en identiteit
Industrial column	Bedrijfskolom

INK/EFQM	INK/EFQM
Intelligence pyramid	The intelligence pyramid
International Market Research	International Market Research
International Pricing Strategy	Internationale prijsstrategie
ITIL V3	ITIL V3
Karasek's Job Strain Model	Karasek Job Strain Model
Knowledge management	Kennismanagement
Kraljic Matrix	Inkoopmodel Kraljic
Lead time/net time	Doorlooptijd/nettotijd
Levers of Control	Hefbomen van controle (beheersing)
MaBa Analysis	MaBa-analyse
Managerial Grid	Managerial Grid
Mergers and Takeovers	Fusie en overname
Multichannel marketing	Multichannel marketing
Organisation Chart	Organogram
Organisational Climate Index	Organisatieklimaatindex
Organisational growth, Greiner	Groeimodel Greiner
Organisational Management	Organisatiebesturing
OSO model	OSO-model
Pareto Analysis	Pareto-analyse
Performance matrix for family businesses	Prestatiematrix van familiebedrijven
Physical Distribution	Fysieke distributie
PMT, Abell & Hammond	PMT Abell & Hammond
Positioning	Positionering
PRINCE2	PRINCE2
Product Life Cycle	Productlevenscyclus
Progress reporting	Voortgangsrapportage
Purchasing Process	Inkoopproces
Ratio Delay Studies	Multimomentopname
RASCI Matrix	RASCI-matrix
Research method	Onderzoeksmethoden
Resource Based View	Resource Based View
Sales Funnel	Sales Funnel
Segmentation	Segmentering
SERVQUAL	SERVQUAL- of Gapmodel
Seven-S model	Zeven-S model
SIT Method	SIT-methode
Situational Leadership Theory	Leiderschapsstijl Hersey & Blanchard
SIVA	SIVA-model
Six Sigma	Six Sigma
Stakeholder Management	Stakeholder Management
Strategic Alignment Model	Strategisch Afstemmings Model (SAM)
Strategy Clock	Strategic Clock
Strategy Map	Strategy Map
Supplier Selection	Leveranciersselectie
SWOT	SWOT-analyse
Talent Branding	Talent Branding
Target Marketing	Doelgroepbenadering Kotler
Team Buying Team Selling (TBTS)	Team Buying Team Selling (TBTS)
The Ten Steps Plan	Het Tien Stappenplan
Two Factory Theory	Two Factory Theory
Value Chain, Porter	Waardeketen Porter
Value Stream Mapping	Value Stream Mapping